Routledge Revivals

The Origins of Civilization in Greek and Roman Thought

The extent to which thinkers in Greek and Roman antiquity adhered to ideas of evolution and progress in human affairs has been much debated. Did they lack any conception of process in time, or did they anticipate Darwinian and Lamarckian hypotheses?

The Origins of Civilization in Greek and Roman Thought, first published in1986, comprehensively examines these issues. Beginning with creation myths – Mother Earth and Pandora, the anti-progressive ideas of the Golden Age, and the cyclical theories of Orphism – Professor Blundell goes on to explore the origins of scientific speculation among the Pre-Socratics, its development into the teleological science of Aristotle, and the advent of the progressivist views of the Stoics. Attention is also given to the 'primitivist' debate, involving ideas about the noble savage and reflections of such speculation in poetry, and finally the relationship between nature and culture in ancient thought is investigated.

The Origins of Civilization in Greek and Roman Thought

Sue Blundell

First published in 1986
by Croom Helm Ltd

This edition first published in 2014 by Routledge
2 Park Square, Milton Park, Abingdon, Oxon, OX14 4RN
and by Routledge
711 Third Avenue, New York, NY 10017

Routledge is an imprint of the Taylor & Francis Group, an informa business

© 1986 Sue Blundell

The right of Sue Blundell to be identified as author of this work has been asserted by her in accordance with sections 77 and 78 of the Copyright, Designs and Patents Act 1988.

All rights reserved. No part of this book may be reprinted or reproduced or utilised in any form or by any electronic, mechanical, or other means, now known or hereafter invented, including photocopying and recording, or in any information storage or retrieval system, without permission in writing from the publishers.

Publisher's Note
The publisher has gone to great lengths to ensure the quality of this reprint but points out that some imperfections in the original copies may be apparent.

Disclaimer
The publisher has made every effort to trace copyright holders and welcomes correspondence from those they have been unable to contact.

A Library of Congress record exists under LC control number: 85029061

ISBN 13: 978-0-415-74820-9 (hbk)
ISBN 13: 978-1-315-79662-8 (ebk)
ISBN 13: 978-0-415-74821-6 (pbk)

The Origins of Civilization in
GREEK & ROMAN THOUGHT

SUE BLUNDELL

CROOM HELM
London • Sydney • Dover, New Hampshire

©1986 Sue Blundell
Croom Helm Ltd, Provident House, Burrell Row,
Beckenham, Kent BR3 1AT
Croom Helm Australia Pty Ltd, Suite 4, 6th Floor,
64-76 Kippax Street, Surry Hills, NSW 2010, Australia

British Library Cataloguing in Publication Data

Blundell, Sue
 The origins of civilization in Greek and Roman
 thought.
 1. Philosophy, Ancient
 I. Title
 180'.938   B505

ISBN 0-7099-3212-X

Croom Helm, 51 Washington Street, Dover,
New Hampshire 03820, USA

Library of Congress Cataloging in Publication Data

Blundell, Sue.
 The origins of civilization in Greek and Roman
thought.

 Bibliography: p.
 Includes index.
 1. Civilization, classical—philosophy.
2. Man—origin. I. Title.
DE60.B58   1986   938'.001   85-29061
ISBN 0-7099-3212-X

Printed and bound in Great Britain
by Billing & Sons Limited, Worcester.

CONTENTS

Preface ix

PART ONE: THE ORIGINS OF THE HUMAN RACE

1. Mythological explanations 3
2. The theories of the Presocratic
   philosophers 24
3. Later theories 54
4. Evolution and the survival
   of the fittest 73

PART TWO: PATTERNS OF CULTURAL HISTORY

5. Values and cycles 103
6. Golden Age Theories 135
7. Theories of progress 165
8. Hard primitivism and the
   noble savage 203

CONCLUSION 225

SELECT BIBLIOGRAPHY 228

INDEX 231

PREFACE

The aim of this book is to survey and appraise the very numerous and very various Greek and Roman texts which deal with two related questions: how did the human race come into existence? and how, and at what cost, did it acquire its present cultural status? The subject is indeed a vast one, since there are few writers who do not have something to say on the matter, at least where the second question is concerned; so that I have been forced in the second part of the book to concentrate by and large on those authors who have tried to present an overview of the human race's cultural history. There are thus many omissions; but I think that the texts which I have chosen do serve to represent the main patterns of ancient thought on the question of cultural development. I regret very much that these texts could not have been examined in more detail: in particular, I would have liked to look more closely at the authors' analyses of various facets of civilisation, such as technology or language. But this would have led me into new and ever-more-complex areas, and it seemed best to confine my attention to the broad evaluations of culture which emerged from their histories. The opinions which people hold about where they have come from and where they are now are at any time a vital element in human consciousness: the conclusions which I have reached about ancient opinions on this subject are necessarily tentative, but I hope thought-provoking.

There are many authors whom I have never met to whom I owe thanks for helping to inspire or to shape this book: of these I would like to mention four in particular. First and foremost, the Roman philosopher Lucretius, whose short history of human civilisation first led me into this absorbing subject. And next A.O. Lovejoy and G. Boas for their exhaustive work <u>Primitivism and related ideas in antiquity</u>; and W.K.C. Guthrie, for his book <u>In the beginning</u>: both of these encouraged me, while I was writing my doctoral thesis on Lucretius, to explore on my own account the territory which they had so ably mapped out.

Among the people whom I <u>have</u> met, and who have helped me considerably, may I express especial thanks to Paul Godfrey, whose opinions on mythological questions were invaluable; to Joan Stratford, Caroline Heijne and Nick Bailey, who typed the manuscript; to the library staff at the Institute of Classical Studies in London; and above all to Bob Sharples, of University College, London, who read the whole of the manuscript and never complained: he corrected many errors, and is in no way responsible for the ones that remain.

Part One

THE ORIGINS OF THE HUMAN RACE

Chapter One

MYTHOLOGICAL EXPLANATIONS

Greek and Roman cosmogonical myths - stories which seek to explain the origins of our world through the personages and events of mythology rather than in a direct, empirical way - are derived from sources which range in time from the eighth century BC to the fifth century AD. That is not to say that they are numerous, for Greek and Roman mythographers seem more often to have concerned themselves with the problems presented by our environment as it exists now, rather than its possible ancestry. Even less common are the anthropogonical myths - the myths which account for the origins of the human race - for again it is human life in the here-and-now which is the object of concern. Explanations of human origins often make their appearance in an incidental way, and many problems are encountered when one tries to piece together any kind of consistent picture. Certain trends of thought do, however, emerge and it will be the purpose of this chapter to examine them.

A COMMON LIFE WITH THE GODS

Homer is our earliest source, but from him we derive only the briefest of allusions. In Book 14 of the Iliad, Oceanus, the divine river which encircles the earth, is spoken of as the 'begetter of the gods' (line 201) and is associated in this act of creation with the water-goddess 'mother Tethys'; in a later passage he becomes the 'begetter of all' (line 246). It is perhaps not absolutely necessary to read the human race into the 'all' of the second reference, but later authors certainly made this interpretation (1), and if they are correct we are presented with what in Greek myth is a unique version of human origins (2). Another reference, equally brief, is to be found in Book 20 of the Odyssey, where Zeus is reproached for having no pity on men, even though he himself begets them (line 202). Obviously, there is some inconsistency here, but what is most significant about these two allusions is that human beings are seen in both cases as the offspring of the gods. The passage from the Odyssey makes the further point that though they are divine in origin, humans live a life which is not like that of the gods, since it is full of misery and pain.

The same picture emerges from a study of Hesiod, who is our oldest source for a cosmogonical myth of any detail. In the Theogony, he describes how in the beginning there was Chaos, and out of Chaos there arose broad-bosomed Gaia (or Earth) who gave birth to Ouranos (or Sky), the Mountains and the Sea. Sky then spread himself over Earth and the result of their union was the birth of the Titans, the Cyclops and the Hundred-handed Giants. So that these could see the light of day, Earth and Sky had to be forcibly separated through the agency of Kronos, the youngest of the Titans, who castrated his father with a sickle. This violent overthrow of father by son was repeated in the next generation, when Kronos insisted on swallowing his children because of a prophecy that he was fated to be overcome by his son. One child, Zeus, was rescued and lived to vanquish his father and become king of the gods (116-210, 453-506).

Implicit in this story of the struggles among the gods is an account of how an ordered cosmos gradually developed out of an original chaos. But there is no reference here at all to the creation of the human race, which in the next episode is simply assumed to exist. In the course of a crucial confrontation at Mekone, the Titan Prometheus tricked Zeus into choosing the less favourable of two portions of ox, thus ensuring that in future human beings would offer in sacrifice to the gods only the bones of an animal, not its flesh. To make human beings suffer for having gained this advantage, Zeus then deprived them of fire; when Prometheus stole fire and took it down to earth, Zeus responded by creating the first woman (535-584).

Hesiod introduces this episode with the words, 'for when the gods and mortal men were separated (or distinguished) at Mekone...'. It seems clear that more is at stake here than a simple explanation of sacrificial practices among the Greeks. Gods and humans, it is implied, had up to this time been in the habit of dining together and had enjoyed a common life. The institution of the practice of sacrifice converted humans into meat-eaters and thus marked them off from the gods: from this time on they would be mortal, subject to hunger, pain, fatigue and death. Indeed, Zeus' withdrawal of fire would have temporarily reduced them in status still further, since humans would have been forced to eat the flesh they had acquired in a raw and uncooked state, as animals did. When Prometheus restored fire to them, they were re-established in a position mid-way between gods and animals, and the gift of woman confirmed this position.

Hesiod's story, then, tells us nothing about the physical process of creation, but confirms what Homer has said about the original status of the human race. Human beings were once the equals of the gods, but are now condemned to a life of misery and pain. Like the story of the Fall of Man in the Old Testament, it explains why human beings cannot be free from suffering.

This notion of a common life shared by gods and humans is confirmed by other passages from Hesiod. In the Works and Days we are told that 'gods and mortal men are born from the same source' (line 108), and that the first race of mortals, the Golden one, 'lived like the gods' (line 112); while a fragment of Hesiod's verse recalls a time when 'banquets then were shared, seats were shared by immortal gods and mortal men'(3). Other myths tell a similar story. Up until the fateful day when the Arcadian mortal Lykaon sacrificed a human baby to Zeus, the men of that time were the guests of the gods and ate at the same table (4); and another human Tantalus used regularly to dine on Mount Olympus, before being repudiated by the gods because when returning their hospitality he cut up his own son Pelops and served him up in a stew. (5) Again, sacrifice marks the point when the human race becomes distinguished from that of the gods and ceases to enjoy divine privileges.

TREES AND STONES

In Hesiod's Theogony, Earth is pictured both as the parent of the gods and the starting-point for the development of cosmic order. There is no suggestion here that the human race was created out of the earth or indeed that it was created in any way at all. Nevertheless, some evidence does exist for a mythical tradition going back beyond Hesiod which traced the origin of humankind to products of the earth, to trees or stones. When in Book 19 of Homer's Odyssey

Mythological Explanations

Penelope asks the disguised Odysseus about his ancestry, she adds 'for you are not sprung from an oak of the ancient story, nor from a stone' (line 163). This is a proverbial expression which occurs in other ancient works (including *Iliad* 22.126) and which in this context at least appears to refer to a myth about the origin of the human race. Of the trees, it is the oak-tree that seems to have been most favoured as a possible progenitor of human beings. Among the mythical peoples who have tree-connections are the Dryopes, whose ancestor Dryops had been concealed as a new-born baby in a hollow oak-tree (*drus*), from which he took his name (6). Echoes of a similar myth are to be found in later Latin authors, among them Vergil, who makes Evander recount to Aeneas the story of a local people 'born from tree-trunks and the hardy oak.' (7) But the ash-tree too might be a contender: in the *Works and Days*, Hesiod tells us that Zeus made a bronze race 'sprung from ash-trees' (145); and the mythographer Palaephatus records the belief that 'the first race of living men was born from ash-trees' (36). The notion seems a homely one, although it is perhaps not altogether inconsistent with a belief in the divine origins of the human race, since trees had certainly been regarded as sacred in prehistoric Greece, and may, as in Crete, have been worshipped as deities (8).

The 'stone' element in Homer's proverb finds support in the well-known story of Deucalion and the flood, for which a fragment of Hesiod is our earliest source (9). Deucalion and his sister/wife Pyrrha were the sole survivors of a great deluge (10), sent by Zeus as a punishment for a range of variously specified acts of impiety on the part of the human race. After the waters had subsided, the favoured pair managed to recreate human beings out of stones. There is, of course, a geophysical link between stones and the earth, a connection which is made explicit in the version of the story given by Ovid. When Deucalion and Pyrrha, gazing on an empty world, prayed to the goddess Themis to tell them how they might restore their race, she replied that they must throw behind them the bones of their great mother. Horrified by such a suggestion, Pyrrha begged to be excused; but Deucalion eventually realised that their great mother was none other than the earth and that the bones of her body were stones. So they did as they were told, 'and in a short time by the will of the gods the stones thrown by the man's hand took on the form of men, and women were created from those thrown by the woman' (411-413). A similar theme, with similar earthy connections, emerges from the localised story of King Aeacus, whose prayers for the repopulation of his island Aegina, devastated by a plague, were answered when a shower of ants fell from the branches of an oak-tree onto the ground and rose up again as human beings (11).

MEN FROM THE EARTH

References to trees or stones as the progenitors of the human race are scanty, but suggest a long-established tradition. Even more scanty are the hints received from early myth that the earth may have been responsible in a more direct way for the original production of the human race: in book 7 of the Iliad, the curse uttered by Menelaus 'May you all turn to water and earth' (line 99) seems to be a prayer for dissolution into constituent elements; and Hesiod's statement that 'gods and men are born from the same source' could be seen as reference to the earth. But these may be compared with a large number of stories about particular individuals or groups of people being born from the earth. A full account of these earth-born men has been provided by W.K.C. Guthrie (12) and it will be sufficient here to mention just a few instances. One such is Pelasgus, the legendary ancestor of the Pelasgians, the earliest inhabitants of Greece: the poet Asius, writing in the seventh or sixth century BC, says of him that 'the black earth brought him forth, so that the race of mortals might exist' (13). Similarly Aeschylus, who makes Pelasgus an early king of Argos, calls him gegenes (born from the earth) (14). Cadmus, the founder of Thebes, was said to have stocked his new settlement with inhabitants when he planted a serpent's teeth in the ground and there sprang up from these a crop of armed men (15); and one of the early legendary kings of Athens was Erechtheus, whose links with the earth are established by the significant chthon (earth) root in his name: Homer tells us that 'the grain-bearing ploughland gave him birth' (Iliad 2.547), and Euripides describes an end which echoes his beginning, for the earth swallowed him alive when Poseidon struck it with his trident (Ion 281-2).

Many of these stories of earth-born men seem to be connected with the early history of various of the Greek peoples, and the point has often been made that they more than likely should be assigned to the category of 'charter' myths, that is, myths that validate the customary practices or institutions of the society that produces them (16). One's claim to the land on which one was living, the argument goes, would be proved beyond doubt if one could provide oneself with an earth-born ancestor, for then one would be autochthonous in the literal sense of the word, 'sprung from the earth itself'. It does indeed seem quite reasonable to suppose that such myths reflect an attempt to provide a pseudo-historical justification for an existing state of affairs. One can see a comparable process taking place on a conscious level in the historical period, when myths about earth-born ancestors are exploited as the basis for a quite blatant patriotism: in the case of Socrates, who tells us that when the earth was giving birth to creatures of every kind, the land of Athens concentrated its activities on man, as he was the most intelligent of the animals (17), the attempt is a facetious one; but the orator Isocrates is being perfectly serious when he argues that the Athenians' forbears 'were not of mixed origin, nor invaders, but on the contrary, alone among the Greeks, were autochthones, possessing in this land the nurse of their very existence and cherishing it as fondly as the best of children cherish their fathers and mothers' (Panathenaicus 124-125).

But the myths of earth-born men are too complex for us to believe that they were purely and simply the product of a desire to assert one's territorial claims. That, once invented, they were used, consciously or unconsciously, to promote this end we may well imagine; but the proliferation of motifs, and the existence of 'earth-born' myths which have no apparent charter function, suggest a more profound origin. What one can certainly say is that these myths demonstrate the currency from quite an early date of ideas about the earth as the generator of human beings. Moreover, these ideas do not necessarily conflict with the notion, derived from Hesiod, of the original divine status of the human race, since Earth was the ultimate parent of all the gods.

By the fifth century BC at the latest, it had become a poetical commonplace to speak of Earth as the human race's mother and Sky as its father. Usually this was just a metaphorical expression of our dependence on the earth's productivity and on the rainfall which promotes it (18); but Euripides takes it a stage further, when he writes, 'the tale is not mine, but my mother's - how Sky and Earth were one form. But when they had been separated apart from each other, they brought forth all things, and gave them up into the light: trees, birds, beasts, the creatures nourished by the salt sea, and the race of mortals'(19).

THE CREATION OF WOMAN

As we have seen, the cosmogonical myth in Hesiod's Theogony does nothing to reinforce these suggestions of an account of human origins linked to the productivity of the earth. In the Theogony human beings are just assumed to exist; in Hesiod's other major work, the Works and Days, the author in recounting the story of the Five Races merely mentions in passing that the Golden and Silver Races were created by the Olympian gods collectively, and the Bronze and Heroic Races by Zeus himself (109-158), adding the hint about ash-trees already noted. No further information is vouchsafed to us; but on the other hand both the Theogony and the Works and Days do provide us with quite a detailed account of the creation of the first woman. In the Theogony Hesiod describes how when Prometheus presented his gift of stolen fire to men, Zeus retaliated by masterminding the invention of the first woman, who was moulded out of earth by the craftsman-god Hephaistos, and adorned in glittering raiment by Pallas Athene. Thus he contrived for men a 'beautiful evil', for from her are descended all the generations of woman, who through their greed and laziness cause men nothing but grief and misery (lines 570-612). In the Works and Days we are treated to the more familiar version of the story. After the theft of fire, Zeus ordered Hephaistos to mingle earth and water and to create the lovely shape of a woman. Other deities showered her with attributes, both mental and physical, and she received the name Pandora, or 'All-gift', because all the Olympians presented her as a gift to men (20). Epimetheus, the brother of Prometheus, then foolishly agreed to accept the gift on behalf of mankind. Up to this time, men had lived free from evil, toil and disease; but Pandora took the lid off her jar and out flew all these curses. Only hope remained inside, and Pandora was forced by the will of Zeus to shut the lid on that (lines 59-105).

The gift of Pandora is delivered to men after Prometheus' deceptions have first of all reduced them to animal status, and then raised them up to an intermediate position between animals and the gods.

9

Mythological Explanations

The information that the first woman was constructed out of earth and water recalls to mind the two progenitors of the cosmos, Earth and Sky; but the physical ingredients are incidental to the main theme of the story, which is Pandora's reinforcement of the intermediate status of the human race. For she herself is a thoroughly ambiguous creature - lovely to look at, with a face like a goddess; but at the same time earthy, bestial and rapacious. By her seductions she pulls man back up to the level of the gods, but at the same time she thrusts him down among the animals - and so in the end she leaves him where he was, forever balanced between the two. With her coming, man's exposure to mortal sufferings is confirmed; and his mortality is reinforced in another way, for the institution of marriage and child-bearing ensures that in the future the only kind of immortality which human beings will be able to achieve will be through procreation. From now on the human race is responsible for its own continuing existence - cut off from the creativity of the gods, it now has no choice but to maintain itself through the double-edged gift of sexual union.

PROMETHEUS

In most of the myths examined so far which posit an earthly origin for the human race, people are pictured as springing up from the earth like plants, or as developing out of the products of the earth. The chief exception is Pandora, who did not grow spontaneously, but was deliberately manufactured out of earth and water: from the very beginning, she was a tool in the hands of the gods, totally subordinate to their designs. A similarly passive origin for the human race in general is not suggested, as far as our sources permit us to judge, until the latter part of the fifth century, when Aristophanes refers to human beings as 'figures moulded from clay' (Birds 686). No clue is given here as to the manufacturer, but by the next century the Titan Prometheus was beginning to emerge as the most favoured candidate.

In the Theogony, Prometheus is the agent through whose acts the separation of the gods and the human race is achieved; he is associated also with the more physical side of creation, in that his trickery leads to the manufacture of the first woman, and it is his brother Epimetheus who unwittingly presents Pandora to mortal men. He turns up too in another creation story, for he is the father of the Deucalion who survived the flood and recreated the human race. But Prometheus' links with physical creation seem for a long time to have remained undeveloped: at first the accent was on the distinctive identity which he conferred on the human race by his crucial gift of fire. So in the fifth century he was depicted as a civiliser and a saviour, but not as a creator. In the <u>Prometheus Bound</u>, generally attributed to Aeschylus, we are treated to a long recital of the Titan's services to humankind (lines 436-506), but we hear nothing of the ultimate service of creation (21); and in Plato's <u>Protagoras</u>, it is the gods who create human beings, while Prometheus bestows on them fire and technical skill (320D-322A).

The earliest surviving references to Prometheus as creator of the human race occur in the fourth century BC, in fragments of Heraclides Ponticus (22) and Philemon (23), where he is mentioned briefly as having fashioned the first men. Later this aspect of his achievements became commonplace, and we find him using familiar materials to carry out the work - earth and water (or clay), the same ingredients as were used by Hephaistos in the manufacture of Pandora. The Hellenistic poet Callimachus uses the expression 'the clay of Prometheus' as a circumlocution for 'men' (24); and Apollodorus, the second century mythographer, tells us that Prometheus moulded men out of water and earth, and then gave them fire (<u>The Library</u> 1.7.1). Ovid goes into more detail: one theory of human origins, he says, is that when the earth was new and had only recently been separated from the aether, it still retained in it some divine seeds; Prometheus then mixed it with rainwater and from this moulded human beings in the image of the gods (<u>Metamorph</u>. 1.80-83). The second century satiric writer Lucian in one of his sketches describes how Prometheus fashioned the shapes of men out of mud, but was assisted in his work by Athene, who breathed into his models and made them live (25); and in the same century the traveller Pausanias informs us that visitors to Panopeus in Phocis have pointed out to them in a ravine two huge stones which are the colour of clay and emit a smell very like the skin of human beings, which the locals say are the remains of the clay used by Prometheus to fashion the whole of mankind (10.4.4).

THE ORPHIC THEORY

A number of Greek cosmogonical texts, most of them

deriving from Neoplatonist sources of the fourth to sixth centuries AD, are associated with the religious movement known as Orphism, which drew its inspiration from the poetry attributed to the mythical singer Orpheus. To what extent the Orphics constituted an organised sect, and how far back their cosmogonical theories can be traced, are still subjects of great controversy (26), and it is by no means certain that one can cite their myths as examples of an archaic and distinctive set of beliefs. The most significant anthropogonical myth mentioned in connection with the Orphics is linked to the story of how the Titans lured the infant Dionysus away with toys, tore him to pieces, and then boiled and roasted and, in some versions, ate his flesh: for this crime they were blasted with a thunderbolt by Zeus (27). The earliest references to this myth in a specifically Orphic context are to be found in the first century BC, in the works of Diodorus and Philodemus; and the anthropogonic aspect, which emerges from the information that the human race was born from the soot created by the burning up of the Titans, appears only in an Orphic poem quoted by the sixth century Neoplatonist Olympiodorus (28). That the anthropogonical myth is in fact much older than this is suggested by a number of texts, some of them Orphic, which refer to the human race as being sprung from the Titans or has having inherited from them a tendency towards either evil or good; but we cannot be absolutely sure of the link between the two notions (29).

But whatever the date of the myth's inception, it remains valid as an expression of human beings' anxiety about their relationship with the divine. As in the Hesiodic story of Prometheus' activities at Mekone, sacrifice marks the point when the human race assumes an independent existence. Clearly, however, there must be some difference between a myth which sees the sacrifice and eating of animals as a crucial factor in determining the status of the human race, and one which finds the root cause of human existence in the sacrifice and eating of a god. In mainstream mythology, the act of sacrifice, while providing a channel of communication between gods and humans, at the same time commemorates and confirms their eternal separation. The Orphic story, according to a number of commentators, could on the other hand be seen as presenting us with an analysis of the human constitution which distinguishes within it an element derived from Dionysus, and in this way as emphasising the links that are still retained with the divine. Olympiodorus, at any rate, interprets the story in this light, and sees this as the reason for an Orphic stricture against suicide; and his view has been adopted and elaborated on by some modern scholars. But Linforth and West have both dismissed Olympiodorus' analysis as a piece of Neoplatonist speculation with no positive basis in the Orphic source (30); and their reservations seem thoroughly justified. The precise significance of the Orphic story may well elude us, but there are two points which at this stage seem worthy of emphasis. Firstly, if in the Hesiodic story the consumption of animal flesh effects our separation from the gods, but at the same time ensures that we do not descend to the level of animals; then it could perhaps be said that the eating of divine flesh in the Orphic anthropogony points to a more thorough and precipitate fall from grace. And secondly, there is an emphasis in the Orphic acccount on the earthy origins of the human race which is entirely absent from the Hesiodic version. In the Orphic story, human beings are born from the ground, from the soot created by the burning of the Titanic gods; and these gods are themselves ambiguous, for though divine they too are the children of Earth, they bear a name which may be connected with a Greek word for chalk or gypsum (titanos), and in some versions of the Orphic story they cover themselves with gypsum when luring away the infant Dionysus (31). The Orphic myth, then, while in some respects parallel to the story told by Hesiod, presents some strikingly different features.

A summary must now be attempted of the seemingly disparate themes which have emerged from a study of Greek and Roman anthropogonical myths. The oldest and most influential of the Greek creation myths - the one presented by Hesiod in the *Theogony* - offers no explanation of the physical origins of the human race, but instead gives us an account of how human beings, who once lived a life like that of the gods, came to be separated from the divine. But in other myths, no less archiac, we encounter the seemingly peripheral but clearly persistent notion that human beings were born from the earth, either directly or with trees or stones as intermediaries. This idea, while in no way contradicting the divine connections of the human race, certainly views the human constitution from a different angle. Different again is the Orphic perspective, which combines the concepts of a fall from divine grace and a rise from

13

earthy origins. Later mainstream myth, dateable to no earlier than the fifth century BC, concentrates on the earth element of the older anthropogonies, but instead of picturing human beings growing up spontaneously, now makes use of a motif which at first applied only to the creation of the first woman, and sees the whole of the human race as having been moulded out of clay like a terracotta figure. By the fourth century BC, Prometheus, the key figure in the Hesiodic separation story, has become the craftsman who shapes the human race.

Two major problems arise from this synopsis:
1. why does the main Hesiodic myth ignore the physical creation of the human race?
2. what is the relationship betwen the Hesiodic and the 'earth-created' theories?

One answer to the first problem has been suggested by Peter Walcot in his investigation of the influence on Hesiod of Near Eastern mythology (32). He believes that there is, in fact, no gap in the Hesiodic myth. For him, the Pandora story fulfils, in its two versions, two very different functions: in the <u>Works and Days</u> it is used to explain the necessity for hard work; whereas in the <u>Theogony</u> it represents the culmination of the story of the creation, by accounting for the origin of at least one of the sexes. Why the female sex should have been lighted on is explained for him by the close parallels which he discerns between the Pandora story and an Egyptian myth which might well have been transported to Greece during the Mycenean era. In this myth, the ram-headed craftsman-god Khnum was pictured as shaping the first living beings on a potter's wheel, and was associated also with the fashioning of new pharaohs, each of whom repeated the creation miracle by establishing order out of chaos. One striking visual representation of the fashioning of a female pharaoh might, he believes, have made sufficient impression on the Greeks as to give rise to the story of Pandora.

This solution is hardly satisfactory. It ignores the climactic part which the Pandora story plays in the account of the separation of gods and humans, and fails to explain, other than in terms of mere possible absorption, why the creation of one of the sexes should have been highlighted while the existence of the other was just assumed. Geoffrey Kirk (33) also rejects Walcot's solution, and in providing his own answer turns to the Mesopotamian mythology of which there are certainly many echoes in Hesiod. He points out that a number of Mesopotamian myths do describe the creation of the human race, but from a perspective which stresses the master-slave relationship between gods and humans. In Sumerian myth, for example, the water-god Enki, with help from his mother Nammu (the primaeval sea) and from the goddess Ninmah (probably the mother earth), creates human beings by mixing clay with his own blood: this scheme is devised specifically so that the human race may furnish the gods with a regular food-supply. And in the Babylonian Creation Epic, Enuma Elish, the storm-god Marduk proposes to his father Ea that humans should be created expressly as servants of the gods: the rebellious god Kingu is slaughtered for this purpose and his blood provides the material for the human race (34). Kirk suggests that the Greeks, with their highly developed sense of freedom, would have found this notion of slavery to the gods a repugnant one, and so in their absorption of Mesopotamian creation stories would have rejected this one distasteful element. The story about the creation of woman, however, was retained, since it had the function of explaining, not the relationship between gods and humans, but the subsidiary relationship between women and men. Hence a creation myth developed in which the existence of men was simply assumed, but which preserved an incongruous account of how women came into being.

Kirk does not in this analysis address himself to the problem of why from at least the fifth century BC on, when Greek notions of freedom were arguably more highly developed than they had been at any earlier time, the notion of divine manufacture began to be one which the Greeks <u>were</u> capable of stomaching; and this must constitute, I believe, a major objection to his theory. It must also be said that, although a number of elements from Mesopotamian myths do seem to have been absorbed into their Greek counterparts, there is certainly no one clear-cut model for the Hesiodic story. We should perhaps be asking ourselves, then, not why Greek myth-makers rejected just one of the very many elements which they failed to absorb, but why they allowed themselves to accept the elements which they did. One possible answer is provided by the structuralist thinker J-P. Vernant (35), who argues that the <u>Theogony</u> is a poem 'in which everything takes place at the level of the gods', and that for this reason 'we learn how the gods came into being, not men'. We are dealing here, he believes, with a myth about the origins of the gods and their struggles for sovereignty, in the course of which an ordered cosmos emerges and, with the victory of Zeus, is established on a permanent and unshakable footing. The evolution of divine power and the evolution of the universe are seen as inextricably linked; the initial separation of Sky and Earth has to take place so that the gods can come into being, and the universe which then takes shape represents both the framework and the prize for the gods' subsequent battles for supremacy.

In all this, there is no room for an account of the origins of the human race. The story is a god-centred one, and when men make their first appearance, in the episode where Prometheus apportions the sacrificial victim, the focus is not on how they came into being, but rather how they came to be different from the gods whom they so closely resembled. Prometheus' action has the effect of defining their status as mortals, and of emphasising the gulf that must henceforward always exist between them and the blessed immortals.

By way of elaboration on Vernant's theory, I would suggest that the separation between gods and humans that is effected at Mekone represents the culminating point in the process of progressive differentiation by which the universe has been brought into being. When Earth is separated from Sky at the beginning of the story, the universe can begin to take shape and the gods can come into existence because they have been given something over which they can rule. Similarly at a later point in the story, the separation which robs the human race of divine status sets the seal on Zeus' victory by providing him with a new field for the exercise of his divine power. Vernant is right, I believe, when he says that an account of human origins would be inappropriate here. The <u>Theogony</u> is a story about how an order which is inherently linked with divine rule came to be established in the universe: in the course of it the myth-maker comes up against the question, not of 'where did we come from?', but of 'why do we belong to the realm of the ruled and not to that of the rulers?' By explaining how the human race, like other parts of the universe, came to be separated off from the realm of active divine leadership, the myth seeks to provide an answer to the problem of why human beings have to endure all the sufferings of mortal life instead of enjoying the privileges of divinity and immortality. And here, perhaps, we have a clue as to why Greek myth-makers were not interested in taking up the suggestions about human origins made by the Mesopotamians. The Babylonian Creation Epic provided them with part of what they were looking for by presenting them with a pattern of divine succession linked to cosmic order: but its story of the physical creation of the human race offered no satisfying solution to the question of why human beings are not divine, because it did not envisage a situation when they ever had been. Greek myth-makers (perhaps because at that stage in their history they were more inclined to be despondent about the human condition than their counterparts from the more advanced Mesopotamian civilisations) looked at the problem negatively: we could so easily be divine, they thought, why aren't we? what went wrong? The angle of vision is from high to low, from divine to human: the outlook could be said to be pessimistic.

We now come to the second problem, of the relationship between the Hesiodic myth and the stories of earth-born humans. One possible explanation of the discrepancy has been suggested by E.E. Sikes (36), who thinks that racial differences may have accounted for the existence in Greece of two conflicting sets of beliefs about human origins. The earth-created stories, he says, may have been very ancient ones which circulated in Greece prior to the arrival of the Greek-speaking peoples. When the Greeks entered the country, they brought with them an alternative theory, encompassed in tales about heroes and legendary kings who were descended from the gods, tales which stressed the relationship between gods and humans. (Sikes does not mention the Hesiodic myth in this connection, but it too can be included, perhaps with more accuracy than the tales actually referred to by Sikes, in the genre of myth which emphasises the divine origins of the human race.) These two theories, Sikes believes, continued to exist side by side, and a single poem like the Odyssey could in separate passages reflect both of them. Class-consciousness eventually produced a kind of reconciliation of the inconsistency: descent from the gods was an acceptable theory where it applied to rulers and kings, but the majority of ordinary men and women must be envisaged as having been created out of the earth. H. Lloyd-Jones (37) echoes this notion of class-distinctions, and like Sikes refers to the legend of Deucalion, in which Deucalion himself (who has his own descendants) is the son of a god, Prometheus, but creates another class of human beings by turning stones into people. For Lloyd-Jones, this is symptomatic of a comparatively humble view of mankind's place in the universe: the large nucleus of men and women have been created from

17

'inferior material'.

Sikes' theory of the different racial origins of the two sets of beliefs cannot on current evidence be either confirmed or contradicted. Perhaps however, for our present purposes, a knowledge of the precise source of a belief is not overly significant. What strikes me as being more significant is the question of the consistency of the two sets of beliefs, and this is where I would differ from both Sikes and Lloyd-Jones. There is, I believe, no contradiction between the theory of divine origin and the theory of creation from the earth, such as would necessitate the class differentiation posited by these two writers. I would suggest that both sets of myths tell the same story in that both examine the relationship between the human race and the gods on the one side, and between the human race and the animal/vegetable kingdom on the other. Both assign the human race to an intermediate status between the two: the only difference is that the angle of vision is reversed from one myth to the other. The Hesiodic myth explores the problem of how it came about that human beings ceased to be gods, why they moved downwards towards the animal kingdom; while the earth-created stories tell us that human beings came out of the ground like plants and animals (38), but rose to be something very different. In the former the accent is on descent, on the passage from a high to a more lowly status; in the latter, it is the ascent which is stressed, and the passage is from a low to a more elevated status: but in both myths the status acquired is one which is not only in-between, but which participates in the character of both extremes. This ambiguity is ensured, I believe, by the nature of the agents who bring about the passage from one state to another. In the Hesiodic myth, Prometheus and Pandora are the key figures who are instrumental in the downfall of man. Both are themselves ambiguous, for both are in one way or another deceitful, and both have within them elements of the divine and of the non-divine, though to a different degree. Prometheus is primarily a god, descended from gods, but his championship of the human race against his own kind marks him out as separate and doomed. Pandora, on the other hand, though she has been created by the gods and looks like a goddess, is made out of earth, she has human speech and strength, and a shameless mind. Between them, these two ensure that the human race shall be less than gods, but will never descend to the level of animals: Prometheus, one might say, will always pull it up again towards the gods, while Pandora will thrust it down; and so the human race hovers between the two, never quite sure in which direction it is moving.

A similar ambiguity is manifested by the agents in the story of Cadmus and the crop of armed men, to quote just one example of an earth-created story. Here, Cadmus himself and the serpent are the two intermediaries in the growth of men from the earth. Cadmus is descended from gods, ultimately from Zeus, but there are mortals too in his lineage, and there is even a hint of an animal strain in his blood, since Zeus had taken on the form of a bull and Io that of a cow when the seduction was performed which produced Cadmus' forebears. The serpent, of course, is very definitely an animal, but he is also an offspring of Ares the war-god. The crop of armed men for which these two are responsible rise up from the earth: we could say that they rise towards the level of the gods, for the gods themselves were born from the earth. But they will never reach that level, because the ambiguous nature of the two intermediaries will keep them, once more, hovering forever mid-way between earth and heaven, mid-way between animal/vegetable status and divine status (39).

My suggestion, then, is that both the 'divine origin' set of anthropogonies and the 'earth-created' set point to the intermediate and ambiguous position which the human race occupies in the universe. But the two perspectives are, it has to be admitted, very different. Can any reasons be found for either simultaneous or historical shifts in emphasis? The evidence would certainly seem to indicate that the earliest myths concentrated on the divine origins of the human race, and that those which did posit creation from the earth often referred to particular groups of people rather than the whole species. Taking up the charter myth theme, I would offer the tentative idea that when human beings were looking at themselves as members of a particular political or social group, and were asserting their claims over possible rivals, then they were more inclined to be conscious of human capacities and achievements and hence to adopt the optimistic perspective which emphasised their rise from an animal status; whereas when they were assessing themselves as members of a species, they were more disposed to be pessimistic, and to ponder on their fall from divine grace. With the passage of time and the increasing control over the environment which technical and social change brought, the self-confidence which had at first manifested itself in the charter myths became more marked: coupled with an increased knowledge of the physical resemblances between humans and animals, it produced a frame of mind more ready to accept for the whole human race a theory of origins which stressed both the original animal-like status of human beings and the ascent from that status. This would account, I believe, for the emphasis on earth-created anthropogonies which becomes discernible in the fifth century, and certainly by the end of that century it would seem that people had become self-confident enough to accept a belief which made the ascent of the human race seem an even more formidable one: the adoption of the notion that the gods had actually manufactured the first human beings out of earth suggests to me, not a lapse into slavishness, but on the contrary a terrific assertion of the human capacity for striving upwards. But it should be noted that this myth, too, leaves the human race in an intermediate position between the gods and the earth, and that before too long Prometheus was again being seen as the intermediary in this process, now raising people up instead of causing their downfall.

Finally, I wish to say something about the Orphic anthropogony, which it seems to me differs from both the mainstream sets of beliefs. The fall from a divine level, and the rise from the earth, seem to be equally stressed in this story. What we may be presented with here is a pattern whereby the human race in the course of creation has been assigned to a station which is utterly removed from that of the gods; but since in our descent from the divine no barrier (such as the eating of animals) has been interposed between us and utter bestiality, perhaps we can assume also that no corresponding barrier need be encountered in our subsequent rise from that condition towards the level of the gods. The Orphic message would thus be a more hopeful one, suggesting that we can (through Orphism, or the worship of Dionysus) regain the level of participation in divinity. Certainly the well-attested Orphic ban on sacrifice and the eating of meat (40) could be interpreted as holding out such a prospect of salvation: by renouncing the criminal blood-letting which was responsible for our original degradation, we can effect an ascent which will wipe out our inheritance of bestial wickedness.

NOTES

1. See, for example, Plutarch's Moralia 938D.
2. But the idea that the world arose out of primordial waters is to be found in both Egyptian and Babylonian creation myths: see Ancient Near Eastern Texts relating to the Old Testament (ANET), edtd. by J.B. Pritchard (Princeton 1955), p.6 and p.61. Water also has a fundamental part to play in Greek scientific accounts of the origins of life: see below, Chap. 2.
3. Fragmenta Hesiodia, edited R. Merkelbach and M.L. West (Oxford, 1967): fragment 1, lines 6-7.
4. Pausanias, 8.2.4.
5. Pindar, Olympian Odes 1. 35-51.
6. Schol. ad Apollon. Rhod. 1. 1283; Tzetzes ad Lycoph. 480.
7. Aeneid 8. 315; see also Juvenal, 6. 12.
8. See W.K.C. Guthrie, The Greeks and their Gods (London, 1950), p.62-63.
9. Fr.234 Merkelbach - West. The story is referred to also by Pindar, Ol. 9.43f.; Plato, Critias 112A and Timaeus 22A; and Aristotle, Meteor. 352A32. It is told in full by Ovid, Metamorph. 1.262-415.
10. Myths about a great flood were current in Mesopotamia as early as the third millenium BC, and from there seem to have spread to many parts of the Near East. The fact that the Greeks had their own version of this myth is generally seen as evidence for Near Eastern influence, since Greece is not of course particularly subject to flooding.
11. See Hesiod fr.205 Merkelbach - West; Ovid, Metamorph. 7. 614ff.; Strabo 8.6.16; Apollodorus 3.12.6; Pausanias 2.29.2.
12. W.K.C. Guthrie, In the beginning (London 1957), chapter 1.
13. Quoted by Pausanias, 8.1.4., in discussing the Arcadians' claim that Pelasgus was the first inhabitant of their land.
14. Aeschylus, Suppliants 250-251.
15. See Euripides, Phoin. 638ff.
16. See, for example, G.S. Kirk, The nature of Greek myths (Harmondsworth 1974), p.273.
17. Plato, Menexenus 237D-238A.
18. See Aeschylus, fr.43 (Nauck); cf. Vergil, Georgics 2.325-327.
19. Euripides, fr.488 (Nauck); cf. fr.836.
20. For the ambiguity of this explanation, see P. Pucci, Hesiod and the language of poetry (Baltimore and London 1977), p.97-98. Pandora is

herself a gift, but she has also received gifts from the Olympians, and brings terrible gifts to men.

21. M. Griffith, in The authenticity of 'Prometheus Bound' (Cambridge 1977), has put forward a convincing case for the play's being the work, not of Aeschylus, but of an unknown author of the second half of the fifth century BC.

22. fr.66 (Wehrli).
23. fr.89 (Kock).
24. fr.192.3 (Pfeiffer); cf. fr.493.
25. Lucian, To one who said 'You are a Prometheus in words' 3; cf. by the same author Prometheus 11-17 and Dialogues of the gods 5.
26. For a summary of current theories, see L.J. Alderink, 'Creation and Salvation in Ancient Orphism', American Classical Studies 8 (Chico, 1981), p.7-23; see also the most recent work, on Orphism, M.L. West's The Orphic poems (Oxford, 1983).
27. See Onomacritus, quoted by Pausanias, 8.37.3.; Diodorus Siculus 3.62; Philodemus De piet. 44; Clement of Alexandria, Exhortation to the Greeks 2.15-16; Plutarch, De esu carn. 1.996B-C. Another Orphic anthropogany emerges from the information that a golden race of mortals was created by the god Phanes, a silver one under Kronos, and a foolish one by Zeus: see fr.140-2, 225 and 233 (Kern). This version could well have been adapted from Hesiod's myth of the races: West (Orphic poems, p.68-113) believes that it came into existence in about 500BC.
28. fr.220 (Kern). It seems certain that the fifth century Neoplatonist Proclus is referring to the same story when he speaks of the punishment of the Titans and the birth from them of all mortal creatures: see fr.224.
29. See I.M. Linforth, The arts of Orpheus (Berkeley and Los Angeles, 1941), p.331-364, for references and discussion. West (Orphic poems, p.140-175) believes that the myth referred to by Olympiodorus is a relatively old one, and may have grown up in the late fifth century BC.
30. Linforth, p.358-364; West, Orphic poems, p.164-166.
31. See Nonnus, Dionys. 6.169 (fr.209, Kern). West (Orphic poems, p.154-5) thinks that the whitening of the faces with gypsum may derive from an initiation ritual. This would not rule out a connection with an earth-born theory of human origins.
32. Hesiod and the Near East (Cardiff 1966), p.55-79.
33. Greek myths, p.272-274.

34. For the Sumerian myth, see S.N. Kramer, *Sumerian Mythology* (New York, 1961), p.69-72. For the Babylonian Creation Epic, see ANET, p.68.

35. 'Sacrificial and alimentary codes in Hesiod's myth of Prometheus' in *Myth, religion and society*, edtd. R.L. Gordon (Cambridge, 1981), p.57-79: see especially p.62-3. The essay first appeared as 'Sacrifice et alimentation humaine a propos du Promethee d'Hesiode', *Annali della Scuola Normale di Pisa* 7 (1977), p.905-40. See also M. Detienne and J.-P. Vernant, *Cunning intelligence in Greek culture and society*, trans. J. Lloyd (Hassocks and Atlantic Heights, 1978), p.57-105.

36. *The anthropology of the Greeks* (London, 1914).

37. *The Justice of Zeus* (Berkeley, 1971), p.33-35.

38. The belief that animals could be born out of the ground was a widespread one, and persisted in later scientific thought in the idea of spontaneous generation: see below, p.62-65.

39. Some people will recognise here an echo of C. Levi-Strauss's theory of dioscuric pairs as mediators between two conflicting terms: see *Structural anthropology*, trans. C. Jacobson and B. Grundfest Schoepf (Harmondsworth, 1977), p.219-225. The theory, I need hardly add, is a controversial one.

40. See Plato's *Laws* 6.782C.

Chapter Two

THE THEORIES OF THE PRESOCRATIC PHILOSOPHERS

Greek anthropogonic myths can be subdivided into two broad categories: there are myths which posit a 'fall of man' situation, a demotion from an original divine status; and myths which describe on the contrary, an elevation in status, with human beings pictured as rising up from the earth. In later mythology, the emphasis was on the latter of the two categories, and the information was often added that the earth from which the human race was produced was wet, or had been 'fertilised' by rain falling from the sky. By the fifth century, these two ingredients, earth and water, were beginning to be recognised by the myths as being of fundamental importance. But by this time, philosophical speculation about the origins of the human race was also well under way, and here too the interaction between dry and moist elements features very prominently.

The credit for being the founding father of Greek philosophy generally goes to Thales, who is the first in the series of sixth and fifth century BC thinkers who are known collectively as the Presocratic philosophers. Thales came from Miletus in that part of Asiatic Greece known as Ionia, and was active in the early years of the sixth century BC. Greek philosophy, then, is often said to have 'started' soon after 600BC. But the transition from mythological to philosophical explanations of the world is far from being a straightforward one. Much debate in this century has centred on the question of what this transformation involved: what were the differences between mythological and philosophical modes of thought, and what differences in the way the world was perceived did these modes of thought produce? Somewhat less frequently, the even more hazardous problem of what brought about these changes has also been raised.

Opinions on these subjects have altered a great deal since Burnet in 1892 depicted Presocratic scientific philosophy as a radical breakthrough, whereby rational thought for the first time in history was applied to the problem of how the world worked. For Burnet, there were no links of any significance between mythological and philosophical answers to this problem. Philosophy for him was a new and distinctive phenomenon, which had its roots in superior Greek rationality. (1) Few scholars today would be prepared to be as dogmatic as Burnet on this subject. It is recognised by many people nowadays that there is continuity of one degree or another between myth and philosophy. The real turning point for this recognition came with the work of F.M. Cornford, who attributed to Greek mythology a higher level of rationality than had previously been conceded, while at the same time denying the absolute rationality of early philosophical speculation. Many of the a *priori* assumptions of mythological cosmogonies were, he believed, taken over without question by the first Presocratics, who reproduced in their theories of world origins the processes of differentiation and recombination pictured in myth. This is not to say that early philosophy had not advanced along the road of rationalisation - to see the formation of the world as a natural rather than a supernatural event was a remarkable achievement. But it could not be called truly scientific, since it was far from employing the empirical methods of observation and experimentation which science demands. (2)

Numerous other interpretations have been produced since Cornford first put forward these startling views. The similarities between mythological and Presocratic cosmogonies are now hard to deny, but many would say that Cornford, in countering Burnet's thesis, succeeded in throwing the baby out with the bathwater. A rescue operation has been performed on Presocratic science, and most scholars today would argue that it does embody certain significant developments in rational thought.

Precisely what these developments are will probably never be agreed. But one of the more uncontentious points is that philosophy, in shedding the anthropomorphic features of the mythological cosmogonies, shook off the habit of seeing the parts of the world as supernatural powers, and instead began to conceive of them as physical entities possessing comprehensible physical qualities. To many, the methodology behind this development is of even greater significance. The cherished and unassailable dogma preserved in the myths of a traditional oral society was now replaced by open and frank speculation, which proceeded on the basis of critical discussion of foregoing theories. The need to argue hypotheses and back them up with evidence suggests a link with current political developments, with the transition from aristocratic to more democratic forms of rule, and the growing habit of political debate which this entailed. On the nature of the evidence which the Presocratics employed, not all would agree: but some scholars at least maintain, contrary to Cornford, that they did make use of sensory observation, in the testing if not in the formation of their hypotheses. (3)

It is important, I believe, that an examination of Presocratic anthropogonies should take place in the context of this debate about the transition from myth to philosophy. Not that we can expect a light of any great intensity to be thrown on the subject by our study of this particular branch of Presocratic thought - especially since in this area the evidence is even more fragmentary than usual. But as the connections with myth seem particularly strong where the anthropogonies are concerned, it will be as well to bear in mind the main tenor of the discussion.

As far as Thales' cosmology is concerned, we really have only two pieces of information to go on: that he believed the primary substance of the world to be water; and that he thought that the earth rested on water. (4) From this, we might hazard a guess that Thales saw human life as having developed originally out of water; and a further guess, that he was influenced in these beliefs by Homer's references to Oceanus. But they would be guesses, and probably not worth discussing any further. About Anaximander, who was also operating in Miletus in the first half of the sixth century and who was said to have been Thales' pupil, we know a great deal more, since he left works which seem to have survived at least until the time of Theophrastus. He is the first Greek philosopher about whose description of the origins of the world we can begin to form a coherent idea, and our examination of Presocratic anthropogonies starts therefore with him.

ANAXIMANDER

Like Thales, Anaximander thought that the world was derived from a single material principle, but he probably differed from Thales in that he made no attempt to define this principle. For him, it seems, the original state of matter was an undifferentiated mass of infinite (or at least enormous) extent, which he called the apeiron or 'the unlimited'. In this primal mass no separate component parts or elements were at first distinguished. But gradually the world as we know it emerged from the mass, by a process which it is next-to-impossible to recover from our sources, but which seems to have involved the progressive differentiation of inherently hostile opposites – the hot and the cold, the wet and the dry. First of all, a sphere of flame ('the hot') was formed which enclosed the nascent world like the bark of a tree; inside it were the air and, at the very centre, the earth (both, one can presume, representing 'the cold'). Next, the ball of flame around the world burst apart into circles of fire, each of which constitutes one of the heavenly planets: they are visible to us only at certain points because of the air or mist in between, which has 'breathing-holes' in it through which the heavenly bodies can be seen. The final stage in the process came with the differentiation of 'the wet' and 'the dry'. The heat of the sun slowly dried up the water with which the earth had originally been mixed, leaving large wet patches which formed the seas. (5)

Our sources nowhere inform us that the first living creatures came into existence when this drying-out process had just begun, and the earth was still substantially mixed with water. But in view of the consistency with which they tell us that the first animals were all born in water, it seems more than likely that this was the case. And with this original dampness is linked one of the most bizarre aspects of Anaximander's theories. Here are two of the relevant quotations:

> Anaximander of Miletus believed that there arose from heated water and earth either fish or creatures very like fish: in these men grew up, and the embryos were retained inside them until puberty; then at last the creatures burst, and men and women who were already able to nourish themselves stepped forth.
> (Censorinus De die nat. 4.7).

> Again, (Anaximander) says that in the beginning man was born from creatures of a different kind, because other creatures soon become self-

supporting, but man alone needs a long period of nursing: hence he would not have survived if he had been like that right from the beginning.
(Ps.-Plutarch Strom.2).

Comparison has, of course, often been made between this idea of the fishy origins of the human race and the Darwinian theory of evolution. It need hardly be said that we cannot impute to Anaximander a fully worked-out evolutionary theory. Indeed, there is probably no evolution there at all, if by that word we mean a process of biological transformation. The passage from Ps.-Plutarch quoted above does, indeed, seem to suggest that human beings originally possessed a different biological form, and this idea is put over rather more forcibly by a statement in Hippolytus (Ref.1.6.6.) that 'man in the beginning came into existence resembling another creature, that is a fish.' But the Censorinus passage seems to state quite clearly that human beings have always had the same biological identity as they have now, and that what we must envisage for the first humans is rather a prolonged embryonic existence, with fully recognisable people emerging during the life-cycle of individuals of the first generation. Such a conclusion is supported by a passage from Plutarch (Symp.8.730E) which ascribes to Anaximander the belief that 'men originally came into being inside fishes.' The more graphic detail supplied by Censorinus and Plutarch suggests that they may have been closer than Hippolytus and Ps.-Plutarch to what Anaximander originally wrote. And a reference in Aetius to the generation of other animal species makes Censorinus' and Plutarch's interpretation seem the more likely one. Aetius (5.19.4) tells us that according to Anaximander 'the first animals were born in moisture, surrounded by prickly barks': barks seem much more like a protective covering than a prior biological form, and if we can assume that humans and other animal species came into existence by a similar process, we can probably assert that Anaximander was quite innocent of any notion of biological transformation giving rise to new species. (6) (Although it should perhaps not be forgotten that Ps.Plutarch and Hippolytus were evidently not innocent of this notion, wherever they thought they got it from.)

Nevertheless, there are, I believe, some notable points of comparison between the Anaximandrian and Darwinian theories. Anaximander does not have the idea of survival of the fittest, in that the passages betray no suggestion that he may have posited the destruction of ill-equipped species. But he certainly was able to conceptualise such a process - he certainly knew that unfit species, if they had existed, would have been wiped out, and was able to draw from that concept and from his observation of the survival of a manifestly unfit species - the human race - the conclusion that human beings must have developed rather differently in the past than they do now.

We cannot be sure that Anaximander described the original generation of animals as taking place when the earth was still covered with water but was just beginning to dry out. But two expressions in particular used by our sources made this seem very probable: Aetius says that after a period of development inside the barks the first animals 'came out on to the drier part'; and Hippolytus tells us that 'living creatures came into being from moisture evaporated by the sun'. If we are right in our assumption, then we can easily see why Anaximander lighted on fishes as the creatures who would nurture inadequate human infants: even grown-ups would not have survived in a world that was mainly sea. And this suggests another tentative anticipation of Darwin. Anaximander must have realised, not just that the first human babies would have required protection and feeding, but that human beings of any age were less well-equipped physically than any other creature to cope with large-scale environmental changes. The close links which Darwin perceived between human biology and the physical environment are foreshadowed, then, in Anaximander.

But there is, of course, a major difference. Darwin saw that the success of biological transformation was determined by adaptation to a changing environment. Anaximander does not ignore adaptation, but he makes it work backwards. He can tell us quite clearly why human beings must once have been contained within fishes, but he does not explain why they should ever have developed a separate and independent existence. One might seek about for causes of this change, but this, I think, would be to distort the pattern of his thought. For him the human race is an inevitability, an end-product whose existence is predetermined by its cosily cushioned beginnings.

This brings us to the question of Anaximander's methodology. We have to accept, I think, Cornford's statement that in constructing his anthropogony Anaximander was employing certain a priori premises about the generative power of natural substances. (7) But it would not be true to say that he made no use at all of empirical reasoning. In forming his hypothesis, he certainly put to use his observation that the young of the human species need more nursing than the young of any other animal species. And in choosing fish as the nurses, while he was doubtless guided in the main by his concept of the watery state of the universe, he may well have believed that he had some corroborative evidence: the Plutarch passage makes a comparison between the nurturing of humans inside fishes and the way in which sharks behave; and Anaximander may well have known (as Aristotle some two hundred years later did (8)) that there is one species of shark where the young, once hatched from eggs, are carried around in the mother's body until they are able to look after themselves. What is important about Anaximander's hypothesis is not the <u>value</u> of the empirical evidence which he used to back it up, but rather the fact that he felt he had to use evidence at all. This does indeed seem to mark a significant transition from dogma to argued theory.

The kind of world which Anaximander envisaged when describing the first appearance of animal life was probably one where the sea covered the earth, and there was a layer of slime at the bottom of the sea. As the heat of the sun acted on the sea and began to dry it up, animal life (protected by thorny barks or, in the case of humans and perhaps at a later stage, by fish-like creatures) emerged from the slime. This is a supposition, but it is supported by the evidence of later theories, and by the fact that three of our sources mention moisture or water, one mentions earth and two refer to the action of heat. The formation of animal life is seen, then, as part and parcel of the cosmological process: just as the heat of the sun effects a separation of land and sea, so it effects also a separation of organic life from the inorganic matter which contains it. And as more and more of the sea dries up (9), so some animals are translated from a marine to a dry-land existence.

An astute comparison has been made by Cornford between the whole of Anaximander's cosmogony, and the semi-mythical cosmogony enshrined in <u>Hesiod's Theogony</u>. (10) In <u>Hesiod's</u> story, it is only after Sky has been separated from Earth that the world can come into existence and the gods can be born. Similarly, for Anaximander the world came into being through a process of gradual separation of elemental masses, and one of the effects of this separation was almost certainly the birth of animal life. Obviously, there is at least one important difference between the two cosmogonies: according to Cornford, it was because Anaximander had no use in his system for the personal gods that he substituted for their creation the creation of humans and animals.

But the substitution is a vital one, and cannot, I think, be explained away quite so easily. It is part and parcel of a more fundamental difference between the two accounts, that is, the transition from a supernatural to a natural explanation of the origins of the world. Separation and interaction certainly have a role to play in both: but for Hesiod the parts of the world are not just divine, they are also possessed of a mind and are capable of making decisions and acting in a purposeful way; whereas for Anaximander they are natural substances, and possess physical properties which respond to certain ascertainable natural laws. A similar distinction emerges from the way in which the two accounts handle the origins of the human race. In Hesiod's Theogony, the human race is separated off from the race of gods as a result of the wilful actions of certain deities; whereas in Anaximander, it is a by-product of the interaction of natural substances. In Hesiod, one might say, human beings (as ex-gods) suffer a diminution of mental powers: in Anaximander (as compounds of water and earth), they make incomparable gains. Indeed, one of the problems posed by Anaximander's anthropogony (and one which as far as we know he did not attempt to solve) is how rational beings could have been created out of inorganic and mindless matter. Mythology encountered no such difficulty, because it saw the whole world as being rational and purposeful: Anaximander, by translating human origins to the level of a natural process, may have cut himself off from any such solution. (11)

The natural substances mentioned by our sources for Anaximander's anthropogony are water and earth, and the agent in their interaction is the heat of the sun. This reminded Cornford of the union of Sky and Earth recounted by Hesiod; but perhaps a more significant mythological parallel is to be found in the stories of human beings created out of mixtures of earth and water. In Hesiod, the first woman, Pandora, is created in this way, and the deity who performs the task is Hephaistos, the god of fire. Later myths envisage the same origin for the whole human race, and make Prometheus, who brought fire down to earth, the agent in the process. One cannot say for sure that Anaximander has been influenced by this trend in mythological thought, since as far as the Prometheus myth is concerned it appears to be later in origin than Anaximander himself. What one can say, I think, is that the optimistic perspective adopted by later myth is present also in Anaximander. In the first chapter I have suggested that myth presented two views of how the human race acquired its existing status; and that the one which propounded an elevation from a vegetable- or animal-like condition became more acceptable as time went on. Anaximander's anthropogony, I believe, demonstrates a similar access of confidence: it is prepared to countenance a process whereby human life has the same origins as animal life, and comes out of inorganic matter; and it is prepared to countenance this because it recognises that such an origin is no slur, but is rather a proclamation of the human capacity for advancement.

Mythology and early philosophy, then, were probably both affected by a change in attitude towards the human condition. But still there are differences. The myths I have mentioned make use of inorganic materials, but the agent in the creation of the human race remains a divine and purposeful one. Anaximander, in substituting the action of heat for the figure of Hephaistos or Prometheus, is not just de-personifying myth; he is removing human biology from the domain of supernatural and unpredictable powers, and placing it within the orbit of natural processes. He offers us a much fuller statement of human advancement than mythology can achieve, because he tells us that our status as rational and thinking creatures has been acquired independently of any conscious and controlling agent.

The idea, then, that human life arose out of heated water and earth was one that Anaximander had in common with mythology, though with certain fundamental differences. It was also one that was to become standard in Presocratic thought, as we shall see.

XENOPHANES

Like Thales and Anaximander, Xenophanes was born in Ionia, in Asiatic Greece, but left there around the middle of the sixth century BC and thereafter led a wandering life. In other ways more fundamental than this, he seems to have differed sharply from his Milesian predecessors, most strikingly in the area of theology. Anaximander's system has little room in it for the gods, and none of the surviving fragments reveal that he had any great interest in questions of divinity. Xenophanes, on the contrary, seems to have meditated on the subject most profoundly. His observation that men make gods in their own image, and that animals would do the same if they were physically capable of it ('Ethiopians say that their gods are snub-nosed and black, the Thracians that theirs have light blue eyes and red hair'; 'But if cattle and horses or lions had hands or were able to draw with their hands ... horses would draw the forms of gods like horses, and cattle like cattle.' DK B16 and B15) demonstrates both a remarkable insight into the relativism of much religious belief, and a very early exploitation of comparative anthropology. In place of anthropomorphic gods, Xenophanes himself seems to have posited a single motionless deity, which he identified in some way with the matter of the universe. But whatever its theistic component may have been, Xenophanes seems to have produced a cosmogony which in some ways was very similar to Anaximander's. He believed that 'everything was long ago covered in mud'. Since then, the earth has obviously dried out, but the process is a cyclic one, and the earth is at present being dissolved once more by the sea. Periodically, in fact, it is reduced entirely to mud, and when that happens the whole human race is destroyed but is subsequently recreated. This theory differs from Anaximander's in at least one respect, since the latter believed that the earth in his own day was drying up, not getting wetter. But Xenophanes' cycle must have included a similar 'drying out' phase, and Anaximander's own theory <u>may</u> have been a cyclical one. (12)

Xenophanes produced some remarkable evidence to show that the earth had once been mixed with water but had since dried out and hardened: 'shells are found inland and in the mountains, and in the quarries of Syracuse he says that an impression of a fish and of seaweed has been found; again in Paros the impression of a bay-leaf has been found in the depth of the rock, and in Malta flattened shapes of all kinds of marine creatures.' (13) Like Anaximander, then, Xenophanes believed that he had to use argument to back up his theory; like Anaximander, he drew his arguments from observable phenomena - and in his case, phenomena of an unusual kind, whose understanding would require a degree of research and of sophisticated reasoning. Using the information he had obtained about fossils, he provided the evidence which (so far as we know) was lacking in Anaximander for the original muddy condition of the earth.

It was from this primeval mixture of earth and sea that Xenophanes believed, along with Anaximander, that human life first emerged. 'For we all came forth from earth and water'. (DK B33). Present again are the two vital inorganic ingredients which made their first appearance in mythology and which Anaximander had taken over and elevated into the realms of natural science. No reference to the action of heat on these substances can be culled from the scanty fragments of Xenophanes, but in view of his belief in the drying out of the earth, he may well have seen this as an important factor.

THE PYTHAGOREAN PHILOSOPHERS

The brotherhood founded in Southern Italy by Pythagoras in the latter years of the 6th century BC must have been very different from the philosophical school which had grown up in Asiatic Miletus. In the latter, we may imagine, a tradition of scientific naturalism had been established, whose methodology laid emphasis on criticism and debate. The doctrines of the Pythagorean brotherhood, on the other hand, combined a devotion to the principles of mathematical order with a religious mysticism whose tenets included a belief in the transmigration of souls; and the emotional response which Pythagoras evoked among his followers ensured that any later elaboration or alteration of his teachings could only gain acceptance by being ascribed to the master himself. Consequently, it is generally very difficult to differentiate the thought of Pythagoras from the thought of later members of the brotherhood; and the thoughts in any case are not always easy to understand.

However, one thing that seems certain is that the fifth century Pythagoreans, at least, were interested not so much in the matter of the universe as in its structure: as Aristotle says, 'they have therefore made no mention of fire or earth or of other bodies of this sort ...' (<u>Met</u>. 990 A17). For them the universe was the product of number and the principles of number; and by this they seem to have meant, not simply that structural change in the universe was expressible in abstract numerical terms, but that numbers were actually capable of generation, and brought the sensible world into existence. The notion is a vague one (at any rate, in our sources) and its significance need not be

The Theories of the Presocratic Philosophers

discussed here (14): enough has been said, I hope, to make it appear unlikely that the Pythagoreans would have had anything much to say about the material origins of the human race. And so it strikes us as odd that one of the many taboos attributed to Pythagoras, a stricture against the eating of beans on account of some mysterious affinity with humankind, should be explained by Porphyry in the 3rd century AD as follows:

> ... when the first origin and birth of all things was in confusion, and many things were at the same time mingled together, sown together, and rolled together in the earth, birth and separation gradually took place, animals being born and plants growing up at the same time. Then from the same putrefaction men were born and beans sprouted.
> (<u>Life of Pythagoras</u> 44) (15).

Here we seem to be on familiar Ionian territory, with the newly-created earth, when it was still mingled with other elements and hence in a soggy condition, giving birth by a gradual process of separation to plants and animals. In view of what Aristotle has said about the Pythagoreans' lack of interest in the material composition of the world, it seems surprising that the master should have described the origins of human life in these terms. Pythagoras was possibly more of a materialist than his fifth-century successors; though it is not altogether easy to see how he would have reconciled this theory of original generation with the belief in the immortality of the human soul, which <u>can</u> be attributed to him with some certainty. At any rate, Porphyry is a late source, and far from reliable: the problem is probably not worth a great deal of consideration.

EMPEDOCLES

One of the most striking practitioners of early Greek philosophy was Empedocles, who came from Acragas in Sicily, and was active around the middle of the fifth century BC. Many fanciful tales grew up in ancient times about his life and death, and he was credited with a wide range of vocations - including those of politician, prophet, doctor and orator. On the basis of the fragments of his work which survive, we are certainly able to say that he embraced within his complex personality the attributes of poet, philosopher and religious mystic.

All of the extant fragments come from two long hexameter poems, called On Nature and Purifications. As far as we can tell, the former was a scientific work which sought to explain in materialistic terms the physical workings of the universe; while the latter had all the appearance of a religious tract, and espoused with visionary fervour the doctrine of the transmigration of souls, and the vegetarianism with which it is often associated. One immediate Empedoclean problem, therefore, is the relationship between these two widely differing works, which many critics have seen as inconsistent and irreconcilable. (16) This problem has no immediate bearing on the anthropogony, and fortunately need not detain us here.

In his scientific treatise, Empedocles was seeking to provide an answer to the contentions of a recent thinker, Parmenides of Elea. Parmenides had thrown an almighty spanner into the works of Ionian natural science by resorting to logic in order to prove that movement and change are impossibilities, and that for this reason the world and all its multifarious phenomena do not in fact exist. For him, reality consisted of a single, uncreated, unchanging and indestructible entity which he called Being. (17) One of Empedocles' objects, then, was to rescue the world of the phenomena while at the same time taking account of Parmenides' critique. This he did by delineating a system which embraced within it the existence of both the One and the Many. This system puts forward as the ultimate realities of the universe four material 'roots', earth, water, fire and air (called 'elements' by Aristotle and subsequent writers); and two controlling forces, Love and Strife, which have the power to combine or separate the elements. The phenomena which our senses perceive come into existence through the mingling together of the elements, and are destroyed through their dispersal: change is continual, but, in that the process of change is constant and repetitive, there is an overall metaphysical stability and permanence.

This much is relatively uncontroversial. But the precise nature of the operations of Love and Strife, and of the cyclical pattern which they give rise to, is the subject of much debate, and this is where the second major Empedoclean problem lies. Since the question of the anthropogony is closely linked to the larger question of the cosmic cycle, a summary of the controversy must be attempted. The various interpretations can be grouped together under two main headings. According to the one which up until the 1960s was thoroughly orthodox, and which still attracts authoritative support, the cyclical development of the world involves four stages: (1) Love gradually gains ascendancy over Strife, and under its influence all the elements are increasingly mingled, until (2) Love is in complete control, and the whole universe consists of a sphere in which the elements are indistinguishably fused together; then (3) Strife gradually ousts Love and disrupts the sphere by separating the elements; until (4) Strife is in complete control, and the elements are all separate. This can be labelled the 'two-world system', since at stages (1) and (3) a world like ours comes into existence and is then destroyed: we ourselves are living during the phase in the cycle when Strife is in the ascendancy. (18)

In the last twenty years, a number of scholars have produced interpretations which challenge this orthodox one. There are many differences between them, but what they share is a belief in a 'single-world system' involving an endlessly repeated cycle of 3 stages: (1) the sphere is shattered by Strife and the elements are separated; whereupon (2) Love gradually gains mastery over Strife and mingles the elements together; until (3) the sphere is reconstituted. Our world comes into being at stage (2); it is a world in which Strife and Love are both operational, with the basic cosmology being (to one degree or another) the product of Strife's powers of separation, while Love's combinatory powers give rise to the lesser phenomena. (19)

It is impossible in a work of this kind to review the mass of evidence and argument which has been produced to back up these two alternative interpretations. And to do so would lead, I am afraid, to no serious conclusions on my part; for I must confess at this point that I find myself incapable of deciding between the two. The fragments, it seems to me, could bear either meaning (and possibly others as well): their wording, ripped out of its framework, is arcane and elastic, and the comments of the doxographers can similarly be twisted to suit one's predilections. We shall probably never know the truth about Empedocles' cosmic cycle. This is a pity, particularly in the present context, since the zoogony is closely linked to the cosmogony. It appears, on the available evidence, to be an interesting one, but its parts cannot, with any confidence, be fitted together into a coherent whole. Still, we must review those parts, and get from them what we can, and perhaps consider whether they throw any light on the cosmic cycle.

The most complete account of the zoogony is given by Aetius, writing in the first or second century AD. He tells us that according to Empedocles:

> the first generations of animals and plants were in no way complete, but consisted of limbs which were not joined together; the second appeared when the limbs were joined together, and were like fantasy creatures; the third were the generations of the whole-natured forms; the fourth were born no longer from homogeneous substances like earth and water, but now from each other, in some cases through 'the condensation of their nourishment, in others because feminine beauty caused the excitement of the sexual urge. The distinctions between the various species of animals were the result of the nature of the mixture ... (5.19.5)

Aetius here gives no indication of the stage or stages in the cosmic cycle at which these creatures were generated; but an innocent reader might naturally assume that he is referring to phases in animal development which followed on from each other, and which perhaps occurred early on in the world's history. Supporters of the 'two-world system', however, have been forced (drawing on the evidence of other fragments which will be discussed shortly) to adopt a two-fold generation of living creatures to fit in with their two worlds. Again, there are many differences of detail; but a broad division exists where this interpretation is concerned between two principal views. Some scholars believe that the generation of separate limbs and their coming together as monsters took place in the world created when Love was in the ascendancy; while whole-natured forms and regular men and women were the product of the world increasingly dominated by Strife. (20) Others think that all four phases of creation occurred in each of the two worlds, although in the world under Strife they happened in reverse order (finishing up with separate limbs). (21) The 'single-world system' on the other hand involves no such problems. Adherents of this interpretation have no alternative but to locate all four phases of generation in the world that takes shape under the growing influence of Love. Each phase in this case represents a higher degree of elemental mixture, with the creatures produced by sexual intercourse standing in this respect at the top of the evolutionary tree.

Separate evidence for each of the first three of the four stages listed by Aetius is provided by the fragments. That Empedocles believed in the fourth stage can, one assumes, be taken for granted; though how and when sexual reproduction came into being is another matter.

First stage: separate limbs

'Here many heads without necks sprang up, bare arms wandered about without shoulders, eyes roamed by themselves in need of foreheads' (DK B57).

Aristotle and Simplicius make it quite clear that the generation of these separate limbs took place 'under Love'. (22) From Aristotle we learn also that the limbs were produced out of a mixture of elements, and were composed of bones and flesh, so were certainly not unlike the conventional limbs with which we are familiar. (23)

The same process is probably referred to in a number of other fragments, from which we glean the additional information that it was the mingling together in the earth of certain proportions of water and fire which caused the limbs to grow. See, for example, fragment 96 - 'And the grateful earth received in its broad melting-pots two parts out of the eight of shining Nestis, and four of Hephaistos. And they became white bones, wonderfully joined together by the glueing of Harmonia.' - where Harmonia stands as a symbol of Love, and water and fire are personified as Nestis and Hephaistos. (24)

This process, we may imagine, took place in the early stages of Love's ascendancy, when she was just embarking on her long-term mixing project, and was beginning to get to work on the cosmic masses - earth, sky, planets etc. - created by Strife. We know from another fragment that water was mixed with earth through the medium of rainfall; whether Empedocles had a similar naturalistic explanation for the addition of fire to the mixture, it is impossible to say, but lightning could have been the answer.

The limbs which were manufactured in this way presumably came into being within the earth. There are similarities here with Anaximander's theory - for him too, animal life first emerged from the earth, and was the product of an interaction between earth,

39

water and fire. But in fact the process envisaged by Empedocles appears to be the reverse of the one envisaged by Anaximander. For the latter, it was the separation of previously intermingled elemental stuffs which gave rise to animal life - animals can thus be seen as among the last vestiges of a vast cosmic mixture. Empedocles, on the other hand, sees animals as the product of a coming together of separate elements derived from different parts of the cosmos - and thus approaches the mythical notion of a union between Earth and Sky. And for him these animals are the precursors of a cosmic fusion which is to come.

There are no fragments which allude to the creation of separate limbs under Strife. (25) It is not impossible to imagine how Empedocles might have envisaged such a process - it could have been similar to the one outlined by Anaximander - but since there are no references to it, it seems bootless to invent it. From this we can surmise, either that separate limbs were not part of animal development in the world under Strife (as most 'two-worlders' do), or that there was no world at all under Strife (which is to be a 'one-worlder').

Second stage:
the coming together of the separate limbs
Aristotle says of the much-quoted 'neckless heads' that they were later on joined together in the earth by Love. (26) That these wandering limbs sometimes combined in such a way as to produce the fantasy creatures referred to by Aetius at the second stage is confirmed by Simplicius, who tells us that the separate heads, hands and feet created under Love came together to form monsters that were half-man and half-ox. (27) Empedocles was clearly notorious for these creatures - Aristotle mentions them, too, and Aelian supplies a more extended quotation:

> many creatures were produced with a face and breast on both sides; there sprang up man-faced animals of the ox-family, and on the other hand creatures that were basically men with ox heads; there were creatures made up partly of male and partly of female attributes, fitted with shadowy parts. (DK B61)

But did the separate limbs always combine to form unviable monsters? Or were more conventional creatures sometimes produced? According to Censorinus, human beings were created through the joining together of limbs from the earth (4.8). And Simplicius, when discussing the 'man-faced animals of the ox-family', adds the information that 'as many of these parts as were fitted together in such a way as to be able by chance to ensure their preservation, these became animals and survived' (28). Sometimes, it seems, the law of averages saw to it that chance combinations were productive of viable animals (including humans).

Support for this interpretation can perhaps be derived from the basic Aetius passage. Aetius seems at first to be describing four successive stages of animal generation, each producing a different kind of creature, and culminating in regular animals. But when we reach the fourth stage, we find him describing the method of generation (sexual reproduction) rather than its end-product - he omits completely to tell us that regular animals now appeared for the first time. Can we assume therefore that they have been appearing all along the line (except at the first stage, where generation, as Aetius tells us, was not complete)? And that Aetius has been outlining successive methods of generating regular animals, rather than successive kinds of animals? Thus, animals would have been created first from separate limbs, then from the 'whole-natured forms', and finally from sexual reproduction. If this was the scheme outlined by Empedocles, then it must be admitted that Aetius has not made it terribly clear. But that regular animals appeared at least at the second stage seems to be born out by Censorinus and Simplicius.

As with separate limbs, so with the monsters, our sources all refer to creation under Love; none suggest that they were created under Strife. But do we have any information as to when this might have taken place - was it in our world, or in some other? Nothing direct, but it is hard to escape the conclusion that Empedocles was here seeking to provide a scientific explanation of the composite creatures like minotaurs, centaurs, and so on, which featured so heavily in mythology. And surely he must have believed that it was in an earlier epoch of his own world that these miraculous beasts had appeared: for no folk memory could possibly have been preserved of them if they had inhabited a world which had been utterly obliterated by the formation of the sphere. (29)

So far, so good. A credible account of how animal life might have been generated in a world increasingly controlled by Love seems to be emerging.

41

As Love gradually extended her mixing activities, she first of all produced separate limbs, and then joined them together in random fashion: sometimes monsters were created, sometimes creatures capable of survival. And surely, we are tempted to say, it was under Love that these viable creatures began to reproduce themselves by sexual intercourse. So a pattern emerges whereby Love mixes first the elements, then the limbs, and finally the sexes. And if I am right in assigning the monsters to our world, then we have to assume that ours is the world increasingly dominated by Love. As far as the zoogony up to this point is concerned, we know of no world under Strife.

Aetius' first, second and fourth stages can all be accounted for in this hypothetical reconstruction. But it is the third stage which must give us pause.

Third stage: the 'whole-natured forms'

More information about the mysterious 'whole-natured forms', located by Aetius at the third stage of generation, is provided by fragment 62:

> Come now, hear how fire, as it was separated, drew up the night-born shoots of men and tearful women; for this is a story which is neither irrelevant nor fanciful. First there sprang up from the earth whole-natured forms, having a share of both water and heat. These the fire sent up, desiring to reach its like. They displayed as yet neither the lovely form of the limbs, nor the voice, which is the organ proper to men.

These creatures, though lacking limbs and language, are nevertheless called whole-natured - perhaps because in spite of being shapeless lumps they were organic and viable wholes (rather like embryos). That they were destined at some stage to develop into men and women is unmistakably implied by the first part of the fragment - which tends to confirm the suggestion already made that Aetius is talking about methods of generation, rather than creatures generated.

When we come to consider the process by which the 'whole-natured forms' were produced, it is difficult to avoid a comparison with Anaximander. Like the latter's earliest animals, the 'whole-natured forms' had earth, water and heat in their make-up, and were drawn out of the ground by the attraction of external fire. Anaximander almost certainly placed his zoogony in a period when the world was still coming into existence though a process of separation. And Empedocles too speaks of 'fire as it was separated'. It is hard to believe that we are not seeing here a picture of a cosmos being formed through the separation of the elements - which as far as Empedocles is concerned is a cosmos under the influence of Strife. This seems to be borne out by the reference to 'night-born shoots': at this time the sun would not have been fully fashioned because fire was still leaving the earth to join it.

And so the 'two-worlders' assign the 'whole-natured forms' and the men and women who succeed them to the world that comes into being under the increasing dominance of Strife. Love was still active in the early stages of this world and was responsible for the residual mixture of elements still present in the earth; but Strife was gaining ground, and as it did so the harmonious creatures born from the earth gave way to human beings distinguished by sex and forced to resort to copulation in order to reproduce themselves. Not a consummation devoutly to be wished - as the tearful women will testify.

What can a 'one-worlder' say in answer to this? That 'whole-natured forms', like separate limbs, were produced in a world where Love was beginning to mingle together the elements; but that fire was rebellious and under Strife's influence was still trying to keep itself separate and join the main body of fire in the heavens. Or that in trying to join its like, fire was not necessarily obeying the commands of Strife: such an impulse could easily be the work of Love and the separation caused by that impulse was not after all a separation of elements - for fire carried with it portions of earth and water, and this indeed was the essence of the creative process. (30) The men and women produced as a result were an improvement on the 'whole-natured forms', for they had limbs that were lovely and language that was their hallmark. In any case, we should not necessarily see psychological or aesthetic improvement as one of Love's achievements - as any 'two-worlder' who thinks that monsters are a manifestation of Love's growing power would have to admit. (31)

And so it could be. The pattern of animal generation in the one world ruled by Love would then embrace: separate limbs, coming together to form mostly monsters, but occasionally viable animals;

whole-natured forms, which in some way or other gradually transform themselves into men and women (and probably other animals); and finally sexual reproduction. No-one to my knowledge has come up with an explanation of the supposed physical basis for these developments; or with an insight into why Empedocles should have wanted the 'whole-natured forms', when he had already accounted for regular animals in another way. Perhaps he thought that regular animals generated from 'whole-natured forms' had a better chance of survival, being more numerous. But I must confess, along with Solmsen, that fragment 62 still carries with it for me a lingering suggestion of two worlds.

All this has been said at great length and the conclusions are far from definite. Most of the evidence which we possess for Empedocles' zoogony points to the creative power of Love. Only fragment 62 carries any very definite suggestion of an animal kingdom produced by the operations of Strife: if we could happily dismiss it, then we could with more confidence deny the existence of animals under Strife, and so call into question the existence of any world at all under Strife which could properly be called such. But fragment 62 is not easily subdued and must leave some doubt in most people's minds.

Leaving aside at last the question of Empedocles' dubious cosmology, what else do we learn from what we can piece together of the zoogony? Certainly that Empedocles had a remarkable mind and was responsible for some new and striking insights into the subject of animal origins, including very probably a recognition of the part played in animal development by the survival of the fittest, which will be discussed in a later chapter. (32) But what are perhaps more noticeable are the numerous similarities between Empedocles' theory and those of earlier Ionian thinkers, in particular Anaximander. In Empedocles, we find the same naturalistic approach to the origins of the human race.

The original mode of generation outlined by him was precisely the same for human beings as it was for other animals - indeed humans are scarcely distinguished from animals in Empedocles' thought, and so close are the physical links between them that a mixture of species is seen as by no means impossible. The relationship between living beings and the physical environment is also stressed, and the creation of animals is·directly related to large-scale changes taking place in the cosmos as a whole, changes brought about by the action of forces which Empedocles chooses to call Love and Strife, but which seem to be mechanical in operation. Inorganic substances - water and earth - are seen as the source of organic life, and the process of creation, involving the action of heat, is natural and non-purposeful. And emphasis is placed on the gradualness of animal development - human beings and other animals are subject to biological change, and did not spring fully-formed from the hand of some divinity.

All in all, what we derive from Empedocles' anthropogony, as from Anaximander's, is surely a sense of the rise of the human race. Born from the ground, indistinguishable from other animals, cobbled together out of spare parts or articulated out of shapeless lumps, we are unable to point to anything in our origins which destines us for technological or intellectual accomplishments. It is to the animals-we-once-were rather than to the gods-we-once-were, that Empedocles wants to direct our thoughts in this account; and viewed from this perspective, our current status seems to have been achieved through ascent. Indeed, if Schofield is correct (33), and the almost equal mixture of elements in our blood heralds the perfect mixture of elements in the sphere, then we are in our intellects (located in the blood) the precursors of the one perfect and divine thinker. We were once animals, we are on our way to being divine - this is one of the messages which could be derived from what survives of Empedocles' poem <u>On Nature</u>.

Of course, we have lost a lot of that poem, and 'two-worlders' would certainly say that for human beings in our own day and age (as opposed to the ones created under Love) the reverse message was being trumpeted. And whether you believe in one world or two, you have to accept that in a cyclical theory there are always two ways of looking at things. If we are on our way to being divine, then we are also on our way to a fall from divinity. This, I believe, is the perspective which receives most of the emphasis in the other poem, <u>The Purifications</u>, of which more later.

ANAXAGORAS

One of the most brilliant of fifth century thinkers, Anaxagoras was born in Clazomenae in Asiatic Greece, but spent most of his active life in Athens, and more than anyone else was probably responsible for importing Ionian science into that city. Certain aspects of his physics have given rise to considerable debate among modern scholars; but unlike the controversy surrounding Empedocles' cosmology, this debate has no direct bearing on the main outline of his anthropogony, and need not detain us here. It is generally agreed that Anaxagoras saw the basic matter of the universe as consisting of innumerable seeds, controlled by a single motive force which he called Mind and which he probably envisaged as a corporeal substance. Our world came into being when Mind started a rotation of the seeds, as a result of which the ones that were predominantly dense, moist, cold and dark came together in the centre, and those which were predominantly rare, hot, dry and bright flew outwards towards the circumference, to form the aether. In the centre, the seeds which were to make up the earth were gradually separated off from those which were to form the seas.

Our sources afford only a few hints as to Anaxagoras' beliefs about the origins of animal life, but from some of them at least a familiar picture seems to be emerging. Diogenes Laertius attributes to him the theory that 'animals were born from moisture, heat and an earthy substance, but later on from each other' (34), which paints an Ionian-style picture of an earth whose productivity was at its peak when it was beginning to be separated off, through the action of heat, from the water with which it was originally mixed. Animals were born from the earth, then; but, if another set of references is to be believed, the original mixture alone was not responsible for their creation.

According to Theophrastus, Anaxagoras thought that 'air contains the seeds of all things, and that these seeds, when carried down with the rain, produce plants' (Hist. Plant. 3.1.4.); while the late second century Christian bishop Irenaeus makes him apply the same process to animals: 'Anaxagoras, who was called an atheist, put forward the doctrine that animals were created by the fall of seeds from the sky to the earth' (2.14.2). Anaxagoras saw an affinity between plants and animals - 'a plant is an animal rooted in the earth, according to Plato, Anaxagoras and Democritus and their schools' (35) - and may well have thought that the two were originally created in the same way. Did Anaxagoras envisage then, prior to the rising up of human beings from the earth, a dropping down of some vital ingredient from the sky? And could this ingredient have incorporated Mind, of which he must have believed that living beings had a share - '...there are some things in which there is Mind as well' (DK B11)? If this was so, then Anaxagoras provided the explanation which was lacking in Anaximander of how animate beings could be created out of inanimate matter; and at the same time, along with Empedocles, came closer than any of the Ionians to the mythological picture of living creatures born from a union between Earth and Sky, and thus mediating between the inanimate and the divine. That he held this belief is perhaps borne out by the fact that the poet Euripides was reputed to have been a pupil of Anaxagoras; and that Euripides himself was the creator of a myth which made Earth and Sky the parents of the human race, and specified body and soul as the respective ingredients derived from each of them. (36) But we should bear in mind that Theophrastus might well be referring to Anaxagoras' theory of the creation of plants <u>in the present day</u>, rather than in the original creative process; and that Irenaeus is a late source, and as a Christian might have possessed a predisposition for misinterpreting pagan thought. We cannot be sure that Anaxagoras gave rainfall a place in the original creation of living beings: though even without it, he must have seen Mind as being somehow present in the mixture.

ARCHELAUS

Archelaus was an Athenian philosopher active in the latter half of the fifth century BC, said to have been a pupil of Anaxagoras and an associate of Socrates. We have little evidence for his views in general, although it is assumed that he took over Anaxagoras' basic system, while making some fairly far-reaching changes to it. The cosmogony, for example, is in some ways a novel and peculiar one. Archelaus seems to have believed that in the beginning it was water that collected at the centre of the world, and that this was then 'burnt-up' to form both air and earth.

But still, the recipe for the generation of living creatures is the same as it has been so often before: water mixed with earth and then heated. Archelaus' theory of animal origins in fact supplies us with some of the details which we have perhaps lost from Anaxagoras: 'He says that when the earth was first getting warm in the lower region, where the hot and the cold were mixed together, many animals began to appear, including men, all with the same life-style and all of them feeding on the slime. They were short-lived, but later on they began to be born from one another' (Hippolytus, Ref. 1.9.5.). Here we have a detail which has not been encountered before - a reference to the nourishment which nascent animals and humans drew from the slime that had produced them in the first place (37). And Mind too must somehow have been present in the mixture - 'he says that Mind is inborn in all animals equally, for each of the animals, as well as man, makes use of Mind ...' (Ref. 1.9.6.) - but unfortunately our sources are no more enlightening than those for Anaxagoras as to how it got there.

DEMOCRITUS

Democritus of Abdera, who was also active in the second half of the fifth century BC, is a figure of fundamental importance in the history of scientific thought. His theory of the atomic nature of matter was passed on (with some modifications) to Epicurus and his followers, and thence to natural philosophers in seventeenth century Europe. But we possess no account of his zoogony other than two brief references in writers of the third century AD. Lactantius in passing tells us that he 'thought that men emerged from the ground like worms ...' (Inst. Div. 7.7.9.), while according to Censorinus, 'Democritus of Abdera held that men were first created from water and mud. The view of Epicurus is similar ...' (De die nat. 4.9.). The latter suggests that Epicurus may have derived his theory of human origins, like his atomism, from Democritus. At any rate, further discussion of Democritus' beliefs will best be postponed till we arrive at the theories of Epicurus, for whom we have more solid information.

By the late fifth century, the theory was firmly established that the first human beings were born from the ground, that earth and water were the substances of which they were composed, and that heat was an agent in their manufacture. The contiguity of water and earth was generally attributed to the unfinished state of the cosmos, though Empedocles and possibly Anaxagoras thought that rainfall was responsible for bringing the two together. No other basic hypothesis, so far as we know, was ever put forward in scientific philosophy.

The Theories of the Presocratic Philosophers

The parallels between this theory and certain mythological accounts of human origins cannot be denied. The set of anthropogonic myths which identified the human race as a product of the earth included in some of its versions (particularly the later ones) stories of earth and water mixed together by a god with fiery associations, or of rainfall dropping from the sky and fertilising the earth. The links with animal and plant life were stressed in this set of myths; and similarly in Presocratic philosophy, humans were scarcely distinguished from animals and, in Empedocles and Anaxagoras at least, were brought into close relationship with plants. Myth and philosophy alike saw humankind as an integral part of the material cosmos, developing and growing along with it. And, one is tempted to add, just as the mythographers pictured the cosmos as a living being, so too did some of the early Presocratics fail to recognise any distinction between inanimate and animate matter. Only with Anaxagoras and Archelaus do we get any hint of a factor exclusive to living organisms - a factor which they called Mind.

But for all this, these Presocratic theories are remarkable for the fact that they leave little room for the operation of purposeful and self-willed supernatural powers. Creation takes place on the level of natural substances and natural, mechanistic processes. Even in Empedocles, the most metaphysical of all these philosophers, the divine characters are instantly recognisable as the personifications of natural phenomena, and the difference between this and true mythology is at once apparent. Mythographers work down from the level of the gods to that of the world, and so the world becomes full of gods. Scientific philosophers, on the contrary, work upwards from the world to the gods and so the material universe is elevated into a divine, all powerful entity. When reading myth, we are not at all surprised that human life should have been created out of the vibrant stuff of the cosmos; but when reading the Presocratics, we are left with a question on our lips - how can the human race have come into being out of all this lifeless matter?

That said, there must surely have been an interaction between Presocratic thought and the later mythological anthropogonies. As scientific philosophy gained ground so the alternative mythical notion of the human being as a fallen god faded from the scene, and the earth-created myth came to the fore. What the science and the myth have in common is a notion of the rise of the human race - out of the matter of everyday things, out of the matter which they share with animals and plants, human beings grow and strain upwards. In myth, they grow towards the gods who invested the matter with life; in science they grow, perhaps, to become gods themselves. In either case, it is a self-confident and expansive society that can reflect on its origins in such a fashion.

NOTES

1. J. Burnet Early Greek Philosophy (London 1928; fourth edition, London, 1930), p.1 - 30.
2. See especially F.M. Cornford Principium Sapientiae (Cambridge 1952).
3. For some of the views on this topic, see: A.G. Vlastos, review of Cornford's Principium Sapientiae in Gnomon 27 (1955), p.65-76: reproduced in D.J. Furley and R.E. Allen, Studies in Presocratic Philosophy, vol. 1 (London 1970), p.42-55; K.R. Popper, 'Back to the Presocratics' in Conjectures and Refutations (London, 1963), a revised version of an article first published in Proceedings of the Artistotelian Society 59 (1958-9), p.1-24: reproduced in Furley and Allen, Vol. 1., p.130-153; G.S. Kirk, 'Popper on Science and the Presocratics', in Mind 69 (1960), p.318-39: reproduced in Furley and Allen, Vol.1., p.154-77; G.E.R. Lloyd, Magic, Reason and Experience (Cambridge, 1979), p.226-267, J. Barnes, The Presocratic Philosophers (London, 1982), p.47-52; and J.-P. Vernant, The Origins of Greek Thought (English trans. London, 1982), esp. p.102-132. Both Vlastos and Popper agree with Cornford in accepting that Presocratic hypotheses were not arrived at empirically, as a result of observation; but deny (Popper in the strongest terms) that a priori reasoning is inimical to science. Kirk and Barnes believe that the Presocratics did use observation, but Barnes is less sure about their employment of the critical method. For the political background to the advent of philosophy see Lloyd and Vernant.
4. See H. Diels and W. Kranz, Die Fragmente der Vorsokratiker (Berlin, 1952), Thales A12. This work will hereafter be referred to as DK, and the philosopher's name will be understood.
5. Many points in the reconstruction of Anaximander's cosmogony are the subject of debate. For good discussions, see C.H. Kahn, Anaximander and the origins of Greek cosmology (New York, 1960),

p.75-118; and G.S. Kirk, J.E. Raven and M. Schofield, The Presocratic Philosophers (Cambridge, 1983), p.105-140.
  6. For a much fuller discussion of these points, see J.H. Loenen, 'Was Anaximander an evolutionist?' Mnemosyne series 4, 7 (1954), p.215-232.
  7. Principium p.170-171
  8. Hist. anim. 565B
  9. According to Aristotle (Meteor. 353B6), Anaximander believed that the sea would eventually dry up completely.
  10. Principium p.193-198
  11. Anaximander may have believed that the apeiron was divine: see Aristotle, Phys. 203B7; though we could here be reading Aristotle's own interpretation of its qualities. If Aristotle is right, the basic material principle of the universe could be regarded as conscious and intelligent; but there is no suggestion in the sources for the origin of the human race that an external and purposeful agent was at work.
  12. See above, note 9, for the drying up of the earth, and below, page 115 and 116, for a discussion of the possibility that Anaximander's cosmology was cyclical.
  13. Hippolytus Ref. 1.14.5.
  14. For an account and criticism of Pythagorean numerology, see Aristotle's Metaphysics as cited in DK58B5-13.
  15. Diogenes Laertius gives a number of other explanations of the Pythagorean taboo on beans: they cause flatulence, which shows that they contain a large amount of 'soul'; they are bad for the stomach and cause bad dreams (8.24); they resemble the male genitals, or the gates of Hades, or have a form like that of the universe (8.34).
  16. For good discussions, see Barnes, Presocratic philosophers, p.495-501, and Kirk, Raven and Schofield, p.320-321. Barnes believes that the Empedoclean daimon is corporeal, Schofield that it always requires a corporeal home: neither believes that there is any ultimate inconsistency between the two works.
  17. This belief did not prevent Parmenides from expressing 'mortal opinions' (i.e. false but satisfying opinions) about cosmology. Presumably amongst these opinions was the theory attributed to him by Diogenes Laertius (9.22) that 'there were two elements, fire and earth, the former with the function of craftsman, the latter with that of his

material. The generation of men came about with the sun as first cause'.

18. This theory has been put forward by amongst others: P.Tannery, Pour L'histoire de la science hellene (Paris, 1887), p.304 ff.; E. Zeller, Die Philosophie der Griechen (5th ed., Leipzig, 1892), p.778 ff.; J. Burnet, p.197 ff.; E. Bignone Empedocle (Torino, 1916), p 223 ff.; W.K.C. Guthrie, A History of Greek Philosophy (vol. 2, Cambridge 1965), p.167ff.; D. O'Brien, Empedocles' Cosmic Cycle (Cambridge, 1969), p.156-197; M.R. Wright (ed.), Empedocles: The extant fragments (New Haven and London, 1981), p.40-48; J. Barnes, Presocratic Philosophers, p.308-11.

19. This view, with variations, is put forward by: J. Bollack, Empedocles, vols.1-3 (Paris, 1965-9), especially vol.1, p.97-124; F. Solmsen, 'Love and strife in Empedocles' cosmology', Phronesis 10 (1965), p.109-48 (reproduced in Furley and Allen, vol.2, p.221-264); U. Holscher, 'Weltzeiten und Lebenszyklus', Hermes 93(1965), p.7-33; A.A. Long, 'Empedocles' cosmic cycle in the sixties', in A.P.D. Mourelatos (ed.), The Pre-Socratics (Garden City N.Y., 1974), p.397-425; and Schofield, in Kirk, Raven and Schofield, p.287-299.

20. See Burnet, p.242-244; Bignone, p.565-98; Guthrie, Greek Philosophy vol.2, p.200-11; Wright, p.53-54. There is a disagreement amongst these writers as to whether men and women were produced under Love as well as under Strife.

21. See E.L. Minar, 'Cosmic periods in the philosophy of Empedocles', Phronesis 8 (1963), p.140-5; and O'Brien, p.196-236. O'Brien makes the 'whole-natured forms' the last creatures produced under Love, and the first produced under Strife.

22. The first line of the fragment is quoted by Aristotle three times: In De gen. an. 722 B19-20; De caelo 300 B27-31; and De anima 430 A27-30. Simplicius quotes all 3 lines in In cael. 586.7.

23. In the De caelo passage, see above.

24. See also DKB73 and B98: the latter adds aether or air to the elements which were mingled in the earth.

25. Fr.20, which O'Brien interprets as referring in its second part to a zoogony under Strife (p.218-229), is much more easily understood as a description of the life and death of a single organism. See Wright, p.194-195.

26. See De gen. an. 722 B25-26 and the De anima passage referred to above, note 22.

27. In phys. 371.33

28. In phys. 371.33-372.11. For a discussion of the Simplicius passage in relation to a 'survival of the fittest' theory, see below, page 88-89.
29. Certainly if the daimon is a corporeal entity, it is hard to see how any memory of an earlier world could have been preserved.
30. For the first view, see Kirk, Raven, and Schofield, p.305. For the second, see Solmsen, in Furley and Allen, p.241-242, and Long, in Mourelatos, p.417.
31. See Solmsen, in Furley and Allen, p.241.
32. See below, p.86-89
33. Kirk, Raven and Schofield, p.321.
34. See Diogenes Laertius 2.9.; and cf. Hippolytus Ref. 1.8.12.
35. Plutarch Quaest.phys. 1.911D.
36. For the Earth-Sky myth in Euripides, see above page 8-9, and page 21, n.19. For the body-soul duality in this myth, see Supplices 531-36. For Euripides as the pupil of Anaxagoras, see Vitruvius 8.1 and Aetius 5.19.2-3: interestingly, these references occur when the second fragment noted on page 21 is being quoted.
37. Trephomena could possibly be translated as 'being reared from' rather than 'feeding on'. But another reference in Diogenes Laertius - 'animals were born from the earth when it was warm, and it sent up an ooze resembling milk to serve as nourishment. It produced men in the same way' (2.17) - would seem to lend support to the second translation.

Chapter Three

LATER THEORIES

By the end of the fifth century BC, the centre of the philosophical stage, as far as the Greek world was concerned, had shifted very definitely to the city of Athens, where it was to remain for at least the next hundred years. At about the same time, for a variety of reasons which need not be analysed here, a reaction against purely scientific speculation had set in, and philosophers had begun to direct their thoughts instead towards the question of the human race's special role in the world, and of what this implied about relations between its members. Thus were ethical and political philosophy born.

This line of enquiry is not necessarily inimical to a study of human origins - some philosophers, indeed, would consider it to be very relevant. But from the late fifth to the middle of the fourth century BC, ethical philosophy was dominated by the figures of Socrates and his pupil Plato, who looked outside of the physical world and therefore outside of the historical process for the mainspring of human morality. For them, the moral potential of the human race, depending as it did on the realm of metaphysical values, was not tied up with humankind's biological status, which could thus be largely ignored. In this kind of intellectual atmosphere, we cannot expect to encounter a willingness to study human origins and human development from a purely physical standpoint.

When science re-emerged as a vital discipline in the second half of the 4th century BC, there was a tendency (not by any means universal) for it to be more specialised, and less all-embracing in its scope. With this went an increasing accent on empiricism, on producing theories that were testable by observation or even by experiment, and this produced a tendency, (again, not universal) for science to be more descriptive, and less speculative. Linked with this was a growing consciousness of the utilitarian application of science - though this was probably never a dominant factor in the ancient world. But for all these reasons, scientific thought from the fourth century BC on was never so over-ridingly historicist in its approach as it had been in Presocratic days. It relied less on recapturing the origins of the world as a means of understanding how the world worked; and similarly in seeking to know how human beings worked, it harked back less frequently to the supposed origins of the human race. For an example of how this attitude was beginning to make itself heard as early as the late fifth century BC, we can turn to the literature of medicine, a science that paved the way for others in terms of being specialised, empirical, and utilitarian:

> I am not going to claim that man is all air, or fire, or water, or earth, or in fact anything, except what his body is obviously composed of: let those who want to discuss such matters.

declares one of the Hippocratic writers (The Nature of Man 1), in a reference to late Presocratic wranglings. A large number of later scientists followed his example, and steered clear of 'such matters'.

The theories of human origins that were produced in later times tended to be the products of wider philosophical systems, rather than of science as such. Most of them relied heavily on the by now orthodox notion that animal life developed out of the earth. It will be sufficient in this chapter to note some of the more prominent examples of this theory, while bearing in mind the fact that an idea, once it has become standard, can be exploited in a wide variety of philosophical and religious contexts. In most Presocratic anthropogonies, the idea of birth from the earth had been coupled with the idea of a gradual development, linked to large-scale changes taking place in the cosmic environment. This was a viewpoint adopted by a number of later thinkers, who appreciated the philosophical implications of this, and deliberately introduced their gradualist histories of human civilisation with studied accounts of human origins. But Plato too could take a man born from the earth and use him to illustrate quite a different story. Earth-born people, especially when their souls come from elsewhere, do not necessarily point to an evolutionary interpretation of human civilisation and of human morality.

I begin my survey with a writer who should strictly be included among the Presocratics, since he was probably some twenty years older than Socrates, but who was one of the pioneers of the new ethical approach to philosophy.

PROTAGORAS

Protagoras was one of the most famous of the Sophists, the loosely defined group of teachers who came to prominence in late fifth century Athens as purveyors of a popularly demanded education in rhetoric, politics, conduct and life in general. Protagoras was clearly more principled and more profound than many, since he seems to have escaped the opprobrium which was beginning to build up even then against the Sophists, and in spite of his openly professed religious agnosticism was a highly respected figure in Athens. Our knowledge of his beliefs is derived from a few fragments, and more especially from the dialogues of Plato, in particular from the one which is named after him and in which he is a central character. There has been much discussion as to how far what he says in this dialogue represents his own beliefs, and how far it is merely a view of things imposed on him by Plato (1). This is a question which comes particularly to the fore when one considers the account which he gives in the dialogue of the origins of human society, an account which will feature in the next few chapters. For my part, I tend to believe that in some of its later sections, this account has been given a distinct, but not over-riding Platonic bias; but this is a problem which need not concern us at this stage. What is more significant here is the evidence it offers for the currency of the earth-born theory of human origins.

In what, as the character of Protagoras announces in introducing it, is a deliberately 'mythological' account of the origins of life and civilisation, he tells us that at one time there were no mortal creatures, only gods. 'When the appointed time came for (mortal creatures) to be created, the gods fashioned them within the earth out of a mixture of earth and fire, and the substances compounded from earth and fire'. He goes on to describe how two of the Titans, Prometheus and Epimetheus, were given the task of equipping the animals thus created with

Later Theories

appropriate powers, and how Epimetheus provided all the other animals with the means of defending and supporting themselves, but left humans out. Prometheus was then forced for the sake of human survival to steal fire and technical skill from the gods. (2)

The story of how the human race acquired its distinctive technological bent will be looked at later. The creation story is my concern here, and this to my mind can be regarded as the genuine Protagorean thing. Before commencing his tale, the character of Protagoras has offered to present his views either as a reasoned argument, or in the form of a fable, and when his audience has left the decision to him has chosen a fable as likely to be more enjoyable. So right from the start we are invited to take the mythological trappings of the story with a pinch of salt. It seems quite unnecessary then to discover anything here to conflict with Protagoras' well-known agnosticism (which Plato in any case could surely not have denied). Having stripped the story of its gods and Titans, we are left with the familiar theory that human beings shared their origin with other animals, and were born from the earth out of a mixture of elements (the 'substances compounded of earth and fire' are generally assumed to be air and water). This is a thoroughly Presocratic notion, and one to which Protagoras could easily have subscribed. It is worth noting in passing that, even in a pseudo-mythological context, Prometheus still adheres to the role of civiliser, and has not yet assumed the mantle of creator.

SOCRATES

Socrates was the teacher who more than ayone else in the late fifth century BC was responsible for steering philosophical debate away from a material universe of which humankind was but a part, and towards a conception of the human race which put it in direct touch with a metaphysical world of divine and eternal values. We should not be surprised, then, to find that there is very little about the physical origins of the human race in Socrates' teachings. But before passing him over, we should note the fact that in the biographical account which he gives of himself in Plato's Phaedo, he tells us that in his youth he was addicted to natural science, and was fascinated by questions such as whether 'when the hot

Later Theories

and the cold take on a kind of putrefaction, then animals are produced' (3). That someone who is reputed to have been a pupil of Archelaus should have got involved in such debates is quite understandable. The way in which the question is mentioned perhaps suggests that, while the theory of 'elements in the earth' was already well-known in Socrates' youth, it was still not altogether standard. Again, in Plato's Menexenus, Socrates recites a speech which refers to the 'earth-born' theory, though here it seems to owe more to popular mythology than to natural science:

> At the time when the whole earth was sending up and giving birth to living things of every kind, animals and plants, our own land was unproductive and free of wild animals: she made her choice of living things, and brought forth man, who is superior to the others in intelligence, and alone respects justice and the gods.

He goes on to say that in those days it was only in Attica that the earth produced grain, the characteristic food of humans, since the earth like any other mother naturally provided food for her own offspring: 'For in pregnancy and childbirth, the earth does not imitate a woman, but a woman the earth' (4). This speech, as Socrates readily admits, is a parody of the patriotic speeches that were common in his day, full of nationalistic platitudes drawn from folk-lore. It tells us very little about Socrates' real views, but like the passage already quoted, does give an indication of the climate of belief at the time. (5).

PLATO

Plato, the most famous of Socrates' pupils, not only had a resounding impact on philosophical trends in the fourth century BC, but has exercised an influence which has reached down the ages. More of a scientist than his beloved teacher, he was nonetheless not particularly interested in the material composition of the world: like Pythagoras (by whom he was greatly influenced), he was much more concerned with its form and structure. For him, the workings of the world, the revolutions of the planets, the succession of night and day and the endless cycle of the seasons were significant largely because they demonstrated an order and regularity which supported his belief in

Later Theories

a moral and rational soul as controller of the universe. Human beings, through their own souls, were linked with the principle of divine reason, and this was the most important fact about them: their material origins were seen as somewhat irrelevant.

Nevertheless, we do have from Plato two versions of the origins of human life, which, though they are set in discussions of two quite different subjects, do present a reasonably consistent picture.

In the Politicus, one of Plato's characters explains that the history of the world is a cyclical one (6): there is an epoch when the workings of the world are under the direct guidance of the deity, 'when God himself goes round with the world and helps to roll it'; followed by an epoch when 'God lets go' and the world begins to revolve in the opposite direction, without any divine guidance. This sudden reversal is naturally accompanied by vast cosmic catastrophes, and by widespread destruction of life, so that only a remnant of the human race survives. At the outset, these survivors still retain a recollection of the divine order under which they once lived; but gradually this memory is lost, and people become more and more prone to disorder and discord, until finally, when the world is on the brink of destruction, God 'takes his place again at the tiller' and the direction of the world is once more reversed.

We, needless to say, are living in the epoch of growing disorder. The previous epoch, when God had control of the world, was the blissful era recorded in mythology as the age of Kronos: at that time 'men had neither wives nor children', but were born from the earth. Every process in that era was the reverse of the one familiar to us; and so in those days, people rose from the ground as old men and women, and grew younger and younger until they became babies: then the babies got smaller and smaller, and finally vanished into thin air. Every soul had to go through an allotted number of births, so when one body had vanished, the soul 'fell to the earth like seed corn' and collected another one (buried there in a previous epoch). It was when every soul had completed its predetermined incarnations that God released his control of the world. And at that point people who had been getting smaller and smaller started to grow again, and people who had just risen up from the earth promptly dropped dead. There was to be no more birth from the earth in this new epoch: people were now expected to be responsible for their own existence, and so had to make use of sexual

59

reproduction. But our earliest ancestors were the children of the earth-born survivors, and have handed down to us those legends about an earth-born race which 'now meet with general and mistaken incredulity'.

What are we to make of all this, other than laughter? Plato has inserted this account as an introduction to a serious analysis of the development of human society and culture in our own world. Nevertheless, although the account carries a genuine moral message (which will be discussed in a later chapter), it is hard to believe that we are expected to take the anthropogonic part of it as a serious scientific treatment. Plato himself calls the account a fable or muthos (274E), and one of its main functions seems to be that of leading us gently into a difficult subject.

So did Plato believe in original generation from the earth or not? The next passage to be considered would suggest that in a certain sense he did. And while he is probably not expecting us to accept everything in the Politicus account as gospel, it is worth noting that by suggesting that people sprang from the earth fully-grown, he has avoided the problem of how the first humans managed to survive without parents to protect them. Some of the Presocratics attributed an animal-like condition to early humans as a way of explaining their survival; and then posited a gradual, and possibly haphazard, process of development whereby full human status was acquired. Plato instead (and here surely he is not being fanciful) has humans coming into existence as fully-equipped, intelligent, superior beings, whose special role in the world has already been marked out for them. The key to this difference is the soul. In the excerpts we possess, none of the Presocratics discusses the first humans' acquisition of a soul; some at least (as we shall see) would have said that the soul (or the intellect, or the moral sense) was something which developed in the course of human history. Plato on the contrary sees the soul as a fully-developed entity, the true essence of a human being which marks him or her out as a distinctive creature right from the start.

The second passage comes from the Timaeus, in which Plato combines a scientific account of the workings of the world on various levels (e.g. cosmology, geometrical structure of objects, sense-perception, physiology, pathology) with a cosmogony that describes the original creation of an orderly universe by the Demiurge or Creator (7). He fashioned it from the four elements, producing first earth and fire, then inserting water and air between them; and finally placing in the centre of this sphere a soul, created by a complicated blending of spirit and matter, which was then stretched throughout the whole and wrapped around the circumference. Thus the universe itself was a living being. The Demiurge went on to fashion Time, the seven planets with fixed orbits, the 'visible gods' (that is, the unmoving stars), and the 'created gods' - in this last item Plato accepts the genealogy of Hesiod, for 'to know how they were born is a task beyond our powers, so we must believe those who have told the story before us'.

Finally, we are given an account of the creation of human beings, in which matter and soul are fitted together as they were in the creation of the universe as a whole. This was the result of a deal which the Demiurge made with the created gods. The former fashioned eternal souls from the same materials as the soul of the universe, though not of the same purity. Then, while he rested, the created gods 'borrowed from the universe portions of fire and earth, water and air, on condition that these loans should be repaid', welding them together with 'a multitude of rivets too minute to be seen', in order to make the bodies which were to be the frameworks for the immortal souls. Gradually the souls assumed control of the tumultuous and irregular motions and sensations of the bodies. A soul which succeeded in mastering the contamination arising from its association with the body would lead a righteous life, and on the death of the body would return to the star which was its fellow (there being as many souls as stars). A soul which allowed itself to be contaminated by the body would on its second birth be relegated to the body of a woman, and after that into every kind of animal, until it succeeded in overcoming the violent passions of the body.

Although Plato has warned us (29D) that this is no more than 'a likely story', it is clearly a more serious exposition than the one we have been given in the Politicus. Here we have a prime example of how some of the basic tenets of the Presocratic philosophers can be taken over by Plato, and used as the basis for an anthropogony which is wholly different in its implications. Human beings, Plato tells us, were created from the same elements as had gone towards the composition of the universe; and when their bodies die, the 'loans' are repaid and the elements composing them return to the sum total of matter in the universe. Some at least of the first humans were earth-born (and so we learn that the account given in the Politicus was not entirely fictitious), for the Demiurge, in providing the souls around which the gods were to shape the bodies, 'sowed some of them in the earth, some in the moon, and some in the other instruments of time' (that is, the other planets). Presumably, the bodies were subsequently generated in the same locations as the souls, and so the prospect presented to us is not just one of earth-born people, but also of 'life on other planets'.

Humans born from the earth, from a mixture of elements: this much is thoroughly Presocratic. What Plato adds, of course, is the immortal soul, which connects human beings with the rational and metaphysical mainspring of all existence. In this he shows himself to be much more indebted to the Pythagoreans than to any of the other Presocratics. By stressing the sharp dichotomy between body and soul, he has manipulated the history of the human race to produce a totally inverted message. By their souls, human beings are given the potential for an existence which is distinguished from that of the rest of the animal kingdom; by their souls they are shielded from the implications of any biological development which they may undergo; by their souls they are placed within the orbit of a divine predestination. Human reason did not rise up out of the ground along with the human constitution and develop along with it: on the contrary, reason is at war with our physical constitution, and must seek only to suppress it.

ARISTOTLE AND SPONTANEOUS GENERATION

From Plato's pupil Aristotle we get no account at all of the origin of the world or the creation of the human race. Nor would we expect to, since Aristotle, unusually among ancient philosophers, believed our world and all the species within it to be eternal and uncreated. (8) There might be temporary and local changes in the physical environment, caused by an adjustment in the relationship between the four elements which make up our world (9); but the world as a whole maintains substantially the same constitution, and manifests the same processes throughout eternity.

Aristotle, then, would not appear to be particularly relevant to our theme. He does, however, analyse in detail one physical process which is quite closely related to it - that is, spontaneous generation. Belief in the generation of living creatures without sexual reproduction seems to have been very prevalent in the ancient world, and the existence of such a notion may well have encouraged the widespread theory of original generation from the earth. So it is worth pausing to examine some of the manifestations of this belief.

Aristotle was probably the first thinker to elevate spontaneous generation into a serious scientific doctrine. Certainly, he is the first to provide us with a detailed analysis of its operations. In one work he classifies generation into three types, natural, artificial and spontaneous. The last type, he says, takes place by chance, and sometimes produces the same creatures as natural generation: for there are some animals that can be generated either from a seed or without it. (10) Others, however, can only be generated spontaneously. (11)

Among the animals he mentions as being produced in this way are insects, certain kinds of grey mullet, small fry, eels, and testacea. The locations listed for the generation of insects are numerous - they include dew deposited on leaves, mud, wood (growing or dry), the hairs of animals, flesh, excretions (either deposited or still in the intestines), and even snow and fire. The fire-flies must be regarded as unusual, however, for generally he believes the presence of water to be essential for spontaneous generation. This is because water contains *pneuma* or the breath of life, and *pneuma* contains the stuff of souls: when water which has any corporeal substance mixed with it is heated, a bubble is produced which encloses this soul-principle; the corporeal matter then hardens all round it to form a body. The most common location for the generation of animals other than insects is damp earth or mud, where earth represents the corporeal matter from which the animal's body is formed (12).

Earth, water and heat - the same elements are present here as in the Presocratic theories of the original generation of animals. From Aristotle we obtain the detail which we would love to find in them about the role played by each of the constituents; and an explanation of how inanimate matter could have given rise to living organisms. The body-soul distinction is maintained, as in Plato, but in Aristotle it is maintained within the framework of physical processes, without resort to an external divinity.

Not surprisingly, it is in connection with spontaneous generation that Aristotle mentions the original creation of animals. If human beings and animals were ever earth-born, he says, 'as some people allege', they must have either had the form of larvae to begin with, or have been born out of eggs, since they must either have contained their nourishment within themselves (as larvae do) or else have derived it from an egg: food, he assumes, could not have flowed to them out of the earth, as it flows from a mother. Aristotle himself, suspending his disbelief for a moment, concludes that larvae are more of a possibility than eggs, since in the present day one can still witness the spontaneous generation of creatures with the form of larvae, but never of eggs. He does not, however, accord any kind of credibility to this hypotheses; his belief in the eternity of the species would have prevented him from seriously entertaining it. (13)

Aristotle's pupil Theophrastus disputes the operation of spontaneous generation in some instances. Frogs, he says, do not fall from the sky in showers of rain: his sensible suggestion for what really happens is that the frogs are already underground, and are forced out when the rain runs into their hiding-places. But he does believe that flies are generated from dung and rotting materials, and worms from the damp roots of wheat. Like Aristotle, he sees moisture and heat as being important elements in this process. (14)

Few later writers discussed spontaneous generation in the same scientific way as Aristotle and Theophrastus; but the belief by no means went out of fashion. According to Diodorus Siculus, writing in the first century BC, the Egyptians of his own day supported their claim that animal life had first appeared in Egypt by pointing out that the soil of the Thebaid was still productive of very healthy mice: 'some of them are fully formed as far as the breast and front feet, and are capable of movement, while the rest of the body is unformed and remains a natural clod of earth' (1.10.2). Vergil at about the same time advised farmers who should have the misfortune to lose their entire stock of bees to replenish them by beating a young bullock to a jelly, then hanging the carcase up in a confined space: bees would develop as the flesh began to ferment (Georgics, 4.281-314). A little later Ovid also remarked on the number of animals still produced by the prolific land of Egypt, when the slime deposited by the Nile was heated by the sun (Metamorphoses 1.422.-33). At the end of the second century AD, the belief was still going strong, and the sceptical philosopher Sextus Empiricus showed himself to be not over-sceptical in some matters by giving a comprehensive list of animals produced by spontaneous generation: among the more novel touches are ants from sour wine, beetles from asses, and gall-insects from figs (Outlines of Pyrrhonism 1.41). Two hundred years later, Augustine could still refer to a theory that frogs dropped from the sky, though this had been rejected by Theophrastus some seven centuries earlier (contra Faustum 6.8). Indeed, the belief in spontaneous generation has a much longer history than this, for it was not until the nineteenth century that the notion of animal life developing in our own day and age out of inanimate matter was finally banished.

THE EPICUREANS AND DIODORUS SICULUS

Towards the end of the fourth century BC, the atomic theory of the Presocratic philosopher Democritus was taken up in a somewhat modified form by Epicurus, who made it the basis of the comprehensive philosophical system developed by him in his school at Athens. Like Democritus, Epicurus believed that all matter consists in the final analysis of an infinite number of invisible atoms moving about in an infinite void, and that all the differences in quality which we encounter in perceptible phenomena are to be accounted for by differences in the size, shape or disposition of the atoms constituting those phenomena.

We have so little in the way of original works of Epicurus that it is not surprising that in those that do survive we find no record of his views on the origins of animal life. A late Roman writer, Censorinus, tells us that '(Epicurus) believed that when mud was heated, first of all there grew up in it things like wombs, rooted in the earth, and when these had given birth to infants they produced from themselves a milk provided by nature ...' (De die nat. 4.9). Epicurus may have derived this idea, like so much of his science, from Democritus - Censorinus certainly suggests that he did by his preceding words about the similarity between the beliefs of the two philosophers. But we cannot be sure: Censorinus may never even have read Epicurus; finding an account of the wombs in a later Epicurean philosopher,

Lucretius, he could have just assumed that it had been inherited from the master. (15)

Lucretius, the Roman poet of the first century BC, is today the best known of the exponents of Epicureanism. In the fifth book of his stirring exposition of Epicurean doctrine, On the nature of things, he paints for us an Epicurean picture of the origins of our world. This came into being when some of the atoms whirling around the void got tangled up in a huge atomic traffic-jam. Gradually within this chaotic mass, atoms of a similar kind began to come together. Particles which were heavier and more enmeshed collected together in the centre to form the earth, and squeezed out smoother and rounder atoms. The lightest of these collected at the circumference of the sphere as the aether, and took with them fire-atoms, from which the sun and the moon were formed. Thus, the earth gradually contracted, forcing out from within itself atoms which went to make up the sea and the air: the air-atoms, being lighter, settled above the sea. (16)

Later on Lucretius takes up the theme of how the earth 'has deservedly won the name of mother'. He describes how, at the time when the earth was still exuding heat and moisture, 'there grew up wombs, clinging to the earth by roots', which nurtured embryonic animals. When the time was right, the young creatures inside, 'fleeing from moisture and eager for air', broke out from the wombs, and were then fed by a milk-like sap which flowed from the earth's pores. (17)

Wombs in the earth are a strange idea, but were almost certainly not invented by Lucretius. Democritus and Epicurus have already been mentioned as possible antecedents for this - the latter at least is likely, for Lucretius seems to have adhered quite closely to the teachings of his master. Perhaps also Anaximander's 'fish-like creatures' and 'spiny barks' had some influence, although their function was rather different, since they sheltered animals until they were capable of looking after themselves, whereas Lucretius' wombs operate only for the normal period of gestation. But Aristotle may have been thinking of a similar theory when he played with the hypothesis that earth-born creatures had been born from eggs. (18)

Like Aristotle, Lucretius sees a link between spontaneous generation in his own day, and the original creation of animals from the earth. In fact for him (as a thorough-going empiricist), the former is evidence for the latter: is it any wonder, he says, since even today many animals are formed from the earth when it is moist and warm, that in the days when the earth was young, it should have been capable of producing many bigger creatures? From comments he makes elsewhere on spontaneous generation, we know that it has an atomic basis: it occurs when moisture disturbs the old arrangements of the atoms in the ground, and brings together ones that by virtue of their size, shape, and dispositions are capable of producing animate beings. (19) A similar process must have been behind the original generation of animals, and again we are thankful for the scientific detail missing from the Presocratics.

But of course, there are many similarities between Lucretius' theory and some of the Presocratic versions. Like them, he makes no distinction between human biology and the biology of animals in general; like them he attributes an animal-like existence to the first human beings. For him too, the earth was at its most productive when the cosmos was still in the throes of formation, and animal life developed as part-and-parcel of the overall creative process. And of course the presence of heat and moisture in the earth is as vital to his system as it is to so many others: as with Anaximander, it is the gradual separation of substances (or in his case, atoms) that are going to form other cosmic masses which produces the ideal creative condition. We even have, in Archelaus, an antecedent for the notion of a milk-like slime as food for the new-born creatures. (20)

However, just because we know much more about Lucretius' system than we do about any of the Presocratic ones, we can be much more happy with his explanation of how organic life came out of the inorganic. This is not a feature of the account in Book 5; but again we know from elsewhere that the human soul, like any other phenomenon, is a material entity, and consists of the kind of smooth round atoms which go to make up wind, heat and air. (21) I feel little doubt that, at the time when atoms which were to join the aether, the planets and the sky were still being squeezed out of the earth, Lucretius would have said that the constituents of soul were present in the earth. So here we are far from a Platonic situation, where semi-divine souls are implanted from an external, metaphysical sphere of existence. For Lucretius, the soul, and all that that implies, grows along with the body.

Strangely, it is in the historian Diodorus Siculus that we find the zoogonical account which most closely resembles that of Lucretius. Diodorus,

Later Theories

who tantalisingly was writing at about the same time as Lucretius, prefaces his version of the history of the world with an account of its creation, and of the origins of animal life. In this he tells us that when, in the universal whirl, first the heaven and then the sea were separated from the earth,

> it was like potter's clay and altogether soft. But as the sun's fire shone down upon it, it first of all solidified, and then because of the warmth, it fermented, and some of the wet parts swelled up in many places. Here there arose putrefactions covered with thin membranes ... Finally, when the embryos had achieved their full development, and the membranes had been thoroughly heated, they broke open and produced every form of animal life.
>
> The creatures that had more warmth in their composition became birds, those that had more earth became land animals, and of course the wet ones turned into marine life (1.7.1-6)

There has been a great deal of discussion about the possible sources for this account (and the subsequent anthropology), and a solid body of opinion now exists which says that both Lucretius and Diodorus derived their theories ultimately from Democritus, though via separate channels. (22) There are of course a number of differences between them: Diodorus has more circumstantial detail, and an explanation of the distinctions between the various classes of animal; Lucretius has atomism, a system of nourishment and, elsewhere, a soul. But far more striking are the similarities, and again in Diodorus we notice the absence of any special attention given to the human race, the close links with cosmogony, and the omnipresence of heat and moisture.

THE STOICS

The Stoic school of philosophy was founded by Zeno soon after the rival Epicurean establishment, and like Epicureanism it was still attracting adherents as late as the third century AD. There are many resemblances between the two systems, but on the basic question of the mainspring of human morality and human history they are sharply divided. The Stoic system is an utterly theistic one, according to which there are two ultimate principles of existence, God and matter. God is identifiable with divine reason, which manifests itself as an all-pervasive necessity and providence. Matter is without any qualities other than mass until it is acted upon by God, but under God's impulse it takes on the properties of the four elements, fire, air, water and earth. Using these elements God gives shape to the world and to everything in it; and by penetrating the world in the guise of pneuma, or a mixture of air and fire, he keeps it unified and controls every aspect of it. Pneuma is present in everything, including human beings.

We are given a fair amount of information by Stoic writers on the way in which the world is going to be destroyed - or rather, on the endless destructions by fire to which the world is subject. Rather less is said in our sources about the way in which the world is recreated once it has been destroyed; but it seems that in some way God acts on the primary fire to convert it first of all into air, and then into moisture: part of the moisture is then precipitated as earth, while another part evaporates to form atmospheric air, which in its turn is kindled into planetary fire. (23)

Even less evidence is available to us for the Stoic theory of the origins of life. A familiar note is struck by Censorinus when he attributes to Zeno the belief that 'the human race originally came into being out of the newly-created world, and the first men rose up from the ground with the help of divine fire, that is, through the providence of God' (De die nat. 4.10). As in so many theories, the fire present in the earth helps to raise up the first human beings; as in some of them at least, we can easily imagine that here too the earth provides the corporeal matter, while the fire goes to constitute the soul. The difference here, of course, is that God is present in the fire: the creation of the human race did not for the Stoics arise out of the elemental turmoil which accompanied the formation of the cosmos, but out of the eternal and unalterable presence of God in all things. Human life was not a by-product of a physical process, but was part of a divine plan for the world.

LATIN AUTHORS: EARTH AND SKY

With later Latin authors, it became a commonplace to picture the human race as created from the earth. The belief, as we have seen, did not by this time imply one particular philosophical 'line': it could be adapted to suit varying points of view, as it was by Ovid, when he made it the basis for an explanation of divine kinship. (24) In Ovid and in other writers, the presence of aether or fire in the earth was used to introduce into the theory the groundplan for a soul/body, human/animal distinction. And it is worth noting that at times this could be allegorised into a Father Sky/Mother Earth duality. As for example in one fragment of the work of Pacuvius, an Italian tragedian of the second century BC, who exclaims: 'Look now on this, which around and above holds the earth in its embrace, which we term the sky, and the Greeks call the aether: whatever it is, it gives life to all things, it shapes, nurtures, increases and creates all things, and it receives and buries all things in itself; it is the father of all things, and the same things equally rise up afresh from the same place, and to the same place return on death. The earth is the mother: it gives birth to the body. The aether adds the soul' (fr.86). At the end of the day, the view expressed here is no different from Ovid's, perhaps not even very different from Lucretius' atom-based theory: but the perspective is certainly an unusual one, and emphasises in quite a different way the presence of oppositional elements at work in the human constitution.

The 'earth-born' theory, then, had quickly established itself as the orthodox version of the origins of the human race. The way in which this notion was exploited in order to provide a launching-pad for open-ended, progressivist accounts of cultural history will be examined later. What we should note here is that there were other ways in which it could be exploited. It is not merely that some writers add a soul. Aristotle (in his account of spontaneous generation) and Lucretius add a soul; but the soul which they add is still part-and-parcel of the physical constitution of a living creature; it provides an earth-based impulse which helps to raise that creature above the level of inert, inanimate matter. (25) With Plato and the Stoics and some of the later Latin authors, the source of the soul is quite different: in their theories, it is God who, by penetrating the earth or by manipulating it from afar, injects the soul into previously lifeless matter. In this way, their accounts are much closer to the myths which posit an earth-born origin for the human race (myths which involve earthy matter but divine mediators) than they are to the scientific anthropogonies of the Presocratics and their Hellenistic successors. And if their accounts picture human beings as rising from the earth, this is achieved, in the case of Plato's theory certainly, only after the 'fall' of the soul from a metaphysical and divine state of being to a condition of earthly and corporeal contamination. Where Plato's anthropogony is concerned, we are perhaps nearest of all to the 'fall from grace' version of human origins suggested by Hesiodic Myth.

NOTES

1. For a summary of opinions on this matter, see E.A. Havelock, The Liberal temper in Greek Politics (London, 1957) p.407-9; and Guthrie, Greek Philosophy (Vol. 3, 1969), p.64, n.1.
2. Plato's Protagoras 320C - 322A.
3. Phaedo 96B
4. Menexenus 237D - 238A.
5. Or rather, in the case of the Menexenus passage, the climate of belief in Plato's time, since the context of the dialogue makes it extremely unlikely that Socrates ever made such a speech in real life.
6. Politicus 269A - 274E
7. Timaeus 29E - 44C.
8. See De caelo 279 B4 - 284 B5.
9. See Meteor. 351A - 353 A28.
10. Metaphys. 1032 A12 - B1.
11. Hist.an. 569 A29 - 570 A3.
12. See Hist.an. 551 A1 - 552 B25 and 569 A11 - 570 A23; and Gen.an. 762 A8-34.
13. See Gen.an. 762 B28 - 763 A7.
14. See fr.174 (Wimmer) for frogs and flies; De caus.plant. 3.22.3-4 for worms.
15. R. Philippson believes that Censorinus was using Varro as his source, who may well in his turn have been using Lucretius: see his review of J.H. Dahlmann's De Philosophorum Graecorum sententiis in Philol. Woch. 49 (1929), p.672-6.
16. 5. 416 - 508.
17. 5. 780 - 815.
18. For Aristotle, see above p.64. Other possible contributions to the theory have been mooted by various scholars. Bignone (Empedocle, appendix 4, p.625) sees a link between the wombs and the 'whole-natured forms', though this is perhaps rather fanciful. O'Brien (p.232) thinks that Plato's four 'patterns' - for gods, birds, aquatic animals and terrestrial animals (Timaeus 39E - 40A) - may have

influenced the wombs.
19. See 2. 871-3, 2.897-901 and 2.1150-2.
20. See above, p.48
21. See 3. 231-242
22. K. Reinhardt was the first person to suggest that Diodorus may have derived his cosmogony from Democritus, via the late fourth century historian Hecataeus, who like Democritus came from Abdera: see 'Hekataios von Abdera und Demokritos', Hermes 47(1912), p.492-513. This theory has been accepted by Diels (DK68 B5); by Bignone (p.583, n.2), who believes however that Democritus derived his theory in turn from pre-Atomistic philosophers, including Empedocles; by Philippson, Philol.Woch. 49 who makes Epicurus an intermediary between Democritus and Hecataeus; by Vlastos, who rejects Epicurus as an intermediary: see 'On the pre-history in Diodorus', AJPh. 67 (1946), p.51-59; and by A.T. Cole, who supports Reinhardt's thesis with some very detailed argument: see Democritus and the sources of Greek Anthropology (Cleveland, 1967), p.16, 153-163, and 174-192. Contrary opinions are to be found in J.H. Dahlmann, De philosophorum Graecorum sententiis ad loquellae originem pertinentibus (Diss. Leipzig, 1928), p.23ff; in J.S. Morrison, 'The place of Protagoras in Athenian public life', C.Q. 35 (1941), p.9; in W. Spoerri, Spathellenistische Berichte uber Welt, Kultur und Gotter (Schweizerische Beitrage zur Altertumswissenschaft, 9; Basel, 1959), p.1-33; and in E.R. Dodds, The Ancient Concept of Progress (Oxford, 1973), p.10-11: all believe that pre-Atomistic influences on Diodorus' source must be taken into account.
23. Chrysippus in Plutarch's De Stoic. repugn. 1053B. See also D.E. Hahm The origins of Stoic cosmology (Ohio, 1977), and M. Lapidge 'Stoic cosmology' in J.M. Rist (ed.), The Stoics (Berkeley, 1978).
24. See above, p.11
25. In Aristotle's case, however, this applies only to the souls of animals. Humans would not be generated spontaneously, and the source of their souls was probably somewhat different: see below, p.74-75.

Chapter Four

EVOLUTION AND THE SURVIVAL OF THE FITTEST

No ancient thinker ever produced a theory of biological evolution comparable with the one that is widely accepted today. Not only, of course, were the ancients totally ignorant of the fact that mutation can produce the kind of biological variations which promote the on-going operation of natural selection; but they were probably pretty innocent of notions of biological transformation, in the sense of gradual acquisition by living beings generally of radically new pieces of biological equipment.

But some of the conceptual preconditions for the development of a theory of evolution <u>were</u> present in ancient thought. Victorian popular opinion, accustomed to seeing the human race as a distinctive creation with a hot-line to God, was of course shocked by the notion that human beings had evolved from a long line of animal ancestors; but the idea that human life was just one facet of animal life was nothing new, and was relatively common in the ancient world. Again, some of the ancients were aware, as Darwin was, that large-scale changes in the physical environment must have had a considerable effect on the way of life of animal species. And, though they may have known nothing about the acquisition of new physical characteristics, some of them did at least envisage a long-drawn-out process whereby human beings in particular gradually gained the ability to use those physical characteristics which they already possessed. Finally, there are two notable examples in ancient thought of a 'survival of the fittest' theory. Perhaps most important of all, these four ideas were all capable of embracing a belief in the random and open-ended nature of the changes they mooted. If none of this comes near the modern theory of biological evolution, it nevertheless perhaps deserves to be labelled 'an evolutionary perspective', with the word evolution being used in the more generalised sense of a long-drawn-out and unplanned process of development.

ANTI-EVOLUTIONARY BELIEFS

Before these ideas are examined in more detail, it is worth looking at some of the beliefs to which they were opposed. Ancient thinkers knew enough about biology to realise that many of the physical functions of human beings were identical to those of animals. The obvious physical similarities could not be denied; but, as we saw in the preceding chapter, Plato (and quite probably the Stoics) believed that by virtue of their non-physical equipment human beings were rendered quite unique: the possession of a rational soul had distinguished them from the rest of the animal kingdom since the beginning of their history. It was this emphasis on human reason, and on the moral notions with which it was associated, which was most often used to counteract the idea of kinship with animals. So Hesiod urges us to believe that 'Zeus has ordained this law for men, that fish and beasts and winged birds should devour one another, since there is no justice in them. But to men he gave justice, which is by far the best thing' (Works and Days 276-280). According to Theophrastus (De sens. 25), the sixth century BC scientist Alcmaeon was the first person to define the difference between humans and animals, saying that humans alone are capable of understanding, while animals merely have sensations. In the Timaeus, Plato makes the same point in a more whimsical fashion: having ignored animals completely in his account of the creation, he suggests right at the end of the work that they were formed from degenerate men who had no philosophy, and never looked up at the heavens (91E). Aristotle, of course, is more scientific: in seeking to define the soul, he tells us that not all the soul's powers are possessed by all living things equally - animals possess the powers of nutrition, of appetite, of sensation, and of movement, but only humans, 'and whatever being may be superior to them', possess the power of thought (De anima 414 A29-B20). Elsewhere he explains that, whereas most of the soul's powers grow up along with the body and are inseparable from it, 'thought alone enters from outside and alone is divine' (Gen.an. 736 B27-28). This would seem to suggest a powerful distinction between humans and animals; but Aristotle's position is not a perfectly straightforward one: in the Historia Animalium, he points out that there are many psychological resemblances between animals and humans, and makes it clear that for him all living things are linked together in a single scale of being, where the presence of 'soul' is the connecting thread, and distinctions between animals are produced by quantitative or qualitative differences of psychology (588A).

Other thinkers emphasise the superior physiological qualities which help humans to make use of their superior powers of reasoning. In his Memorabilia, Xenophon relays a conversation in which Socrates lists the attributes which he sees as distinctively human: in addition to theology, forethought, learning and memory, he mentions the upright posture which gives humans a wide range of vision; the hands; the tongue that can make contact with all parts of the mouth; and the sexual appetite that does not diminish with the seasons (1.4.11-14). As far as Socrates is concerned, rather than prompting the thought that human reason may have a physiological base, this all goes to show that human beings have been designed by the gods to lead the best of all possible lives.

One conclusion to be drawn from the assumption of a clear-cut distinction between humans and animals is that animals exist for the benefit of the human race. 'If nature makes nothing in vain', Aristotle says, 'we must infer that animals have been created in order to supply humans with food, clothing and labour (Politics 1256 B15-26). According to Porphyry (De abstinentia 1.4.), opponents of vegetarianism among the Stoics argued that if we gave up eating animals, not only would we deprive ourselves of some very useful resources, but we would be embracing a bestial life devoid of the justice which marks the human race off as a superior species. People have the right to eat animals because only people have reason and justice: if we forgo that right, then we are bound also to forgo the fruits of our reason.

Linked with this idea of a fixed and perpetual distinction between animals and humans is the doctrine of teleology - the belief that the world as a whole, or a particular natural object or series of objects within it, goes through a process of development which has a predetermined end. This end may be seen as preordained by an external, divine agency, but this is not an essential feature of the doctrine: the end may be considered to be inherent in the physical nature of the object considered. Present-day ideas about biological development are by no means free from teleology: we now know that the broad physiological changes which an individual animal will undergo in the course of its life are predetermined by the genetic pattern with which that animal is born. But when we come to consider groups of animals - species, genera, families etc. - then we encounter the modern theory of evolution, and teleology must be abandoned. Random and unpredictable genetic aberrations - mutations - can produce variations which over long periods of time will transform an animal group in an unforeseeable way.

Little or no evidence of these transformations was available to the ancients, and biological teleology of one kind or another was deeply ingrained in their thinking. To some, biological development was a divinely-directed operation. Socrates, in the Xenophon memorial already considered, could not believe that the superb marrying of physiological and psychological traits observable in human beings had come about by accident, and concluded that it must be the work of a divine planner. And Plato in the Timaeus set out his belief that a rational and purposive agency - which he called the Creator - was at work in the universe, and had fashioned the world and all the creatures in it according to a perfect metaphysical model, making it as like the model as possible (39E). For him, all patterns of physical development were willed by an external agency, and were not of any great intrinsic interest.

But the thinker who produced the most detailed teleological doctrine, Aristotle, departed radically from his master when it came to the question of agencies. The predetermined end was for him something that was inherent in nature itself:

> There is a purpose in what comes to be and what exists in nature. In the operation of any human art, there is an end for the sake of which the earlier and successive stages are performed. And as things are produced in art, so they are produced in nature, and vice versa, provided nothing interferes with the process. There is a purpose in artistic production; and there is a purpose in what is produced in nature.
> (Phys. 199 A8-13)

Aristotle does not believe that the rationality of natural processes is the result of intentional planning on the part of a conscious, divine mind. As he sees it, the natural world is an intrinsically rational organism, which exists as such for all time. In the great majority of its operations, it exhibits the same order and regularity which characterises artistic production, because like a human artist it is operating under the impulse of a 'final cause', a goal towards which all the stages in natural development are directed. This is a scheme of things which embraces all the minute physical apparatus of living things. Human beings are the most rational of all the animals, this is their 'final cause', and we must assume that they have been given the physical equipment which will promote this rationality. So it is for the sake of their operation as rational beings that humans have been given an upright posture and hands - rationality is not (as Anaxagoras suggests) a fortuitous outcome of these physical attributes:

> Man, instead of forelegs and feet, has arms and hands. Man is the only animal who stands upright, simply because his nature and essence is divine. The role of the being that is closest to the divine is to be intelligent and to think, and this would not be easy if the body were top-heavy and weighed down, since weight inhibits the operation of the intellect and the general perception ... And since man stands upright ... nature has given him arms and hands ... Nature, like a sensible human being, always assigns an organ to the animal that can use it ... If there is a better way, and nature always does the best she can under the circumstances, then man is not the most intelligent of the animals because he has hands, but has hands because he is the most intelligent of the animals.
> (De part. an. 686 A26-687 A19).

The same planning can be seen at work throughout the plant and animal kingdoms:

> ... it appears that with plants too things are produced which assist the attainment of an end - for example, leaves for the sake of sheltering the fruit. So that if it is by nature and for a purpose that a swallow makes a nest and a spider a web, and if plants grow leaves for the sake of the fruit, and have roots that go down and not up for the sake of nutrition, then it is clear there is a causality of this kind in the things that come to be and exist in nature
> (Phys. 199 A25-31).

There are, Aristotle admits, mistakes in nature just as there are mistakes in art, occasions when natural development fails to achieve the goal it was aiming for. Such aberrations come about through 'the corruption of some principle corresponding to what is now the seed' (Phys. 199 B6-7), and lead to the birth of deformed creatures. But in general, he believes, nature's ends are magnificently fulfilled.

There is much in what Aristotle says that is in accord with modern genetics. What he fails to recognise, of course, is that the mistakes he mentions - the mutations - are heritable, and can lead to biological variation and improvement; and that the accumulation of these accidental improvements over millions of years can produce the superbly adjusted machinery which to him speaks of rationality. The belief that nature is in the long term working towards a clearly-defined predetermined end cannot now be entertained. But in that nature operates to eliminate mistakes that are not useful, and to preserve and promote the ones that contribute towards biological progress, we can perhaps agree with Aristotle to the extent of accepting that there is a trend in biological history, and this trend is for the good.

It is not surprising that the Stoic school of philosophy, with its belief in a world permeated by divine reason, should share Aristotle's doctrine of a purpose in nature. So Seneca, a Roman Stoic of the first century AD, writes of animals' instinctive use of their faculties in this way:

> We were once debating whether animals had any consciousness of their own constitution. That this is the case is proved in particular by the fact that they move their limbs so fittingly and nimbly that they seem to be trained for the purpose ... No animal handles its limbs clumsily, no animal is at a loss how to use its body. They do this immediately on birth. They come into the world with this knowledge: they are born fully trained.
> (Ep.Moral. 121.5-6)

The Stoic explanation of this instinctive behaviour is a teleological one: an animal's automatic knowledge of how to make use of its powers is the gift of the providential and divine reason inherent in nature.

> Nature has passed on (to animals) nothing more than the duty of taking care of themselves and the skill to do so ... Nor is it surprising that living beings are born with a gift without which they would be born to no purpose. This is the first equipment that nature granted them in order to survive - the quality of adaptability and the desire for self-preservation. (121.24)

Teleology is a belief that dies hard, even today; and in the ancient world it was always difficult to evade its grasp, particularly when Aristotle had provided it with so much scientific respectability. But both before and after Aristotle there <u>were</u> thinkers who at the end of the day would have been prepared to say that biological development was something that had come about accidentally, as a result of arbitrary natural occurrences. This is a perspective which must now be examined, in the context of the four ideas which I have already delineated as contributing towards an evolutionary perspective.

HUMANS ARE ANIMALS

Those thinkers who believed in a permanent and significant distinction between humans and animals could not deny that a human being was in physiological terms very like an animal. And in the same way, thinkers who were prone to stress the identity of human and animal life could not of course overlook the vastly superior psychological attributes of human beings. The difference between the two lines of thought is not, however, just one of emphasis. The important question which divides them is a historical one, relating to how human beings <u>acquired</u> those attributes. Teleologists thought they were given by God, or were part of a rational scheme of things: humans had always been, potentially if not in actuality, superior to animals, and had never shared their status. But the others - the 'evolutionists' - believed that humans had at first led bestial lives, and had had the same status as animals; only gradually, as a result of unforeseen events, had they acquired the skills that had raised them above that level.

Many of the anthropogonies examined in the previous two chapters made little or no distinction between animal life in general, and the earliest forms of human life. Among them we can reckon the theories of Anaximander, Xenophanes, Empedocles, Anaxagoras, Archelaus, Democritus (probably), Protagoras (possibly), the Epicureans (especially Lucretius), and Diodorus. All of these writers posited the same overall material conditions for the generation of living creatures, including humans, and offered no genetic explanation for the subsequent career of the human race. Particularly noteworthy is Anaximander, who said that the first human beings emerged out of fishes or fish-like creatures. Even if he did not mean to suggest by this that marine animals had been biologically transformed into human beings (as some ancient commentators evidently believed), but only that human beings in their present biological form had originally been protected by fishes, nevertheless there was clearly here a remarkable recognition of the physical identity between the human race and the rest of the animal kingdom. One cannot imagine that a creature which had spent its formative years locked up inside a fish's abdomen would on issuing into the light of day begin at once to practise the mental feats for which it was later noted. Perhaps even more striking was Empedocles' invention of the 'man-faced animals of the ox family': so little genetic distinction did he make between humans and animals that he thought their species could be mixed, though the results would be incapable of survival. And with Empedocles too we perhaps get nearer than we do with Anaximander to a notion of biological transformation. Under Love's impulse, separate limbs came together to form either monsters or viable animals: if separate limbs could be said to have been living beings, then we could suggest that we have here an example of transformation from one state of being to another. 'Whole-natured forms', too, were in some way the precursors of regular men and women – a reference in Simplicius to the separation and tearing apart of the whole-natured form (382.20) suggests that this may have been a genuine transformation, achieved by their splitting into two. Neither of these 'transformations' would have taken place, of course, over many generations, through the operations of heredity, since neither limbs nor 'whole-natured forms' were capable of sexual reproduction. The 'transformation' would have been perpetrated within the lifetime of a single individual; it would in fact be a case of 'the inheritance of acquired characteristics'. But it is doubtful whether Empedocles could have seen the limbs as being 'alive' in any meaningful sense of the word, and we cannot be sure about the transition from 'whole-natured forms' to men and women. Speculation cannot take us very far, and here more than anywhere we must regret our inability to understand Empedocles' zoogony. But of this we can be reasonably sure - for Empedocles the first human beings were very like other animals, and in the creative process were preceded, chronologically if not genetically, by pre-human forms of life.

Anaxagoras and his pupil Archelaus, like other Presocratics, had their first humans derived from inorganic matter along with other animals: for Archelaus we have recorded in addition the assertion that all animals (including humans) originally had the same life-style. And for these two philosophers the links between humans and animals were not purely physical: Anaxagoras believed, according to Aristotle, that all animals 'both large and small, worthy and unworthy' are equipped with mind (De anima 404 B4-5); Archelaus thought the same, but added that some creatures make use of their mental powers 'more quickly' than others (Hippolytus Ref 1.9.6.). And Democritus clearly did not envisage a rapidly emerging human superiority over the rest of the animal kingdom, for he declared that some of our most important skills - weaving, architecture and singing - have been learnt from animals (Plutarch, De sollert. anim. 974A).

With Protagoras we have a problem, of course, because we do not know to what extent his account of the original condition of animals has been fingered by Plato. In the latter's dialogue, Protagoras describes how the gods, after they had created animals out of a mixture of elements, gave the Titans, Prometheus and Epimetheus, the task of equipping the animals with suitable powers. Epimetheus begged to be allowed to do the distribution, and on the whole he managed very well:

> ... he gave to some creatures strength without speed, and equipped the weaker kinds with speed. To some he gave arms, while to the unarmed he gave some other faculty, and so devised means for their preservation. To those on whom he bestowed smallness, he granted winged flight or a dwelling underground; to those whom he allowed a greater stature, their size in itself afforded protection. And the whole distribution was made on this compensatory basis; in this way he carefully ensured that no species should be destroyed.

Epimetheus also clothed and shod them - with fur or skins, hooves or hard pads, and gave each animal its distinctive kind of food - and those creatures who were destined to make up the diet of others were made more prolific so that they would not become extinct, (Protagoras 320D - 321B).

Taken at its face value, this is a thoroughly teleological account, positing as it does a form of divine creation which ensures by its even distribution of natural endowments the preservation of all the species. Even if we remove the gods from the picture (as I think we probably should), we are still left with a provident and rational nature on our hands. And if we have been led to believe by the zoogony that has gone before that there was originally no differentiation between humans and other animals, then what follows will perhaps disabuse us. For Protagoras goes on to explain that Epimetheus used up all the available capacities on other animals, and forgot about the human race, which was thus left 'naked and unshod, uncovered and unarmed'. Prometheus, in order to give them some measure of protection, stole fire and technical skills from the gods and gave them to humans (321C - 321D). From the beginning, the story can be interpreted as suggesting, the human race was marked off from the rest of the animal kingdom by its possession of a technical bent - and, Protagoras says, by virtue of this special skill it assumed at once a different life-style. This differentiation is emphasised in the story by the fact that Prometheus - 'the forethinker' - rather than Epimetheus, is made responsible for the equipment of the human race.

This is a view of things which we would not expect from a relativist and a sceptic like Protagoras; and at this point we begin to wonder whether Plato is playing entirely fair by him. But we can perhaps rescue him as an evolutionist, if we assume that the delay in the story between the creation and the equipment of the human race constitutes a metaphorical expression of gradualism. (Although of course if we try hard enough we can read anything we like into a myth - perhaps it is better to leave it alone.) What we certainly can say, I think, is that there are still some shades of an evolutionary perspective in the account (so perhaps Plato has not completely misrepresented him): what comes over very vividly from it is the sense of a struggle for survival (a struggle which human beings are in some ways singularly ill-equipped to cope with), and a recognition that survival need be at species level only, and can in some circumstances absorb the destruction of large numbers of individuals.

About Protagoras we can never be sure. But what seems clear is that by the late fifth century BC, fuelled by Presocratic speculations, a debate was under way about the fundamental differences between humans and other animals. Comedy is usually a good indicator of popular controversy: and so it is probably significant that in Aristophanes' Clouds a young man (schooled in new-fangled philosophy) justifies beating his father on the grounds that game-cocks do it, and 'they are no different from us, except they don't put measures to the vote'(1427-9).

The teleology of Plato and Aristotle may have put paid for some time to the identification of primitive humans with animals, but from the late fourth century BC on, this view was revived by the Epicureans and by whatever Hellenistic writers were the source for Diodorus' pre-history. Thinkers in the late first century AD were obviously still fascinated by comparisons between humans and animals, and some at least clearly believed that a knowledge of basic human nature could be derived from the study of animal behaviour: so Plutarch could state that it was common practice for philosophers involved in disputes to 'appeal to the nature of dumb animals, as if to a foreign city, and arrive at a judgement by reference to animals' feelings and habits, as being basic and uncorrupted' (De amore prolis 13.16.1). This interest in animals does not in every case indicate an evolutionary perpective – many would have agreed with Aristotle that there are certain basic psychological traits shared by all living creatures. But it is a view that can and sometimes does prepare the ground for a recognition that the human race had begun its existence in an animal-like condition, and had only gradually and fortuitously achieved a fully human status.

LINKS WITH THE PHYSICAL ENVIRONMENT

Enough has been said in the previous two chapters to show that for many Presocratic and post-Aristotelian thinkers, the appearance of life on earth was a by-product of world creation. The mixture of elements in the earth had not been produced specifically for the purpose of creating living beings (as, for example, is the case in Plato's Timaeus), but had come about as part of the overall creative process. And in that

that creative process was a mechanistic one, so the creation of living beings was mechanistic or accidental. Thus biology was dependent for its very existence on large-scale physical changes.

In the modern theory of evolution, continuing change in the physical environment has created conditions favourable to biological transformation. Ancient zoogonies may contain very little notion of biological transformation; but in some writers at least we can perceive a recognition of the fundamental effect which environmental upheavals have had on the way of life if not on the biological forms of living creatures. Anaximander believed that as the water covering the earth evaporated, terrestrial animals (including humans) broke out of their fishes or their spiny barks and took to dry land. Presumably if pressed he would have had to say that if the earth had not been drying out land animals would never have shed their marine casing. There is, as I have suggested in Chapter 2, a touch of teleology here, a suggestion that nature was planning the preservation in a watery world of incipient land animals. And we should not of course be surprised at this - the belief that the human race in particular is an essential part of creation has always been hard to shake off. What I think we can say is that Anaximander was working his way towards freeing himself from this notion, and was at least able to reject the belief (which Aristotle two hundred years later did not reject) that the biological purposes of nature are worked out within the lifespan of an individual. Our way of life has not been fixed for all time, Anaximander is saying - the earliest representatives of our species started life in quite a different way, because the physical environment then was quite different. From here it is a short step to the realisation that the changes in life-style brought about by changes in the environment are not necessarily forseeable ones.

Again, we cannot say much about Empedocles, because we know so little. But it seems that for him the environment must have been changing continuously, because of the constant intermingling of elements (and, according to 'two-worlders', the constant separation of elements in the alternative cycle) going on in our world. And this physical process had at least in its early stages had an effect on biology - it certainly brought the limbs together into proper creatures, and in some way it also effected a transition from 'whole-natured forms' to men and women.

But the most far-reaching changes in the way of life of a human race which had begun its history in an animal-like condition were the changes brought about by its increasing powers of reason. Ancient 'evolutionists' were aware of the importance in this process of the interaction between humans and the physical world around them; but this is a large topic, which will be touched on in a later chapter. (1)

HUMANS ONLY GRADUALLY ACQUIRED THE STATUS OF FULLY RATIONAL BEINGS

The belief that human beings were in the beginning very much like other animals does not in itself constitute an evolutionary perspective. It must be coupled with the idea that the gradual development of the physical, psychological and social skills which have subsequently raised them above that level was the outcome, not of some divine plan or natural law, but of a random and haphazard interaction between humans and the world around them.

The question of how and why human beings have acquired their present status in the world is one of huge proportions, of course, and cannot be dealt with adequately here. What I want to do now is just to give a broad indication of the lines of thought followed in this inquiry by the thinkers whom I have labelled 'evolutionist'.

No-one in the ancient world would have disputed the fact that the human race was at that time capable of many more things than it had been in the past. What they did argue about (among other things) was whether the rationality which was the key to human achievements had been implanted in humans (by God, or by nature) for the whole of their existence, or whether it had developed gradually. Evolutionists would have said 'gradually'. Anaxagoras and Archelaus, as we have seen, thought that animals and humans started life with the same basic mental equipment, but that - as Archelaus suggested - in humans mental powers had developed more rapidly. The author of the Prometheus Bound wrote that before their acquisition of technological knowledge humans passed a mindless existence in underground caves 'like swarming ants' (432-3). The story told by Protagoras in Plato's dialogue perhaps surprises us because it seems to be saying that humans have always been distinguished from animals by their possession of technological skills; but when Protagoras

85

describes how, at a much later stage, Zeus distributed respect and justice among the first city-dwellers (322C-D), this seems to be a clear statement of the belief that political and social skills, at least, develop only with time. The life led by Lucretius' first humans was, in its feeding and sleeping habits and its lack of a stable domestic environment, like that of wild animals (5.931-2, 946-7, 970); and Diodorus attributed to his primitives 'an unordered and bestial life' (1.8.1): both these writers ascribed the growth of civilisation to a slow and painful learning process on the part of the human race. And Plutarch, in his lengthy digression on animal behaviour, said that humans are by nature like animals, but that the growth in them of reason has led them into many new experiences (De amore prolis 13.16.1.).

How did the development of rationality come about? Anaxagoras thought that it was produced by an accident of physiology - that we have become intelligent because we possess hands (Aristotle, De part.an. 687 A7). Others (such as Democritus) (2) pointed to our experience of physical need - humans being the most ill-equipped of all animals to cope with a hostile environment, we were forced to devise artificial means of protecting ourselves; and with experience came knowledge, and with knowledge came reason. Others again were impressed by the significance of chance events, or by our superior powers of observation. The reasons are complex, and need not be analysed more deeply here. What it is important to note is the emergence of a whole train of thought that saw human achievement as something that was not preordained either by God or by a pre-determined programme of mental development. Our bodies, our basic mental equipment, and our experience of our environment can account for all.

THE SURVIVAL OF THE FITTEST

The most radical and imaginative manifestation of the evolutionary perspective is to be found in the 'survival of the fittest' theories outlined by Empedocles and Lucretius. The assorted limbs produced in Empedocles' first phase of generation came together, we are told, to produce monstrous creatures either with limb deformities, or of mixed species, or of mixed gender. Aristotle refers to these monsters in a section of the Physics (198B17-32) where he is playing devil's advocate, and is putting forward a hypothetical argument for the non-teleological creation of bodily parts. Why should it not be just a coincidence, he asks, that our teeth are so admirably constructed for the consumption of food? And why should we not assume that all our other organs have been put together in the same purposeless fashion? 'Whenever all things fell into place as they would have done had they been created for a purpose, these survived, being spontaneously compounded in a suitable way. But where this did not happen, they perished and are perishing, as Empedocles says of his "man-faced animals of the ox family" ...'.

One thing which one can pretty certainly deduce from this passage is Empedocles' belief that monsters of the kind he had described in fragment 61 perished because they were not physically equipped for survival. (3) Here, then, we have one half at least of a survival of the fittest theory - the negative half of it, the realisation that some creatures were not fit to survive. It differs from Darwin's theory of natural selection, of course, in that Empedocles' monsters would not have survived for any great length of time - probably not for more than one generation: they were obsolete right from the start, and did not become so as a result of changing environmental conditions.

But is the positive side of the theory present here, too? - were more viable creatures being generated at the same time as the monsters? Our opinion on this point depends on whether or not we believe that the hypothetical argument Aristotle is putting forward in the first sentence of the quotation was really derived from Empedocles. Aristotle certainly does not say that it was, and though that would seem a likely conclusion, we cannot be sure. What we can be sure about is that someone (if only Aristotle's 'alter ego', though this seems unlikely) was propounding a theory of a purely mechanical and accidental process of creation, whereby some creatures were by chance given the equipment for survival, and some were not.

Aristotle's counter-argument is probably worthy of note, since it belongs to the teleological theory discussed earlier. It is that the products of nature always (or almost always) appear in the same way, like rain in winter; and this cannot possibly be the result of chance, since things produced by chance are untoward and freakish, like frequent rain in summer (Aristotle had never visited Britain, of course). The minute experimental work carried on by our genetic systems, and the millions of years over which this has operated, were naturally quite unknown to him.

We are not getting very far with Empedocles here, but perhaps the Aristotle passage offers one further clue. What is the significance of the expression 'perished <u>and are perishing</u>'? Possibly the phrase 'as Empedocles says' is to be read loosely as applying only to the past and not to the present tense of the verb (4). But it is not out of the question for Empedocles to have believed that monsters were still being created from time to time in his own day. The material conditions which had once produced a crop of monsters, though undergoing gradual change, would not necessarily have been completely transformed - but now the chance coming together of inappropriate parts would be taking place on the level of reproduction, rather than of generation from the earth (5). Many ancient people did believe that grotesque creatures were being born in their own time (6) and Empedocles could well have been one of them. And if it was part of his theory that the odd monster was still appearing along with regular animals and humans, this would lend credence to the idea that the odd regular creature could at one time have been produced alongside the monsters.

That separate limbs did occasionally come together to form viable creatures is suggested more forcibly by a passage from Simplicius' commentary on Aristotle's <u>Physics</u>: 'Thus Empedocles says that under the rule of Love, first of all the parts of animals were produced by chance, such as heads and hands and feet; then these came together: "Man-faced animals of the ox family and others again sprang up", namely "creatures that were basically men with ox heads", that is, composed from the ox and from man. And as many as these parts as were fitted together in such a way as to be able by chance to ensure their preservation, these became animals and survived, because they fulfilled mutual needs - the teeth tearing and softening the food, the stomach digesting it, and the liver converting it into blood. And the human head, when it meets a human body, ensures the preservation of the whole, but being incompatible with the ox body, it is destroyed. For all things that did not come together in accordance with the right formula perished. Everything happens in the same way, even today. All of the ancient physicists seem to be of this opinion who say that material necessity is the cause of generation; and among the later ones this is also the case with the Epicureans' (in <u>Phys.</u> 371.33 - 372.11)

Simplicius at least (who had certainly read Empedocles) was in no doubt that some of the separate limbs came together in such a way as to form creatures capable of survival, and that these combinations were achieved purely by chance. Some scholars see this as a misinterpretation of Aristotle on Simplicius' part, others disagree. (7) It is true that the Aristotle passage could easily lend itself to misinterpretation; but since there are some obviously genuine features in the Simplicius passage which are not to be found in the Aristotle (such as the reference to the rule of Love), I tend to believe that Simplicius must have referred back to his Empedocles, and got it right. Corroborative evidence for the purely accidental character of Empedocles' creative process can be found in another Aristotle passage - 'one might ask whether or not it is possible that elements moving in an unordered way should come together in some cases in the kind of combinations out of which bodies put together by nature are composed? I mean like bones and flesh? This is the sort of thing which Empedocles says happened under Love, for he writes "many heads without necks sprang up"' (De caelo 300 B26-30). And that Empedocles saw chance combinations as resulting sometimes in the appearance of regular animals is confirmed by Censorinus (4.7-8) and by Philoponus (314.7-315.6).

If Simplicius' account is correct, then Empedocles was responsible for a remarkable insight into the operations by which biological efficiency is achieved. Purely mechanical physical processes produce biological variations which are entirely fortuitous - but non-survival ensures that only the efficient varieties go on to reproduce themselves. This is really quite close to the modern theory of evolution. But it lacks, as ever, the knowledge that variation can be created in the course of sexual reproduction, and that inefficient varieties can with changing circumstances become efficient ones. And hence Empedocles never grasped the idea that natural selection is a continuing process, and can lead to the transformation of existing species. For him, selection had to be confined to the very first beings in creation - once sex took over from the unrestrained intermingling of elements, a limit was placed on biological improvement.

Doubts must remain about the interpretation of Empedocles' zoogony, but there can be no doubt about Lucretius: his is the clearest expression of a 'survival of the fittest' theory afforded us by the ancient world. Having explained how the earth produced every kind of animal from wombs, Lucretius goes on to say that at that time many monsters were also created, which were of mixed sex or deformed in some way, - lacking hands, feet, eyes or mouths, or 'locked together in their whole body'; but that these soon died out - 'they could not reach the desired blossoming of maturity, or find food, or be joined together in the act of love' (5.837-48). Obviously, these monsters perished fairly rapidly - it seems unlikely that any could have survived for more than one generation. But at the same time viable creatures were being born from the earth: so we have here both the negative and the positive sides of survival of the fittest.

Lucretius' belief in monsters was very probably derived from Empedocles, whom he much admired; although there are differences between the two theories - separate limbs play no part in Lucretius' version, and he refutes in some detail the inclusion of animals of mixed species among the monsters. (8) Whether or not the monsters had also appeared in the lost works of Epicurus, it is impossible to say - Lucretius could well have borrowed them from Empedocles on his own initiative. (9)

Empedocles, of course, saw monsters as the product of a mingling together of elements. As an atomist, Lucretius would have thought differently. In his zoogony, he makes no mention of the atomic basis of creation, but we can assume that the chance coming together in the earth of unsuitable atoms was responsible for the appearance of unviable creatures. This conclusion is supported by his more general theory of the experimental creation of worlds (5.416-31): from infinite time past, he has told us, atoms moving about in the void have been accidentally uniting in unfruitful combinations; it is purely by chance that they sometimes come together in such a way as to form the beginnings of earth, sea, sky and living creatures. 'Survival of the fittest', then, operates on a cosmic level: we can easily imagine that the same atomic process continued when the world was newly formed, and that monsters were the products of chance atomic encounters. This experimental view of creation is, of course, anti-teleological, since it precludes the possibility that there is any predetermined end involved in nature's creativity. Elsewhere Lucretius rejects biological teleology more specifically, when he argues that limbs and sense organs were not created to fulfil a function: 'nothing at all has been born in the body so that we

Evolution and the Survival of the Fittest

might be able to use it, but once born a thing creates its own use'. One proof of this is derived from his empiricism: until a thing has been created and used, there can be no concept of its usefulness, and therefore no purpose in its creation - 'seeing did not exist before the light of the eyes was born' (4.823-857).

Lucretius (and his precursor Empedocles) may well have believed, like many people in the ancient world, that monsters were occasionally born even after sexual reproduction had replaced generation from the earth. Monstrous births were in fact of great religious and political importance to the Romans, since they were regarded as portents of future disaster. Livy recounts several instances of such prodigies in the course of the Second Punic War - for example a colt born to a cow, and an abnormally large child of uncertain sex; and to the troubled early years of the second century BC assigns several alarming births, including a lamb with two heads, a pig with a man's head, and a colt with five feet (23.31; 27.37; 32.1&9). Pliny the Elder tells us that hermaphrodites had once been regarded as portents, but by his own day had become only objects of fun (N.H. 7.3); but he also relates the occurrence of two rather more prodigious births - of an elephant and of a snake to two human females. Lucan lists among the portents which heralded the Civil War between Pompey and Caesar the birth of infants with limbs that were monstrous in their shape or their number (1.522-83), and Tacitus says that shortly before the Emperor Claudius' death a pig with hawk's talons and half-bestial children were born (Annals 12.64). Lucretius would doubtless have rejected as physical impossibilities the births involving mixed species, but may well have believed - quite rightly - that creatures of uncertain sex, or deformed in their limbs, were still being born in his own day. However, he would not have accepted (because of their incapacity for sexual reproduction) the existence of whole races of monsters; but Pliny the Elder did - among the many he lists are people with one eye, or with back-to-front feet, or with one leg and an enormous foot, or with no noses or no mouths (7.2).

Lucretius' historical monsters could not possibly have survived for very long, even in the absence of any competition from other creatures. But in the next passage he discusses the extinction, not of individual monstrosities, but of whole species. Here, he gets closer to the Darwinian theory of natural selection, in that he recognises that competition is one of the factors in survival; and that the selection process can be rather protracted and can dispose of whole groups of relatively viable animals. 'And it must have been the case that many species of living creatures died out at this time'. Those species, he says, which have managed to survive up to the present day must have been protected from the beginning either by their possession of an inherent means of self-defence, or by their usefulness to the human race. 'The fierce and savage species of lions has been protected by their bravery, that of foxes by their cunning, that of deer by their speedy flight. But lightly sleeping dogs, with their faithful hearts, and the whole species of beasts of burden, and wool-bearing flocks, and horned herds, they are all entrusted to the protection of men. They eagerly fled the wild beasts and sought safety and regular food, which we give them as rewards for their usefulness.' But those species which possessed none of these qualities, 'all these fell a prey to others, entangled in the fateful trammels of their own being, until nature brought their species to destruction' (5.855-77). The non-survival of whole species was not, so far as we know, a feature of Empedocles' zoogony.

But Lucretius is as far from the modern theory of evolution as Empedocles is, in that again there is no awareness that mutation plus sexual reproduction can lead to biological transformation, and to the emergence of new species. In fact, there can be no doubt that Lucretius would have rejected such a notion. One of his proofs that animals of mixed species could never have existed is his (erroneous) observation that, although the earth today produces many grasses, crops and trees, we never see their species being mixed; 'but each of these things grows by its own process, and all preserve their distinctions by a fixed law of nature' (5.916-924). In disposing of the idea that existing species can be naturally mixed, he also closes his mind to the thought that one species can emerge out of another.

This theory of the fixity of the species was seen by Lucretius as a deduction from an atomic law of combination. Elsewhere he has argued that all compounds are made up of atoms of different classes (that is, of different sizes and shapes), but that there is a limit to the combinations of classes which can be achieved: every class of atom is not capable of combining with every other class. If this were possible, you would see animals of mixed species coming into existence, but as it is, everything keeps

Evolution and the Survival of the Fittest

to its own species, because every species is characterised by distinctive atoms, which when brought together make distinctive arrangements and perform distinctive movements. In living things, these distinctive atoms are passed on from parent to child, and they then proceed to absorb compatible atoms from the nourishment that is consumed. But it is not just living things that conform to this atomic law: every atomic compound, including the land, the sea, and the sky, is kept distinct by the limit on combination (2.700-729). (10)

All this is very brilliant; but he was wrong, of course, about the species being fixed. Living organisms are infinitely more complex than Lucretius imagined, and between them and inorganic matter there is one fundamental difference: on the route from the atom to the whole living organism, one encounters the self-copying gene, and the gene does not always copy itself exactly.

One should not leave the subject of evolution without a reference to the light-hearted explanation of human love given by the comic poet Aristophanes in Plato's Symposium (189C - 193D). When human beings were first created, Aristophanes recounts, they were in the form of circles or 'spherical wholes', and had two faces, two sets of genitals, four ears, four arms, four legs, and so on. They should in fact, as it later emerges, be pictured as two people joined together at the front, but with their faces and genitals on what we would call their backs. Among these creatures there were three sexes, the male, the female, (with two identical sets of genitals), and the hermaphrodite (with one of each). They could all walk backwards and forwards, since there was no such concept for them; and when they wanted to run they turned rapid cartwheels, using all eight of their limbs.

These circle-people can scarcely be said to represent a more primitive form of life, since it was their outstanding physical ability, coupled with their mental precocity, which, according to Aristophanes, made them unfit for survival. The gods' position was threatened by their ambition, so Zeus decided to weaken them by slicing each of them in half down the middle. Apollo was given the job of twisting their faces round to the side which had just been bisected, so that they might view the signs of their fall from grace.

From this time on, each of the new human beings longed to be reunited with his or her other half, and when by chance they met they would rush into each other's arms. Soon they began to perish from hunger and neglect, because they tried to do absolutely everything together. Eventually, Zeus took pity on them, and moved their genitals round to what were now their fronts, so that they might at least have sexual intercourse, and by satisfying their desire for each other in this way could then get back to the business of life. Those that had been hermaphrodites in their circular existence now became heterosexual, the others were homosexual. We now come to the message of the story: 'it is from this distant time that love for each other has been ingrained in the human race, the love that restores us to our ancient state and attempts to weld two into one, thus healing human nature'. When any of us has the good fortune to meet our other half, the result is overwhelming love and life-long partnership.

This fantasy provides us with the only clear-cut example of biological transformation to be found in Greek and Roman literature - apart, that is, from the common 'goddess and bull mating to produce Minotaur', or 'weeping nymph turned into willow tree' style of transformation to be found in mainstream mythology. As with the transformations posited for Empedocles, Aristophanes' version was not effected through the operations of sexual reproduction: here again we have a case of the inheritance of acquired characteristics. And it is not just their acquired physiology which we descendants of the circle-people inherit; for we too, though we are not ourselves the product of a bisection, spend our lives, according to Aristophanes, engaged in the search for our 'other half'.

But this transformation is the very reverse of the ones encompassed in the modern theory of evolution, and the process in general is the very reverse of the evolutionary process envisaged by some ancient thinkers. For it does not represent biological improvement, but rather deterioration; it does not secure a rise from an animal-like condition, but instead signifies a demotion from a status that rivalled that of the gods. Aristophanes' humans have moved downwards from the level of the gods towards that of the animals, just as in a visible and tangible way a Minotaur or a willow-tree nymph is a compromise between divinity and bestiality or vegetation. These humans participate in fact in the same fall from grace as is outlined in Hesiod's Theogony.

It has often been suggested that Plato is here parodying Empedocles' 'whole-natured forms', who may well have been spherical, and whom Simplicius suggests may at some stage have been split in two. (11). There could also be a parallel with the monsters put together from separate limbs, some of whom had 'faces and breasts on both sides', or genitalia that were partly male and partly female. The object of the parody, if parody it is, may not be a very specific one: others have pointed out that Plato could well have had in mind the monsters or hermaphrodites which are a common feature of myth. (12) But, as far as I know, mythology offers us nothing quite so close to the Aristophanic story as does Empedocles' belief in monsters or 'whole-natured forms' as precursors of human beings, and I must admit to finding the Empedocles theory somewhat tempting.

I want to add something finally, in anticipation of what is to follow, about value judgements. The acceptance of the principle of gradualism in human development - the belief that human beings began their history in an animal-like condition, and only slowly and haphazardly acquired a fully human status - does not necessarily imply a philosophy of progress. Just as there are people today who accept Darwinian evolution, but think that the human race might have been better off it had remained in the trees along with the monkeys; so it possible to imagine an ancient viewpoint which accepted gradualism as a fact, but denied the positive value of the process. Such a viewpoint did indeed exist in the ancient world, but it was rare, as we shall see. The inclination to take the current status of the human race as a fixed point of reference was so strong, that judgements on the value of the historical process were generally bound up with beliefs about the diachronic relationship between that point and the outer poles of existence. If we started our history as gods, and bestiality is seen as the opposite extreme of existence, then the judgement is an adverse one. If on the other hand we started out as animals, and have divinity at the opposite end of the scale of existence, then the judgement is favourable. It is fairly unusual (though not unheard of) for a writer to say 'we started as animals, and should have stayed that way'.

It has sometimes been said that the emergence in the nineteenth century of the theory of biological evolution had little or no effect on philosophies of progress. (13) Not only was the seminal work of the progressivist philosopher Comte produced before the advent of the Darwinian theory; but the notion of a necessary and natural law of progress, involving a pre-existent and worthwhile goal, was incompatible with the open-ended and fortuitous character of biological transformation. This may well be the case; but philosophies of progress can take more than one form. Progressivism in the ancient world seldom encompassed the teleological notion of an inevitable social and cultural goal; it was, indeed, often half-hearted and hemmed about with reservations. But progressivism of a kind it was (so I shall be arguing), and it was far more often than not linked with the idea of an unforeseen rise from an animal-like condition.

My point about the ancient tendency to judge in a favourable light any historical process that leads from animals to humans can be illustrated by a brief excursion into animalitarianism, or the belief in the superiority of animals. (14) Comparisons between animals and humans were common in the ancient world, and there was no shortage of writers who were convinced that animals were physically, temperamentally, or even emotionally superior to human beings. But it was unusual for anyone not to accept that the human race's possession of reason had raised it on to a plane above that of the animals. The Cynics did reject this viewpoint, and believed that we should forgo the fruits of civilisation and endeavour to live like animals.

> Do you not see these beasts and birds? How much more free from trouble they live than men, and how much more happily, too? and how much healthier and stronger they are, and how each of them lives for as long as is possible? Yet they have neither hands nor human intelligence; but they possess one good above all which outweighs all disadvantages - they possess no property. (15)

An author of new comedy writing at about the same time, could echo this thought in exclaiming 'Oh thrice blessed and thrice happy in all things are the beasts who have not the power of reason.' (16) But this view is unusual: most thinkers adopted the attitude of the elder Pliny, who while he wrote at length about the advantages of animals and the miseries of the human condition, had to admit that though it is bought at a cruel price 'the first place is given by right to man, for whose sake nature seems to have brought forth all else'. (N.H. 7.1)

Vegetarianism provides another insight into the reaction to the move away from bestiality. In historical terms, vegetarianism could be seen as one facet of the original identity between humans and animals: the primitive abstinence from flesh, the inability to use animals, symbolises the shared status of the two groups. Thus a number of evolutionists tell us that the first humans fed only on herbs and fruits, and mark the invention of cooking as one of the stages in human advancement. But the situation here is complicated: vegetarianism can also symbolise the original divine status of the human race, and meat-eating can be seen as an item in the fall from grace, bringing humans closer to animals. This is a topic which must be considered more closely in the survey of cultural histories which follows.

Perhaps because it never embraced a notion of on-going biological transformation, the evolutionary perspective in ancient thought was rarely confined to questions of physiology. It was a line of reasoning which had far-reaching ramifications for an analysis of social and cultural development. If humankind's status in the world had been fixed for all time, if humans had always had much the same aptitudes and abilities as they possess today, then this suggests that the impetus for change in human affairs must have come from some external force. But if humans are not a fixed quantity, if their power of reasoning grows along with their ability to control their environment, then this prompts the thought that the objects of reasoning - justice and morality - also grow along with the human race; that they are in fact, just like human beings, creations of the historical process. From consideration of the earth from which we grew, or the heaven from which we fell, we move naturally to an analysis of trends in human civilisation.

NOTES

1. See below, chap. 7, for references in progressivist accounts to the imitation of nature.
2. See, for example, DK B144.
3. O. Hamelin argues, not very convincingly, that Aristotle's 'as Empedocles says' refers only to 'where this did not happen', and not to 'perished and are perishing': see Aristotle: Physique II, traduction et commentaire (Paris, 1931), p.149. For O'Brien's counter-argument, see Empedocles p.217.

4. This is the way in which it seems to be interpreted by O'Brien; see note (3).

5. If this <u>was</u> Empedocles' belief, then we would probably have to accept that we are living now under the influence of Love, which was responsible for the first monsters. This would lend support to the 'one-world system' interpretation of Empedocles' cosmogony see above, p.37.

6. See below, p.91

7. Zeller, p.989, n.2, and C.E. Millerd, <u>On the Interpretation of Empedocles</u> (Diss. Chicago, 1908), p.58-59, favour misinterpretation. Among those who believe that Simplicius got it more or less right are Bignone, p.573 n.1, and O'Brien, p.211-216. O'Brien accepts that viable creatures were produced as well as monsters; although he thinks that Simplicius <u>has</u> distorted Empedocles in his attribution to him of so overtly an anti-teleological view of creation. To my mind, the operations of Love and Strife <u>can</u> be seen as purely mechanistic and non-purposeful; and Empedocles himself tells us that within the broad framework established by Love, chance can still be at work (see fragment 75).

8. See 5.878-924. This passage is ostensibly directed at the composite creatures of myth, such as centaurs, scyllas, and chimaeras; but he may well have had Empedocles in mind as well. Plutarch (<u>Adv.Col.</u> 1123B) provides us with more concrete evidence of an Epicurean repudiation of Empedocles, when he tells us that they derided his 'man-faced animal of the ox family'.

9. Bignone (p.629-30) thinks that the last sentence of the Simplicius passage quoted on page 88 provides evidence for monsters in Epicurus, obviously believing that 'this opinion' refers not just to an accidental theory of creation, but more specifically to the dying out of monsters. Even if this were the case, Simplicius could well be using Lucretius and not Epicurus himself as his source for Epicurean beliefs.

10. For a more detailed discussion of the Epicurean idea of limit, and the possibility of spontaneity within limit, see P.H. De Lacy, 'Limit and variation in the Epicurean philosophy', <u>Phoenix</u> 23 (1969), p.104-113. A rather different view of the Epicurean notion of natural law is expressed by A.A. Long in 'Chance and natural law in Epicureanism', <u>Phronesis</u> 22 (1977), p.63-88.

11. Simplicius, <u>in Phys.</u> 282.20. According to one of the textual emendations of fragment 62, the 'whole-natured forms' 'lacked the organ which is

proper to men'. In spite of my best endeavours, however, I cannot see how this can be a reference to hermaphroditism.

12. See K.J. Dover 'Aristophanes' speech in Plato's Symposium', J.H.S. 86 (1966). p.41-50; and O'Brien, p.228. O'Brien believes that when Plato at 193A refers to Zeus' threat to split humans into two again if they do not behave, and make them into bas-reliefs, then he is parodying Empedocles' belief in separate limbs. This is in accordance with O'Brien's theory that all four modes of generation occurred in both cycles, but under Strife in reverse order.

13. By, for example, K. Bock, 'Theories of progress, development, evolution', in T. Bottomore and R. Nisbet (eds.) A History of sociological analysis (London, 1979), p.70-71.

14. For a collection of texts relating to animalitarianism, see A.O. Lovejoy and G. Boas, Primitivism and related ideas in Antiquity (vol.1. of A documentary history of primitivism and related ideas; Baltimore, 1935), p.389-420.

15. Diogenes, in Dio Chrysostom, Disc. 10.16.
16. Philemon, fragment 93 (Kock).

Part Two

PATTERNS OF CULTURAL HISTORY

Chapter Five

VALUES AND CYCLES

Greek and Roman authors frequently coupled their theories of the origins of life on earth with sketches of the primitive existence of the first human beings, and of the subsequent landmarks in the development of civilisation. Speculations about the origins of cultural as well as of biological life probably go back to the earliest Presocratic philosophers, though we have lost most of what they thought on the subject. (1) Certainly by the time of the later Presocratics and the Sophists, prehistory and cultural history had become popular subjects for lectures and treatises. (2) As Detienne has rightly said, in Greece (and indeed in the Roman world), 'a proper history of culture usurped the function of mythical discourse about how things began'. (3) Myths about a rise from the earth or a fall from the heavens continued to express the conflict in and among ancient writers about the history of the human status; but these were increasingly supplemented by more circumstantial accounts of how we got to where we are today.

With the cultural histories came value judgements, and more specifically the desire to assign an ascending or descending scale of values to the historical process. Thus, as Ernest Gellner has said, 'time ceases to be morally neutral' (4), and history is constrained to yield up a philosophy. It is in this aspect that cultural history comes to fulfil the same function as anthropogonic myth; and it is an aspect which is scarcely if ever absent from the picture - I would doubt myself whether in any general history at any rate, time can ever appear to be morally neutral, to the eye of the reader if not to that of the writer. For instance, when Nestor, speaking of the famous heroes with whom he fought in the past, says of them 'they were the strongest of

103

men reared on the earth ... Of the men on earth today, no-one could fight with them' (Iliad I. 266-72), we naturally conclude that Nestor is saying 'everything was better in the good old days', although he (and Homer) could conceivably have meant something quite different. Even more dubiously, when a cultural historian tells us about the invention of cooking, for example, because we find it hard to imagine existing on a diet of raw food, we assume him to be giving an account of human progress. Sometimes the point of view of the author seems blatant, sometimes we are more obviously imposing one on him; but I am not sure we can ever really distinguish between the two situations.

The moral trends which we discern in other people's view of history are not always continuous ones. Most of us would agree that as far as Thucydides was concerned, things had got worse in Athens since the death of Pericles, but that does not mean that he saw history as an entirely or even predominantly regressive process. However, when it comes to the very broad and very schematic (and generally utterly speculative) histories which describe the long-drawn-out process of cultural development, we can generally detect some none-too-complex point of view - the very fact that the author has chosen to write about cultural history suggests that he has one. But it seems to me that what an author is very often trying to do in setting out this point of view is not to answer the question 'at what time - past, present or future - would I locate the best condition of the human race?'; but rather to establish the oppositional criteria by which to judge the present-day human condition. By describing a hypothetical 'best' and 'worst' situation, we endeavour to come to terms with living in a world in which good and evil are inextricably mixed. Some authors seek to do this by the comparative method - by giving an account of contemporary races of people who are pursuing an idyllically 'good' or thoroughly 'bad' way of life (which is a method which will be touched on in the following chapters); some authors choose the historical method, and try to imagine what we have come from and what we are moving towards, (this is the method which is to be the main focus of my attention). For some, 'best' is in the past and 'worst' is in the future, for others it is vice versa. This must indicate philosophically and psychologically important differences, but the judgement on where we are now is the same in either case - we are half-way between good and evil. If we

104

remove the time dimension from the picture, the differences become insignificant.

The points of view expressed (or perceived) in cultural histories can be broadly divided into three categories:

A. That which posits an idyllic early period of civilisation, when life was better than it is now both in moral and in material terms. Since then there has been moral deterioration accompanied by an increase in the effort required to maintain our material standards. This is the point of view which Lovejoy and Boas have labelled 'soft primitivism'. (5) In a historicising context it can be called the 'Golden Age' point of view.

B. That which envisages a primitive era which was both physically hard, and morally bad or neutral. Civilisation is seen as a process of improvement in all spheres of life, a process which has continued up to the present, and which may (but not necessarily so) be continued indefinitely in the future. This can be called the 'progressivist' point of view.

C. That which recognises that life at the dawn of history was more difficult in its physical aspects, but which attributes to it a simplicity and goodness which has been lost with increasing technical sophistication. The term which Lovejoy and Boas use to describe this point of view is 'hard primitivism'. (6)

In chapters 1 to 3, I have tried to suggest that myths and scientific theories about the origins of the human race can be divided into 'fall' and 'rise' categories. These categories obviously have their respective counterparts in the 'Golden Age' and 'progressivist' categories described in A and B, and indeed the two subjects - origins and cultural history - can often be found together in the same author. Both the A-type and the B-type accounts of cultural history (though I would not underrate their philosophical differences) express, I believe, the same view of the human race's intermediate status in the world. C is somewhat different, I think: in chapter 8 I shall be suggesting that the impetus behind 'hard primitivism' is a rejection rather than an acceptance of all the values of present-day civilisation.

Clearly, there are many variations on the three themes outlined above, and many overlappings. Not all authors believe that cultural history exhibits just one of these trends: some, for example, might envisage a process whereby the human race degenerates from an early Golden Age, but then begins to pick up again; others might posit a period of progress followed by a period of regress. And it is fairly unusual for an author to be whole-heartedly committed to just one trend: a 'progressivist' may very well from time to time express doubts about the value of some of the cultural changes he describes. The upward and downward curves, and the ambivalences, are all symptomatic, I believe, of the moral confusion which confronts people when they try to pass judgement on their own contemporaries: they all contribute towards the intermediate positioning of the race. Sometimes the deviations will be sufficient, perhaps, to shatter a definition. But the broad framework of points of view which I have set out provides, I think, a valid and useful platform from which to embark on an analysis.

Although I have suggested (and shall be further arguing in the next two chapters) that the view of the current status of the human race expressed in A-type and B-type cultural histories is the same, clearly they do involve important philosophical differences. These too will be examined in the chapters that follow: what I want to do here is to touch on the question of the historical context for those differences. In the last sixty years or so the value judgements attached by Greek and Roman writers to the historical process have been much discussed. The view expressed by J.B. Bury in 1920, that 'the prejudices of Greek thought on this subject' led them to believe 'that they were living in a period of inevitable degeneration and decay' has since been challenged, and the ancient idea of progress has in more recent years undergone some rehabilitation. (7) It is now widely accepted that belief in the past and future improvement of the human condition was more common among the Greeks and Romans than Bury suspected - a turn-around which may to some extent be linked to our own faltering faith in progress, and our desire to find the concept confirmed in the most ancient of sources. If we bear in mind all the provisos and problems of definition involved, we shall probably have to admit that it is impossible to judge whether primitivism or progressivism was the predominant strain in the thousand-or-more-years'-worth of literature which can be termed 'Greek and Roman'; certainly the balance of opinion among all the non-writers who lived during this time is completely beyond our ken. Rather hesitatingly, I would suggest that the evidence <u>does</u> support two more limited verdicts:
1. that the idea of progress was never so

consistently and unequivocally expressed in ancient literature as it was in European philosophical and scientific writings of the nineteenth and early twentieth centuries, and
2. that, as far as our sources permit us to judge, faith in the human ability to advance was more marked among ancient writers of the fifth century, and of the second and first centuries BC, than at other times.
Whether these two things, if they could be truly known, would be worth knowing, I am not sure: but in case it is of any value, I shall list some of the more obvious social, political and scientific circumstances which link in with these two conclusions. Almost all of them have been remarked on by earlier commentators.

Conclusion 1

While the Greeks and Romans were by no means the technological dunces they have sometimes been made out to be, technological change was obviously not nearly so rapid nor so extensive in the ancient world as it has been in our own age. With the control over the physical environment that technology provides, there comes greater self-confidence, and the conviction that human beings have within their own grasp the capacity to improve their lot. Technology also, of course, helps to alleviate physical hardship, and to produce a sense of well-being, or at least the hope that hardship can be eliminated in the future. Many people in the ancient world would have been cut off from such a hope; and it is perhaps no accident that the earliest Greek version we possess of a 'Golden Age' vision was produced by a gloomy peasant-farmer: since it would never have entered his head to look forward to a time when a combine-harvester was going to do his work for him, he looked back instead to an age when the earth poured her fruits spontaneously into people's laps.

The belief that nature has control over them, rather than that they have control over nature, brings people to a greater awareness of the growth and decay cycles that operate in the plant and animal kingdoms. This awareness was bound to be accentuated among peoples whose economy was always an agricultural one. If decline is inevitable for individual living things, this may well be true of the world as a whole, which was seen by some of the Presocratics, and later by Plato and the Stoics, as a living organism. And bound up with the fate of the world was the fate of the human race, whose cultural and moral condition could scarcely be distinguished from its physical condition, by a people that saw itself as so much in the grip of nature.

Progress is a bourgeois idea (so Ernest Gellner has said), (8) and there was no bourgeoisie as such in the ancient world. People who have careers, who expect their lives to be characterised by a series of upward steps in terms of education, status, job satisfaction and income, might expect the life of the human race to be characterised in the same way. But people in the ancient world did not on the whole have careers - even a successful writer or thinker would not generally expect the outward forms of his existence to change steadily in the course of his life. An exception to the 'no careers' statement would be the army and civil service personnel who climbed the ladders created under the Roman Empire: but few of them took up the literary life.

Religion may be relevant here. Those thinkers who believed that the world had been created by God (like the Stoics, and possibly Plato), may have thought also that the world and all its living creatures were in their best condition at the time when they had just emerged newly-made from the hands of their creator. And there was certainly a strong strain in Greek religious belief which taught that ultimate control of human destiny was in the hands of the gods, and that audacious achievements on the part of the human race might provoke the gods to anger.

It is doubtful whether the Greeks and Romans perceived any historical reasons for belief in a past that was more glorious than the present. The great wealth which had been amassed by the Mycenaean rulers of Greece was not known to them as it is to us, although admittedly Homeric epic, with its concentration on aristocratic life-styles, might have left people with the impression that the population of the heroic age enjoyed a lot more material comfort than was available in later times; and as Gomme has pointed out, even in Thucydides' time (when Athens was one of the most prosperous places in the Greek world), it was still believed that in the prehistoric era Athens had been a place of surpassing luxury (9). But an objection to this kind of motivation is that extravagant wealth, certainly mineral wealth, is not often a feature of an imagined 'Golden Age': the accent is generally on satisfying only one's basic needs, in however lavish a way, and the pursuit of wealth is on the contrary seen as one of the elements in human downfall.

Conclusion 2

Some of the circumstances outlined above would have had more force at certain periods of Greek and Roman history than at others. Hence in the seventh and sixth centuries BC, writers (particularly poets) were more likely to come from the class of people who had close connections with the land, and who were therefore prone to thoughts about the power of nature, etc.

Equally, at that time the technology did not exist which might help to dispel such thoughts. But towards the end of the sixth century BC, changes were beginning to take place which might well have encouraged people to believe that they did have the capacity to impose their own wills on the raw materials provided by nature: improvements were being made in the construction of ships, bridges, and temples; new techniques in sculpture and vase-painting were beginning to give rise to more realistic and human-orientated styles of representation; and the introduction of coinage and weights and measures was beginning to transform the systems of exchange. At the same time, Presocratic science, though its practical applications were probably slight, was at least opening up the possibility of understanding the workings of the physical environment. In the century that followed, technology (and in particular building and naval technology) continued to advance, and one practical science at least - that of medicine - began to have considerable impact.

Science and technology were particularly vigorous in the Hellenistic era inaugurated by the conquests of Alexander the Great. Great advances were made in the areas of geography, map-making, navigation, astronomy, mathematics, mechanics, engineering, medicine, and pharmacology. By the second century BC, the feeling of being able to shape the physical environment may in certain quarters have been becoming quite strong.

Changes in historical outlook may also have been linked with political and economic changes. Early on in the fifth century BC, the Greeks successfully repelled two invasions from the mighty Persian Empire, and were probably beginning to feel a high degree of confidence in their civilisation. In particular the state of Athens (where the idea of progress seems to have flourished more than anywhere else) was taking advantage of the part she had played in the Persian Wars to build up a large and prosperous empire for herself. Wealth was flooding into the city and produced a general rise in the standard of living. At the same time, democratic government was advancing by leaps and bounds, and the physical appearance of the city's public sector was being dramatically enhanced.

In the Hellenistic era, on the other hand, philosophical writings, up until the second century BC, manifest a distinct lack of progressivist thought: instead primitivism and the idealisation of the past were rampant. At the same time, the autonomous Greek city-states had been swallowed up in the huge kingdoms of Alexander's successors, and in an age of absolute monarchy political participation had become for most people an impossibility. The fact that enormous wealth was now amassed in the hands of a small elite tended to produce a desire for a time, not of luxury for all, but of a comfortable freedom from materialistic pressures. As a result a new cult of individualism flourished in many areas of life. Communal hopes and aspirations for the time being died the death, and only revived when the centre of the literary world switched in the second century BC to Rome, where imperialism, wealth and self-confidence were all waxing. Progressivism remained a significant strain of thought there until civil war and the rule of the emperors induced another onset of moral pessimism.

This last judgement perhaps seems at odds with the earlier one, which quoted the rise of technology in the Hellenistic era. One might suggest that the effects of technology take a while to seep into the literary consciousness - that this seeping was only just beginning to be felt in the second century BC. One might suggest a lot of things - other objections could be similarly raised and similarly overcome. The whole concept of zeitgeist is an extremely arguable one, and should not be allowed to detain us for too long.

Before moving on to an examination of the value judgements applied in cultural histories, I want to say something about the cosmic context which they envisaged for human civilisation. The great majority of Greek and Roman thinkers believed that matter was uncreated and existed for all time, (10) but on the other hand the great majority also believed that the world (in the sense of an orderly arrangement of matter into earth, atmosphere and planets) had been created at some specific time in the past. (11) Of these thinkers some thought that the world would one day in the future be brought to an end, others thought that once created the world was eternal. Others again established a kind of compromise between world-destruction and temporal infinity (either past and future, or merely future), by positing the occurrence of cosmic cycles.

The idea of cyclical development is one which crops up frequently in ancient thought. I am never sure myself that the word cyclical (meaning circular) is entirely appropriate - non-linear would perhaps be more accurate; but it is a word which is used by ancient thinkers themselves, and will be readily understood by most people. It can be defined as any movement in either (a) space and time, or (b) time alone, which brings a stated object either (a) to a position that is identical to a position previously occupied, or (b) to a state of being that is similar in one or more of its qualities to a previous state of being; and which is repeated either endlessly or a large number of times. This spatial or temporal return can be brought about either by a gradual process of reversal (in which case it is probably truly cyclical) or by some sudden set-back (in which case it is probably not). It is a common enough idea in ancient thought for it to be worth our while looking at in more detail, particularly in its cosmic or cultural manifestations.

Clearly day-to-day experience of astronomical movements, or of the reproductive behaviour of living things, had a lot to do with the formation of the idea. 'Suns can set and rise again'; (12) spring inevitably turns up at the end of winter; and 'with the funeral rites is mingled the sound of wailing which babies make when they first look upon the shores of light'. (13) If day and night, and the seasons, and the human race itself, are all subject to a law of perpetual renewal, then perhaps this law operates in other areas as well. And it is not just the idea of renewal which experiences of this kind will give rise to; they promote also an appreciation of the phased and gradual changes encompassed within each individual cycle (and are thus characteristic of truly cyclical development). In an individual year, the weather will (in general) get warmer and warmer and the days longer and longer (the 'upward' phase) until a peak of warmth and lightness is reached, whereupon the weather starts to get colder and the days shorter (the 'downward' phase). Perhaps the life-cycle of an individual person is the most telling experience of all: each of us gradually gains in bodily strength and physical (and some would say mental) abilities, until we arrive at middle life, when gradual decline sets in. The combined optimism and pessimism which this thought induces in those who are actually approaching middle life cannot fail to be influential. Thus the concept of phased organic change is likely to get transported into other areas, as we see, for example, in the <u>Epitome</u> of the historian Florus, who compares the history of a single state with the life-cycle of an individual. (14)

Both of the cyclical processes which I have so far referred to (astronomy and reproduction) were known to the ancients as facts. Biological reproduction is obvious; and astronomical cycles were by the fifth century BC thoroughly apprehended, if not understood: Catullus knew perfectly well, of course, that it was the same sun and not a different one which came back every morning. (15) But on the basis of these processes, some more dubious cyclical patterns were constructed. Some scientific writers extended the notion of daily and yearly astronomical cycles, in order to produce the theory of the 'great year', which was seen as the length of time which it takes for all the planets to return to the same relative positions as obtained at some moment in the past. The 'great year' can be found in Indian and possibly Iranian myth; (16) it may have been propounded by Heraclitus (of which more anon), and was certainly described by Plato (17), who seems not to have linked its completion with any notable cosmic events. The precise length of time involved was not given by Plato, but 'great years' of 10,800 and 18,000 solar years respectively were variously ascribed to Heraclitus. (18) By Cicero's time, the idea seems to have been quite a familiar one. (19) Whereas for some people it was probably a purely astronomical concept, others appeared to have believed that the progress of a 'great year', like that of a solar year, produced terrestrial effects, culminating in climatic catastrophes and possibly in the destruction of the world. (20)

An even more speculative notion was produced when the idea of cyclical development was transported by some thinkers into the psychological field. A 'soul-cycle', according to some apostles of reincarnation, was the period of time which it took for each soul to go through a series of rebirths before being reunited with the divine. Both Empedocles and Plato held this belief; (21) according to Herodotus, it was a feature of Egyptian religion; (22) and it may also have been found in Orphic doctrine. (23)

Much more relevant to our present theme are the two theories which posit a cyclical development occurring in the time dimension and affecting the history of the world. The two ideas - cosmic and cultural cycles - are closely related. Cosmic cycles are a physical phenomenon, involving either the perpetual destruction and recreation of the world (recreation cycles), or endlessly repeated cataclysms which, while not destroying the world itself, have a devastating effect on the condition and population of the earth (terrestrial cycles). Cultural cycles embrace a pattern of cultural change whereby civilisation is repeatedly developed, destroyed and then recreated. One can assume, I think, that cosmic cycles inevitably bring with them cultural cycles (although some writers describe only the physical part of the process). But the cultural variety can, theoretically at least, occur without any cosmic intervention: unfortunately, those writers who appear to limit themselves to the cultural process give little or no indication of the causes of the recurrence.

The theory of cosmic (and cultural) cycles is not as common in Greek and Roman thought as is often suggested. To say, as J.B. Bury has, that 'it may almost be described as the orthodox theory of cosmic time among the Greeks, and it passed from them to the Romans', is a gross exaggeration. (24) The majority of Greek and Roman authors betray no evidence of having thought in these terms, and for some at least we know that such a theory would have been out of the question. Still, it is common enough for us to speculate on its intellectual origins. Empirical grounds for the belief (observation of astronomical and reproductive cycles) have already been mentioned; perhaps even more persuasive, for some thinkers, was a deductive line of reasoning, relying on two, apparently incompatible, basic principles: the permanence of matter, and the impossibility of infinite individual existence. Many ancient thinkers found the idea of non-existence of matter difficult to swallow. 'What is' cannot become 'what is not', or vice versa: matter cannot be created out of nothing, nor destroyed into it; and if matter is always available, and the same natural or divine laws continue to operate, there seems to be no reason to doubt the continued existence of our world, or of one like it. But on the other hand, the concept of infinity is a difficult one to cope with, both for the imagination and for the logical understanding;

113

Values and Cycles

and the ancients clearly found it as hard as we do to come to terms with the idea of a world which is infinite in time and is subject to an infinite process of change. If all the things in the world are bound to fall into eventual decay, how can this not be true of the world as a whole? Some thinkers sought to establish a compromise between these two conflicting notions by positing the continued existence, not of our world, but of one like it; or by making our world subject to an endless series of catastrophes. That is, they propounded the theory of cosmic cycles. (25) In this way, they established a conceptual framework within which the principles of permanence and of continued change could co-exist; and they avoided the problem of having to anticipate for our world an infinite process of physical and cultural deterioration or (even less plausible) improvement. And, for those writers who were able to envisage an infinite series of past as well as future renewals, the objection to any creation theory of 'why was the world not created before?' was thus circumvented. (26)

It is perhaps strange that early Greek myth seems to be almost free from notions of cyclical return. It is true that in the stories of Deucalion and the flood, and of Phaeton driving the chariot of the sun-god too close to the earth, we perhaps get a glimpse of a belief in periodic catastrophes: but there is in fact no hint in these stories that disasters such as these are likely to recur. It could be argued that myth is timeless and not concerned with either a past or a future; though I would doubt myself whether either Homer or Hesiod could be said to be innocent of notions of time. Perhaps one could concede that Hesiod, for example, is only interested in the past in so far as it offers an explanation for our present status; and that a theory of cosmic cycles demands a breaking away from obsessions with the here-and-now. Perhaps one could also say that it was only with the speculations of the natural philosophers that an interest in physical and metaphysical processes arose sufficient to make cosmic cycles both conceivable and relevant.

That said, it is in fact from Hesiod's poem Works and Days that we receive the only faint suggestion of an early mythical concept of cyclical return. Here civilisation is seen as having passed through a series of stages, each new stage being marked by the appearance on the earth of a new generation of human beings (106-201), with moral and cultural decline being the overall trend exhibited by

Values and Cycles

the transformations. There is no hint in these lines that this process of deterioration is seen as a repetition of past events, and it certainly seems unlikely that Hesiod could have envisaged infinite past recurrence, since in the Theogony he has described the original creation of the world. When he looks to the future, the poet seems for the most part to visualise only an intensification of present-day degeneration; except that at one point he utters the heartfelt cry, 'would that I were not among the men of the fifth generation, would that I had died before or been born afterwards'. (174-5) For a moment, it seems, Hesiod is prepared to give thought to the concept of cultural cycles, and to imagine a time when the fifth generation will have reached the ultimate in degradation and will be replaced by a new golden race. These would be cultural cycles with very definite moral implications. But Hesiod seems to derive no comfort from the concept, and for the most part his thoughts are wrapped up in his own generation, for which he sees no hope.

Among the Presocratics, Anaximander, Xenophanes, Pythagoras, Heraclitus and Empedocles have all been credited with a belief in cosmic cycles. Some cases are more dubious than others. Anaximander certainly seems to have believed that the sea is being gradually evaporated by the sun and will one day dry up completely. (27) This, coupled with the fact that a number of later sources ascribe to him a belief in 'innumerable worlds' (28) can lead to speculation about a theory of cosmic cycles, of either the recreation or the terrestrial 'periodic catastrophe' variety. But the 'worlds' might have been co-existent rather than successive; they may not have been part of Anaximander's doctrine at all (the sources are very confused); and even if they were, there is no saying that the drying-out process was repeated in every one; so all in all we are really in no position to pronounce on Anaximander as a 'cosmic cyclist'. (29)

More reliable information is available for Xenophanes, who thought that 'a mixture of the earth with the sea is taking place, and that in time the earth is overwhelmed by moisture'. Evidence of previous disasters of this kind was derived by him from the discovery of marine fossils inland. This led him to believe in periodic deluges: 'the whole human race is destroyed whenever the earth is brought down to the sea, and is reduced to mud; then there is another beginning of generation, and this commencement takes place in all worlds' (Hippolytus

Ref. 1.14.5). Our sources provide no reference to a corresponding process of evaporation, but Xenophanes must have believed that the earth gradually dried out, otherwise it could not have grown moist again. Hence we have here an example of a genuine cosmic cycle of the terrestrial type, with the earth being transformed in such a way that it is perpetually brought back to a previous condition. (30) Whether the drying-out of the earth would, like its saturation, have led to the destruction of the human race, we cannot say: it is hard to know how it could then have been recreated, since moisture was considered essential for the generation of life. Perhaps the earth never dried out completely, and a scattered remnant managed to survive.

A similar theory of the cyclical transformation of the earth could easily have been held by Anaximander, but we cannot be sure about this. They certainly would have differed on the point in the cycle reached in their own day, since Anaximander thought the sea was drying up, while Xenophanes said that it was encroaching more and more on the earth. As Kirk has pointed out, (31) they may both have had empirical evidence for their divergent views, since around Miletus (Anaximander's home) the sea was receding, while in Sicily, (where Xenophanes lived) it was thought to be eating up the coastline.

Cosmic cycles of the kind outlined by Xenophanes must surely have been accompanied by large-scale cultural transformations. Of these we hear nothing. But cultural cycles of an extreme kind (with no indication of a cosmic equivalent) are attributed to another group of Presocratics, the Pythagoreans. Porphyrys credits Pythagoras himself with the belief that 'events occur again in certain cycles, and that nothing is ever completely new' (Vita Pyth. 19), while Eudemus, a pupil of Aristotle, is quoted as saying that 'if one were to believe the Pythagoreans, the same things numerically will occur again, and I with my wand will talk to you seated as you are, and everything else will be exactly the same, and it is a reasonable inference that the time too is the same' (Simplicius In Phys. 732.30). We do not know whether these minute cultural repetitions were linked with cosmic turn-arounds: but what seems possible is that for the Pythagoreans they were an outcome of the transmigration of souls. This belief is certainly mentioned by Porphyrys immediately before the theory of cycles; and the Pythagoreans may have thought that souls would be reborn in exactly the same order as in previous incarnations, and would produce people who, if not identical in themselves, would perform identical actions. This seems feasible, since elsewhere we are told that Pythagorean reincarnation takes place at precise intervals of 216 years. (32) The result of such a theory would be a rigorous form of cultural repetition, producing maximum determinism and, surely, a sense of moral hopelessness. It is of course rare. Most cyclical theories would have allowed the operation of a fair degree of chance within the broad framework of the cycle, accounting for at least some variation from one revolution to the next. But the Pythagorean conception is not unique: it is to be picked up later by the Stoics.

Xenophanes and the Pythagoreans (though very different in what they envisage) seem to be fairly well attested as 'cyclists'. Like Anaximander, Heraclitus is a dubious case. In attributing to him belief in a 'great year' (already mentioned), Censorinus links this with a cosmic cycle involving a 'great winter' of floods, and a summer which burns up the world. This and other ascriptions of periodic conflagrations to Heraclitus (33) might be thought to conflict with fragment 30, in which he announces that 'this world was not made by any of the gods or men, but it always was and is and will be: an everlasting fire, kindling in measures and going out in measures'. This could be taken to mean that the perceptible world, whose primary substance is fire, though it is subject to changes in its composition, is as a whole constant and indestructible. This would seem to rule out periodic destruction. On the other hand, the 'world' (the Greek word is kosmos) could be read, I think, if we want to preserve for Heraclitus the idea of cosmic cycles, as referring to the sum total of fiery matter which periodically transforms itself into the perceptible world, and periodically resumes its basic form. It would not then be our world, but it would be a world of fire. Much scholarly controversy has raged around this question of the eternity of the Heraclitean world, and around the question of whether later Stoic commentators were disposed to mis-read into his cosmology an anticipation of their theory of ekpyrosis. (34) I am inclined to accept myself that he could have held a theory of cosmic cycles; I am also inclined to agree with Kahn (35) that our interpretation of his philosophy need not be drastically affected by acceptance or rejection. If cosmic cycles were a feature of his cosmology, we learn nothing from the fragments of his work about the cultural ramifications of such a theory.

Values and Cycles

The Presocratic philosopher who most readily springs to mind when there is talk of cycles is Empedocles. That his cosmology included the idea of cycles brought into being by the operations of Love and Strife seems pretty certain: the controversy about the nature of the cycles has already been discussed. In either interpretation, the cycles are of a recreation type: the 'two-world' system constitutes a true cycle, with the cosmic processes in one half of the cycle being an exact reversal of the processes in the other half; the 'one-world' system represents rather the 'sudden catastrophe' kind of cycle, with the dramatic intervention of Strife, and not a gradual reversal, bringing the universe back to its former condition. The distinction may be represented in this way:

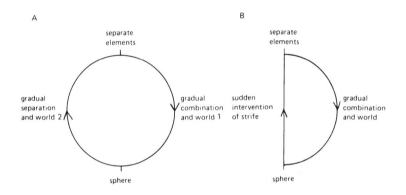

We do not know enough about earlier Presocratic cyclical theories to say whether this distinction should lead us to prefer one interpretation over another. I think it would be true to say that if Empedocles did believe in B, then it would be the first definite example of a 'sudden catastrophe' cycle. But Anaximander and Heraclitus remain imponderables. And in any case, Empedocles' 'sudden catastrophe' would be one that destroyed a hypothetical sphere and not the perceptible world, which would distinguish it from all the theories that came after it as well as those that went before. When dealing with Empedocles, we should not dismiss a theory just because it appears to be unique.

Empedocles' cosmic cycles may have been related to (possibly co-existent with) the cycles of the soul, but there is no direct evidence for this. What

118

Values and Cycles

is more apparent is that there are probably cultural and moral values attached to the various stages of the cycle: these will be examined in the next chapter.

There is no shortage of cycles, both cosmic and cultural, in the works of Plato: they are mentioned in five of his dialogues. But all of the contexts are distinctly 'mythological', and it is impossible to know whether we should take them seriously. The cycles described in the Politicus have already been mentioned: these are cosmic and cultural in their implications, since at the point when God releases control of the world, it begins to revolve in the opposite direction, and is afflicted by catastrophes which wipe out most living creatures; and this reversal is accompanied by a marked falling-off in the cultural and moral standards of the few survivors. Equally fanciful is the disaster syndrome referred to in the Timaeus and taken up again in the Critias. In the former we are treated to a story 'which though extraordinary is absolutely true', passed on, we are assured, by the sixth century lawgiver Solon, who had heard it from Egyptian priests at the city of Sais on the delta. These priests had lectured Solon on how the Greeks were a people with a very short history, because in common with the majority of the human race their ancestors had been practically wiped out by one of the periodic catastrophes which beset the earth. The peculiar position of Egypt on the Nile had protected her from these, and consequently Egyptian temples had accumulated records of human civilisation going back much further than those of other nations. There had been many disastrous floods and fires (caused by a change in the orbit of the planets) in the history of the world, but the Greeks remembered only one of each (Deucalion and Phaeton). In every land apart from Egypt, people had only just begun to develop city-life and the art of writing when the waters or the flames got them again, and all records and most of the inhabitants were lost. But the Egyptians knew what the Greeks did not, that 9000 years ago, before the greatest of the floods, Athens had been a city valiant in war and with excellent laws (Timeaus 21B-23C). Linked to this is the story of Atlantis, a continent where the people led prosperous, civilised, and at first peaceable lives; later on they grew ambitious and imperialistic, and embarked on the conquest of Europe, Asia, and Africa. It was the Athenians who took the lead in resisting their aggression, and through their victories they succeeded in liberating all the territory east of the straits of Gibraltar. Afterwards both the Athenians and the people of Atlantis were destroyed by violent earthquakes and floods, and Atlantis itself sank beneath the sea (Timeaus 24E-25D and Critias 108E-121B).

In spite of the lengths to which countless post-Platonic researchers have gone to establish the historicity of Atlantis, (36) we cannot take the factual part of this story seriously; and hence it is not altogether easy to take its cycles seriously. The same is true of the periodic catastrophes outlined in the Laws, which seem to be a peg on which to hang speculations about the evolution from primitive times of human society. Here a participant in a discussion on the origins of political government suggests that they should adopt a historical approach, and consider the changes which have occurred since one of the 'many destructions of mankind by flood, plague and other causes, which only a remnant survive' (677A). Terrestrial catastrophe provides an amusing and credible starting-point for a sober political analysis: Plato does not commit himself on the point, he merely calls it an 'ancient tale' which 'everyone is disposed to believe'.

If Plato himself was disposed to believe in cosmic cycles, then he may have linked them with the cycles of the soul: in the Politicus, he tells us that God released his control of the world when every soul had completed its allotted number of births. The final allusion to cycles invites the suggestion that there may also have been a link with the 'great year' which he has described in the Timaeus. In Book 8 of the Republic, in trying to imagine how the political divisions grow up which give rise to increasingly inferior forms of state-government, Socrates adopts the posture of a Homeric bard, and prays to the Muses for inspiration. And the Muses 'playing and jesting with us as though we were children, and speaking as though in earnest', tell us that everything which has a beginning must have an end, and that states like plants and animals are bound to fall into decay. In a lecture on the mathematical principles governing the cycles of human birth, the Muses make allusion to the perfect number by which the cycle of divine birth can be expressed - that is the cycle of the world (8.545D-547A). The Muses very sensibly refrain from computing this number; but some commentators have attempted to relate either the perfect number, or the 'geometrical number' which governs human cycles, to the 'great year' of the *Timaeus* and to the cycles described in the *Politicus*. (37) The *Republic* passage is an obscure one, but there does not seem to be much evidence in it to show that Plato attaches any astronomical significance to these numbers: the relationship between them must remain a hypothetical one. Of more significance is the fact that Plato accompanies every single reference which he makes to cosmic cycles with a warning (particularly clear in the *Republic*) that they should not be taken as the literal truth. For him they remain unverifiable and, in terms of their historicity, unimportant.

Aristotle believed that the world was eternal, and so for him cosmic cycles of the recreation type were out of the question. For the same reason, he had liberated himself from the line of argument which said 'matter is permanent, but our world cannot last forever, so there must be cycles.' Nevertheless, this very principle of the world's eternity must have entailed for him both metaphysical and empirical grounds for postulating limited cosmic and cultural cycles. To take the metaphysical grounds first, in one of his works he argues that in an eternal world there must be unlimited coming-to-be; but that the chain of cause and effect must be limited, otherwise it would have no 'source' (the chain would extend infinitely into the past and into the future): the only kind of coming-to-be which is both eternal and has a 'source' is cyclical coming-to-be. (38) This is the kind of change which can be said to come about 'of necessity'. To this Aristotle adds a supportive argument which is in part empirically-based: the movement of the heavens (which he has proved to be eternal) is circular, and this governs the movement of the sun, which in turn governs the seasons; thus circular movement is transmitted from the heavens to the seasons, and since the seasons cause coming-to-be on the earth, this too must be cyclical (*De gen. et corr.* 338A5 - B6).

Aristotle goes on to make a distinction between cyclical movement involving the return of the same individual things (numerical repetition), of which the revolution of the planets would be an example; and cyclical movement involving only the appearance of individuals of the same species (specific repetition), like animal reproductive patterns (*op.cit.* 338B6 - B20). The examples which he quotes in this passage give no indication that he made on the basis of his own arguments any deductions about cosmic changes occurring outside of the cycle of the seasons. But elsewhere it appears that he did. In the

Meteorologica he speaks of the simultaneous drying-up and flooding of different parts of the earth's surface, and says that this takes place 'in an orderly cycle', and is due to the movement of the sun (351A19-B8). We should not conclude from this that the world as a whole is undergoing a process of change: the changes are purely local and temporary, and the basic constitution of the world remains unaltered throughout eternity. But even local changes can be sudden and dramatic, rather than gradual: at fixed intervals, Aristotle says, there occurs in one region or another a 'great winter', with an excess of rain. This may have been linked by him with the notion of the 'great year', since he tells us that the winter is part of 'some great cycle', and it seems more than likely that for him the causes of such a winter would have been planetary (op.cit. 352A17 - 34). The cosmic cycles which Aristotle envisages, then, are confined not just to the earth, but to varying parts of it: it is a movement which takes place in space as well as in time.

These limited cosmic cycles clearly had a cultural impact. 'In all probability every art and philosophy has been developed to its utmost many times, and then destroyed again' (Metaphys. 1074 B 10-12); proverbs are the remnant of a vanished philosophy which, because of their brevity and wit, have survived the great destructions of the human race (fragment 13, Rose); and 'the same opinions come round again among humans not once, not twice, not a few times, but infinitely often' (Meteor. 339B28).

For these cultural cycles we can surmise that Aristotle had an empirical as well as a metaphysical argument: if the world is eternal, then the obvious newness of some of the arts is most easily explained by imagining intermittent cultural wipe-outs; and indeed Aristotle must have known that in some regions civilisations had once flourished which had since been lost. Cycles in the advance of human knowledge must surely have been matched by cycles in social and political development; though in Aristotle's Politics we are given only one hint of a belief in these: when discussing the history of the caste-system, he says 'other things also have been discovered very often, or rather infinitely often, over the long course of time. Necessity itself probably taught the things that are needful; and it seems reasonable to suppose that when once these things are established, one sees the growth of things which contribute towards luxury and refinement. So we must believe that this is the way with political institutions also' (1329B25). Cyclical repetition can probably be assumed to embrace the whole range of cultural phenomena, and to involve regular sequences of development.

Little evidence of cyclical beliefs can be culled from Greek and Roman historians, as one might expect of people accustomed to examine the minutiae of events. Thucydides' claim that his history would be valuable because things that have happened in the past 'will in all human probability happen again in the future in the same or a similar way' (1.22.4) need not point to a cyclical view of history, as has sometimes been suggested. His prediction was based on his belief in the constancy of human nature, but he knew that there was more to history than that: his appreciation of the role played by chance, if nothing else, would have led him to reject the idea of endlessly repeated patterns of events. From other references to repetition, we can assume him to mean that some things, like plagues and revolutions, will recur in the future, but without entailing the same sequence of events, and with a lot of variation in the circumstances. (39)

A later Greek historian, Polybius, seems to have had a much more restricted notion of the possibility of historical change. In introducing an analysis of the origins of political institutions, he takes as his starting-point, like Plato, one of the periodic catastrophes which wipe out most of the human race, along with its customs, techniques and institutions. When among the scattered survivors, social intercourse and notions of morality gradually develop, then true government is born. Government passes through a series of forms, each of which in turn degenerates and gives rise to the next form: thus monarchy degenerates into tyranny, and is supplanted by aristocracy; aristocracy degenerates into oligarchy, and is supplanted by democracy: and democracy degenerates into anarchy, and is eventually supplanted by monarchy. 'Such is the cycle of political organisations, the law of nature according to which the forms of government are changed and brought back to their original condition' (6. 4-9).

A clear-cut example of cosmic (i.e. terrestrial) and cultural (i.e. political) cycles. But there are problems with the account. The cultural cycles do not coincide with the cosmic ones: the reversion to monarchy is seen as the outcome of a natural law of political transformation, and not as the result of a fresh catastrophe. And though Polybius has invited us to see the history of the Roman state as a prime example of this law in action (and has predicted that it will go into a decline), when he goes on to analyse the Roman constitution he seems to be saying that Rome has somehow managed to weld together the best elements from each form of government, and that this has conferred on her an incomparable stability (6. 11-18). As Momigliano has remarked, Polybius may have learnt about cycles from a philosopher, but found himself unable to apply them to his historical narrative. (40)

The cycles envisaged by Polybius were humdrum affairs compared with those of the Stoics, who revived the notion of extreme cultural repetition propounded by the Pythagoreans, and coupled it with a theory of periodic cosmic collapse. According to the latter, the whole world is periodically reduced to fire, in a huge conflagration called ekpyrosis, which represents the return of all substances to the primary element of fire. (41) No sooner has this come about than the formation of a new world commences. In each successive world, every person, every object and every event is a minute repetition of what has gone before:

> For again there will exist Socrates and Plato and every man, with the same friends and fellow-citizens; and he will have the same beliefs and meet with the same experiences and pursue the same activities. And every city and village and field will be exactly recreated. And there will be a recreation of the whole, not once only, but many times, or rather infinitely often, and the same things will be recreated without end. (42)

We know that the Stoics cited empirical evidence in support of their theory of periodic collapse and recreation (43): the grounds for belief in exact repetition must have been more metaphysical, but must remain a matter of speculation (44). Sorabji has pointed out that there was some debate among Stoics about whether a recreated phenomenon was one and the same thing: 'Some even said that a person exhibiting no changes, who was not however the same person, would appear in the next cycle. Others said the opposite: that it would be the same person, but that small changes would be permissible, for example, in respect of freckles'. (45)

Cosmic repetition, while it is attributed to the first three heads of the Stoic school, was not accepted by all its leading thinkers: Panaetius, for example, is said to have abandoned it in favour of an indestructible world. (46) But it was still orthodox enough in the first century AD to be embraced by Seneca, who seems to have viewed as horrifically imminent 'the single day that will destroy the human race', when 'cities that an age has built an hour obliterates'. (47) And in the next century the Stoic emperor Marcus Aurelius seems to experience an understandable ennui at the thought that there will never by anything new under the sun:

> future generations will see nothing new, just as our ancestors saw nothing more than what we do today: if a man reaches his fortieth year, and has any understanding at all, he has virtually seen, because of their similarity, all possible events, both past and future'. (48)

The rival Epicurean school of philosophy did not have a theory of cosmic cycles; but it is perhaps worth pausing awhile to glance at their doctrine to see what the alternatives might be. The Epicureans believed that our world would one day be destroyed; indeed, in seeking to prove this point, they used some of the same arguments as the Stoics. (49) But they also thought that scattered throughout the infinite void there was an infinite number of worlds, some of them at an earlier stage of development than ours, some at a later; and that before our world there had been other worlds, and after our world there would be more to come. (50) The element of chance which was admitted into atomic motion ensured that world-creation was a haphazard process, and that there was no possibility of predetermined and phased recurrence. Other worlds would be created, but we could not predict when, or where, or what they would be like. However, one thing which seems certain is that worlds identical to our own would at some stage come into existence. Lucretius, in his treatise on the mortality of the soul, is quite prepared to admit that the matter out of which an individual human being is composed will one day in the future come together again, as it has done 'often' in the past; without committing himself as to whether this would be the same person, he argues against any consistent identity because there would be no recollection of a former life. (51) The same must be true of any individual world. Though the odds against this happening would seem to be much higher, the infinity of time within which the atoms operate ensures that any compound, including a world, will be recreated infinitely often from precisely the same matter. When a world which has exactly the same atoms in it as some previous world does come about, will the same things happen in it? I think that the unpredictable swerves which atoms make must rule this out. (52)

Among the many disciples of cosmic cycles in the ancient world, there are few who seem inclined to project themselves into the next cycle, and to draw from the future any lessons for their own day-and-age. Perhaps not surprisingly, in view of the inevitability of it all. And there are fewer still who derive any comfort from the thought that, though our world and our civilisation are doomed, others are bound to appear. Again, this is not surprising, since according to most people's beliefs, few people, if any, were going to survive to see it. Where optimism is concerned, one of the few exceptions is Vergil, whose belief (though imitated later) was an exceptional one, and who was hyperbolising anyway. In the famous Eclogue 4, he assumes the stance of one who believes that the new Golden Age is almost upon him and that he is going to be around to witness it. Taking up a prophecy found in the Sibylline books, he rapturously heralds the birth of an unnamed child, whose lifetime will mark the onset of a new age of progressive happiness and virtue. That this revival is associated with the completion of a 'great year' is suggested by the exclamation 'the great sequence of centuries is born anew' (line 5); and that the fresh cycle will to some extent be a repetition of the last one can be deduced from the words: 'then there will be another Tiphys, and another Argo to bear chosen heroes; still there will be other wars, and once more the great Achilles will be sent to Troy' (34 - 36). This line of thought is obviously derived from Stoic theory, but the influence is minimal: the repetition which Vergil envisages is clearly not endless, nor does he show much sign of expecting the new age to be inaugurated by an earth-shattering catastrophe. Someone who had just lived through ten years of civil war probably thought that a cosmic holocaust would be an unnecessary refinement of suffering.

Some of the most elaborate arguments in favour of cosmic cycles comes from Neoplatonist and early Christian thinkers. Plotinus, one of the founding fathers of Neoplatonism, believed that the cosmos contained all the 'reason-principles' (logoi) belonging to the individual souls of living creatures: consequently the number of 'reason-principles' must be limited, and since the species of living things were eternal, there would have to be a recycling of 'reason-principles' and of souls. When all had been used up, then a new age and a new cosmos would begin (Enneads 5.7.1 and 3). (53) The third-century Christian writer Origen, a one-time student of Neoplatonist, followed a similar line of reasoning: God could not have created an infinite number of living creatures, because infinity is incomprehensible; a finite number of creatures implies a finite world, but if the world had a beginning, what was God doing before? It was in answer to this problem that Origen suggested a succession of worlds (De principiis 2.9.1. and 3.5.2.-3). Hardly a satisfactory solution, as Sorabji has shown, (54) since either these worlds must have been infinite in number, or God must have been twiddling his thumbs before he started creating them. Origen's successive worlds were by no means identical, since the crucifixion had occurred in only one, his own (2.3. 4-5). Which makes one wonder why God chose that one for redemption. But Origen was an early Christian thinker, and by the fifth century, cosmic cycles had been expunged from Christian orthodoxy. (55).

In the long run, no special value judgements can be attached to cosmic or cultural cycles. However things develop within an individual cycle, from the standpoint of eternity, creation is always going to be matched by destruction, improvement by deterioration, and good behaviour by bad. In a person devoid of expectations, neither hope nor despair would be the feelings induced by the contemplation of cycles, but only perhaps the boredom so graphically conveyed by Marcus Aurelius' comment. Some people, however, do have expectations of human history - they would like things to get better, and cycles tell them that in the long term nothing ever will. So Augustine, viewing the cyclical process from the perspective of a soul forever caught up in the wheel of reincarnation, was able to castigate the pagan thinkers who imposed this torture on our minds:

> they are utterly unable to rescue the immortal soul from this merry-go-round ... it must proceed on an unremitting alternation between false bliss and genuine misery. For how can there be true bliss, without any certainty of its eternal continuance, when the soul in its ignorance does not know of the misery to come, or else unhappily fears its coming in the midst of its blessedness. (56)

Values and Cycles

Any atheistical humanist (or Marxist) might mourn in the same terms the fate of a human race whose future history is thus marked out for it.

But Greek and Roman purveyors of cycles seldom seem to mourn. Of course, we are handicapped in some instances by the lack of complete evidence, but I would say that of all the writers whom I have discussed in this chapter, only Hesiod, Plato and Seneca exhibit any signs of distress when talking about cycles. Hesiod is a dubious case, and anyway his distress is caused, not by the cosmic outlook, but by the particular point of the cycle at which he finds himself i.e. moving towards its worst phase. Plato's cycles may be fanciful; and the unfavourable comparison which he makes between the 'God-released' and 'God-controlled' phases of his Politicus cycle is, I would suggest, part of an attempt to express the mixed potential for good or evil which exists in our world. (57) Seneca probably has a genuine belief in cycles, and the pain which the belief causes him also seems genuine: of the world which is recreated following ekpyrosis, he writes, 'every animal will be created anew, and there will be placed on the earth once more a human race knowing nothing of evil, born under better auspices. But their innocence too will last only so long as they are new. So quickly does wickedness creep up' (N.Q. 3.30. 8). But if Seneca were a more conventional Stoic, he would be able to reflect more consistently (instead of only intermittently) that the Wise Man can cultivate a soul which will lift him out of the determinism of the cycles. The more orthodox Stoic reaction to cycles is the one expressed by Marcus Aurelius.

Of the other 'cyclists', two more deserve special mention. Empedocles may have been less than impressed by the phase of the cycle in which he himself lived: this will be discussed in the next chapter. But Empedocles is, as ever, a problem, and this is another aspect of his beliefs concerning which I shall have to confess to uncertainty. And secondly there is Vergil, who veers in the other direction - one of the few writers who seems to feel any enthusiasm for cycles. But as with Hesiod, his outlook is not a cosmic one: it is because he believes that he himself is about to witness the start of a new era that he is able to produce a positive response.

From the remaining 'cyclists' we cannot, I think, elicit any value judgements concerning the cyclic process. Viewed in this light, time does indeed have a tendency to appear morally neutral, and the cyclical theorists whom I have not marked out as exceptional will not feature greatly in the next three chapters. There is, I believe, a good reason for this refusal to judge. Thinkers who believe that we are caught in a world where good and evil are mixed can express this idea by putting perfect good in the past and perfect evil in the future, or vice versa. But there is no need to do this if you are a 'cyclist': the theory itself is capable of representing the situation just as graphically - creation and destruction, life and death, good and bad twirl round and round us, and there is never any end to the process. The 'Golden Age' theorist or the progressivist confines his attention to the good and evil in our day-and-age, and has the more limited outlook. The cyclical theorist adopts a cosmic approach, and sees good and evil in the eternal universe.

NOTES

1. See, for example Anaximander DK B4 and Xenophenes DK B18.
2. See Anaxagoras DK B4, B21b, A66, A101-2; Archelaus DK A1, A4; Democritus DK B154, B144, B278, A75, A151, A138; Protagoras DK B8b; for Hippias, see Plato's Hippias Major 285D; for Polos, see Plato's Gorgias 448C; Prodicus DK B5.
3. See M. Detienne, 'Between beasts and gods', in R.L. Gordon, p.219. This essay first appeared as 'Entre betes et dieux', in Nouvelle revue de psychanalyse 6 (1972), p.231-46.
4. Ernest Gellner, Thought and change (London, 1964), p.3.
5. p.9-11.
6. p.9-11.
7. See J.B. Bury, The idea of progress (London, 1920), p.9. For the challenges to his view, see in particular, L. Edelstein The idea of progress in classical antiquity (Baltimore, 1967); and E.R. Dodds, Progress, p.1-25.
8. Thought and change, p.13.
9. A.W. Gomme, A historical commentary on Thucydides, vol.1 (Oxford, 1945), p.103-4.
10. Plato seems to be the only exception, and even about him we cannot be sure: see Richard Sorabji, Time, creation and the continuum (London, 1983), p.268-76.
11. Aristotle and the Peripatetics are the most obvious exception here: see p.62 above.
12. Catullus 5.4.

Values and Cycles

13. Lucretius 2.576-7.
14. 1. Proemium 4-8. Florus is probably innocent of any notion that the historical cycle once completed is subject to renewal: see A. Momigliano 'Time in ancient historiography' in Essays in ancient and modern historiography (Oxford, 1977), p.189. This essay first appeared in History and theory, Beiheft 6 (1966), p.1-23.
15. He would have thought, however, that this was the result of the sun's motion and not of the earth's. Aristarchus of Samos, an astronomer of the third century BC, produced a theory that the earth moved around the sun and revolved on its axis; but it never caught on.
16. See M.L. West, Early Greek philosophy and the orient (Oxford, 1971), p.94 and 191.
17. Timaeus 39D.
18. The former by Censorinus, De die nat. 18.11; and the latter by Aetius 2.32.3. In the Censorinus passage, a number of other writers are credited with belief in a 'great year', but Censorinus may be confusing this notion with other forms of cyclical development.
19. See De natura deorum 2.51 - 52.
20. Among the former, one can probably count Plato, and Cicero's 'mathematicians'; among the latter, Vergil (see Eclogue 4 and p.126 below), and Censorinus (and possibly the thinkers to whom Censorinus refers). A lot of confusion is caused in both ancient and modern discussions of cyclical concepts (including the 'great year') by persistent references to 'starts' and 'completions' - a tendency from which I am not myself immune. A circle has, of course, no beginning or end, that is its whole significance. But on any circle other than a simple diagrammatic one, there may be points which are considered to be of more relevance than others, and the part of the circle which comes after that point may be called its start, and the part which comes just before may be called its end. Even an astronomical circle, though in itself neutral, may in its terrestrial manifestations yield up points which are of special significance to its observers. Thus a solar year can be said to begin on any arbitrary date which is of importance to an individual (on August 4th I shall enter my 38th year), and to finish (only a trifle inaccurately) 365 days later. And in the west in order to record time we choose collectively to say that a solar year begins and ends at about the time of the winter solstice. In the same way, a 'great year' could be seen as neutral, and hence any

starting- or finishing-point would be entirely arbitrary; but it could be seen as having terrestrial effects, some of which might be more significant to us than others. A universal deluge or the destruction of the world would be such an effect, and a year could well be said to finish with the occurrence of such a disaster. There is of course empirical evidence for the climatic effects of solar cycles; none at all (to my knowledge) for the effects of a 'great year'. While a neutral 'great year' is a perfectly logical concept, its supposed terrestrial effects are entirely speculative.

21. See Empedocles, DK B115; and Plato's Phaedrus 248C - D.
22. 2.123.
23. See Alderink, Ancient Orphism, p.73-78.
24. Idea of Progress, p.12. Bury is by no means an isolated offender: the misconception may have started with St. Augustine, who contrasted 'the false cycles discovered by false and deceitful sages' with the 'sound doctrine of a rectilinear course' (City of God, 12.14); and has continued more or less up to the present day.
25. J. Barnes, Presocratic philosophers, p.503-4, postulates on a more scientific basis the same line of reasoning: if time is infinite, but the universe is finite and has a finite number of states which follow one another in causally ordered succession, then those states are bound to recur. It is an argument which is not incontrovertible, but would nevertheless have been attractive.

A parallel argument might be used to support a doctrine of reincarnation: if there is a finite number of souls, but the human race exists for all time, then souls must be recycled. R. Sorabji (p.188) has pointed out that this argument was used by some Neoplatonists; St. Augustine (City of God 12.21) realised that if it were accepted, one could not also believe that all souls would eventually be freed from reincarnation, since the supply would eventually dry up. Plato's soul-cycles probably avoid this problem: Plato seems to think that only a few souls will escape permanently (see Phaedrus 248C).

26. The idea of an infinite past seems to cause more problems than the idea of an infinite future. The evidence for the projection of cosmic cycles into the past is not good for any of our 'cyclists'; and some at least, for example Plato, definitely seem to have believed that there was a point in past time when the original creation of the world took place. Aristotle argued that this was a logical

131

impossibility: see De caelo 279 B4 - 280 A23.
27. See Alexander In meteor 67.11, where he is commenting on Aristotle, Meteor. 353 B6.
28. See Simplicius In phys. 1121.5, and In de caelo 202.14 and 615.16; Ps. Plutarch Strom. 2; Aetius 2.1.3 and 2.1.8; Cicero De nat. deor. 1.10.25; and St. Augustine City of God 8.2.
29. For good discussions, see C.H. Kahn Anaximander, p.33-35, 46-53, and 185-186; and Kirk in Kirk, Raven and Schofield, p.139-140. Kahn is not happy with any of the evidence for innumerable worlds, but thinks that a 'recreation' cycle would not have been out of place in Milesian theory. Kirk similarly rejects innumerable worlds, and thinks that Anaximander would have confined himself to terrestrial cycles, involving the alternate drying-out and saturation of the earth.
30. The 'worlds' or kosmoi referred to in the last sentence of the Hippolytus passage may suggest recreation rather than terrestrial cycles. But as Kahn (Anaximander, p.51-2) points out, this would conflict with Xenophanes' basic monism: the 'worlds', Kahn suggests, could be the habitable worlds which re-emerge after every deluge; or the known worlds scattered over the face of the earth. The same could be said of Anaximander's 'innumerable worlds', though the sources do not always fit in with this interpretation.
31. In Kirk, Raven and Schofield, p.178. Aristotle was aware that the two processes were going on simultaneously in different parts of the world: see Meteor 351 A19 - B8.
32. Theologumena Arithmeticae DK14 A8.
33. Aristotle Phys. 205 A1-4 and De caelo 279 B12-17; Clement Strom. 5. 105; Diogenes Laertius 9.7-9; Simplicius In de caelo 94.4.
34. For ekpyrosis, see below p.124. For some seminal discussions of Heraclitus' cosmology and its influence on the Stoics, see R. Mondolfo, 'The evidence of Plato and Aristotle relating to the ekpyrosis in Heraclitus', Phronesis 3 (1958), p.75-82; G.S. Kirk (ed.) Heraclitus, the cosmic fragments (Cambridge, 1954), p.300-305; G. Vlastos 'On Heraclitus', American Journal of Philology 76 (1955), p.337-66; A.A. Long 'Heraclitus and Stoicism', Philosophia 5 (1975-6) p.133-56; and C.H. Kahn (ed.) The Art and thought of Heraclitus (Cambridge, 1979), p.134-6, and 145-153.
35. Heraclitus p.135-136.
36. For a brief resume of these efforts, see P. Vidal-Naquet, 'Athens and Atlantis: structure and

meaning of a Platonic myth', in R.L. Gordon, p.201-214 (for resume p.202-205). This article first appeared as: 'Athenes et Atlantide' in *Revue des Etudes Grecques* 78 (1964), p.420-44.

37. See J. Adams' 1902 edition of the *Republic*, reprinted in 1965, p.201-9 and 295-305, and M.L. West *Early Greek Philosophy*, p.162.

38. There are, as may be imagined, objections to Aristotle's arguments against infinite causal chains, some of which make use of his own example of fathers and sons: see Sorabji, p.226-231. For a detailed discussion of the interpretation of the passage, see R.W. Sharples, "If what is earlier, then of necessity, what is later"? Some ancient discussions of Aristotle *De gen. et corr.* 2.11, *Bulletin of the Institute of Classical Studies* 26 (1979) p.27-44.

39. See Thucydides 2.48 and 3.82. For a discussion of cyclical time in Thucydides and other historians, see Momigliano, *Essays in ancient and modern historiography*, p.179-204, esp. p.187-190.

40. *Essays in ancient and modern historiography* p.188-189. I think Momigliano is wrong in saying that the implication of Polybius' account is that all peoples go through the same stages of transformation simultaneously. Polybius goes on to imply that different states will change at different times and at different rates (6.9.11). It is true that this is inconsistent with the picture of periodic destructions: these could possibly be interpreted as local affairs (like Aristotle's), but I think the passage does not easily bear that meaning.

I also think that Momigliano is reading too much into the account when he looks in vain for evidence of a cyclical theory in the non-constitutional part of the narrative: Polybius nowhere suggests that events in general will be repeated, only constitutional changes. But with Momigliano's general conclusions I do agree. For a possible explanation of the apparent contradictions in Polybius' Book 6, see C.D. Brink and F.W. Walbank, 'The construction of the sixth book of Polybius', *C.Q.* NS4 (1954) p.97-122.

41. See, for example, Eusebius *Praep.evang.* 15.18. 1-3.

42. Nemesius *De nat. hom.* C.38.

43. See Philo Judaeus, *Aet.* 118-131, which quotes, for example, the argument that the sea is receding around Delos, thus showing that the element of water in the world is growing less. The arguments

cited by Philo may have been used by Zeno, the founder of the Stoic school: see Regenbogen in Pauly-Wissowa Suppl.7, 1539-40.

44. For one suggested argument, see Jonathan Barnes, 'La Doctrine du retour eternal', in J. Brunschwig (ed.), Les Stoiciens et leur logique (Paris, 1978), p.3-20.

45. p.183. For the first view, he cites Origen, Contra Celsum 4.68; and for the second, Origen, op.cit, 4.20 and Alexander In An.Pr. 181.25.

46. See Philo Judaeus, Aet. 76.

47. N.Q. 3.27-30.

48. Meditations 11.1 The aim of this meditation is to persuade the rational soul that it should be happy at any time to relinquish life, because it will have already experienced everything that life and the eternal universe has to offer. Marcus Aurelius may have derived satisfaction from this thought, but the vividness of his language suggests that is was not an unreservedly attractive proposition; and it certainly induces ennui in me.

49. See Lucretius, D.R.N. 2.1105-74 and 5.91-109, 235-415.

50. D.R.N. 2. 1023-89.

51. D.R.N. 3. 847-61.

52. The principle of isonomia (derived from the doctrine that, while there is a finite number of atomic shapes, there is an infinity of atoms possessing any one shape) will also ensure that worlds which are exactly the same as ours though not composed of identical matter will be created an infinite number of times. For isonomia see Lucretius, D.R.N. 2.300-2, 522-40, and 5.526-33; and C. Bailey, The Greek Atomists and Epicurus (Oxford, 1928), p.461-7. For the swerve, see Lucretius, D.R.N. 2.216-93, and Long, 'Chance and natural law in Epicureanism'.

53. It is interesting that neither Plotinus nor his master Plato (in the Politicus myth) seems to have been able to face the prospect of a world without living beings: when they come to an end, so must the world. Most people would put it the other way round.

54. p.186.

55. See Augustine's attack on cyclical theories, City of God 12.12-14.

56. City of God 12.14. trans. Henry Bettenson (Harmonsworth, 1972)

57. For a further discussion of Platonic value judgements, see below, p.149-153, 181-2, 209-213.

Chapter Six

GOLDEN AGE THEORIES

A Golden Age is a time of bliss, when people lead lives free from toil and anxiety and warfare, and nature amply provides for all their wants. It is a concept which tends to furnish a mental solace for all the pain and trouble of present-day life, and as such it can be located either in the past, or in the future, or in some distant place which we have almost certainly never visited - which may in fact be completely imaginary. This last type - the geographical Golden Age - is relatively uncommon, both in Greek and Roman authors, and with us; perhaps because travel in both ages has been too widespread to leave many illusions about the rest of the world. Again, the ancients were not being carried along on a wave of technological revolution into the future, as we often seem to be; and for them the Golden Age was most frequently (though not always) a phenomenon of the past, belonging to the very first generation of the human race. Probably every civilisation has produced historicising idylls of this kind - the Garden of Eden springs to mind immediately. Psychologically, the concept is closely linked with nostalgia, with the human tendency to colour history with all the imagined tints of our own personal youth. And like nostalgia, the Golden Age is generally far removed from reality: it can only exist in our hearts and minds because it never in fact existed.

The Golden Age, then, idealises the past, often in a most improbable manner. And in this way it says far more about the present than it does about the past. It is in fact constructed out of the present, its chief characteristics are inversions of the characteristics of our own day-and-age: thus the picture presented is very often a negative and doubly nebulous one - 'there was _no_ this, there was _no_ that, there was no the other.' We are often left wondering what people actually did in the Golden Age.

So (perhaps as in all history) the value judgements expressed in Golden Age theories are not really judgements about the past, but about the present. We help ourselves to come to terms with the here-and-now by setting up something which is consciously opposed to it, and which is deliberately unreal: by telling ourselves that the only alternative to what we have now is something that is impossible, we become reconciled to our own lives. The Golden Age is very far from being a practical ideal.

Our own use of the expression 'golden age' derives from the ancient world, and it is a useful label for soft primitivist theories. But I must here offer a warning that in a Greek context it is somewhat misleading. It was a Greek writer - Hesiod - whose use of the word 'golden' to describe the first human era established a metaphor which has survived down the years; but Hesiod, and all subsequent Greek writers who made use of the metaphor, spoke of a 'golden race', never of an 'age'. It was not until the second half of the first century BC, apparently, that Latin writers coined the expression 'golden age'; but by them it was employed so frequently that by the end of the first century AD it was being used as a figure of speech to denote any time, past or future, better than their own. Though presumably the force of the metaphor derives from the human admiration for a glittering metal, when 'gold' is applied to a 'race' or an 'age' it is unusual for it to refer to the mineral wealth of the time - when the time is in the distant past, this is hardly ever the case.

Gold is not the only symbol used by the ancients to denote a primitive paradise. The 'reign of Kronos' or the 'age of Saturn' are probably just as common; and as Baldry has pointed out, (1) as far as the Greek tradition is concerned, the notion of a happy life under the rule of Kronos may well have predated the myth of a golden race. Kronos was the god who ruled the world up until his dethronement by his son Zeus, and his term of office is often associated with the standard 'golden' blessings - leisure, peace, plenty and virtue. By the late first century BC, the Roman god Saturn was being identified with Kronos, and the 'age of Saturn' too became synonymous with the Golden Age. His festival - the famous 'Saturnalia' - included features which suggest a temporary importation into the present of 'Golden

Golden Age Theories

Age' characteristics – leisure (in particular for slaves), plenty of food, association with one's betters (slaves dined with masters, just as in the Golden Age humans mixed freely with gods), and the absence of war and punishment (since during the festival wars could not be begun nor criminals punished). There may have been a separate Roman tradition to account for these features; but it seems more likely that the whole Saturnalian apparatus had been derived ultimately from Greece – possibly via the Etruscans. (2)

The characteristics most commonly associated with a Golden Age by any name are:

> creation by the gods;
> close association with the gods;
> absence of agriculture, and freedom from the necessity to work;
> spontaneous production by the earth of crops;
> vegetarianism;
> absence of violence and war;
> absence of shipping and trade;
> absence of technology, particularly mining;
> absence of government and laws;
> absence of family life;
> common ownership of goods and property;
> and mutual affection between humans and animals.

The deterioration which sets in once the Golden Age has ended (during a period which may be divided up into silver, bronze or iron ages; or distinguished by the onset of the rule of Zeus) is characterised chiefly by the introduction of the reverse features:

> departure of gods from the earth;
> necessity for agriculture and hard work;
> hunting of animals and meat-eating;
> mining, money and private property, trade and ships, violence and war;
> laws and punishment;
> family life;
> a decline in moral standards, involving crime, lust, impiety, disrespect for parents, brothers and guests, oath-breaking and deceit.

GREEK POETS AND THE GOLDEN AGE

In Homer's epic, though there are a few examples of a regretful longing for the past (natural during

Golden Age Theories

wartime or odysseys), the attention of the <u>characters</u> is directed generally to the here-and-now. <u>Our attention</u>, of course, is directed entirely on the past, a glorious past, but by no means a Golden Age; and overt comparisons with our own present are absent. It is Hesiod who provides us with our first account of a 'Golden Age' and of the subsequent deterioration. In the <u>Works and Days</u>, in explanation of why the gods keep hidden away our means of livelihood, he recounts the story of Prometheus' trickery, of Zeus' hiding of fire, of Prometheus' theft of the same, and of the baleful gift of Pandora, who brought toil, disease and hardship to the earth (42 - 105). He then goes on to tell 'another myth' about how gods and mortals were originally born from the same source. First the gods made a golden race of men, that lived under the rule of Kronos. They lived like gods, free from sorrow and toil, and never grew old or tired, but spent all their time feasting. The earth bore fruit for them spontaneously, and they enjoyed peace and plenty, until they were covered by earth and became the daemons who ward off evils from mortals. Next the gods created an inferior race of silver, which was unlike the golden one in body and mind. It took a hundred years for them to reach maturity, but after that they did not live very long. They showed hubris towards each other, and did not worship the gods or make sacrifice to them. Zeus hid them away under the earth, where they became the blessed ones of the underworld, and then made out of ash trees a third race of bronze. These were in no way like the silver race. They were terrible and strong, and loved war and hubris. They ate no bread; their armour, houses and all their manufactures were of bronze, and they knew nothing of iron. They destroyed each other, and went to live in Hades. Next Zeus created a divine race of heroes, juster and more righteous. They fought at Thebes and Troy, and some were destroyed in battle; others were transported by Zeus to the Islands of the Blessed, where they enjoyed a carefree existence under the rule of Kronos. Finally, Zeus made a fifth race of iron, which is our own. This race is afflicted with toil, sorrow and old age; but still good is mixed with their evil. However, things are going to get worse before Zeus destroys them. Children will be born with grey hair; fathers will fight with children, guests with hosts, comrade with comrade and brother with brother; there will be no respect for aged parents, or fear of the gods; cities will be sacked; faith and justice will be despised, and hubris praised; lies, perjury and envy will prevail, until Aidos (Shame) and Nemesis finally desert the earth (109 - 201).

What we seem to have here is a combination of myth and history; or rather, a combination of what we perceive as fiction and of what we perceive as fact. While the metals clearly have a symbolic function, and seem to represent a declining scale of values, there is at the same time some historicity in the application of bronze and iron to two of the latter races, as Hesiod himself acknowledges. Griffiths would go even further: he suggests that to Hesiod the gold and silver races would not have been entirely metaphorical, and that a belief in the early use of these two metals was common in ancient times. (3) This might well have been the case, but Hesiod certainly does not say that the metals were used, and the point cannot be firmly established. The gold and silver may have been pure symbols - as Socrates says in Plato's Cratylus, 'golden' means 'not made from gold, but good and beautiful' (398A).

The tradition of an early paradise followed by moral decline may well have been derived from the Orient, as the Garden of Eden myth suggests. West points out that Greek oral tradition up to that time had apparently been dominated by heroic legends which were rather different in their implications; he cites Persian, Babylonian and Indian texts as offering parallels for the metal ages, and suggests that the notion may have reached Greece via Mesopotamia in the course of the eighth century BC. (4) Baldry (op.cit.), while he accepts that the basic idea of a paradise on earth may have been oriental in origin, believes that the specific association with metals was an invention of Hesiod's. But while it is true that the oriental myths which use metals all derive from texts which are later than Hesiod, this does not rule out an earlier origin, and the juxtaposition of metals and heroes in Hesiod certainly suggests a conflation of traditions. The point is perhaps not an important one.

Three problems in particular present themselves from the text itself.
1. Hesiod makes no attempt to marry the narrative of the ages with that of the Prometheus-fire-Pandora myth which he has just recounted. Neither the sacrifice trick, nor the reacquisition of fire, nor the advent of the female sex are mentioned in connection with the demise of the golden race, which disappears from the scene for no apparent reason.
2. The bronze race is not noticeably inferior to

Golden Age Theories

the silver race. They both commit hubris. Indeed, physically the bronze race is superior, if one rates physical strength, which Hesiod seems to do. This is a problem if one is thinking in terms of progressive deterioration.

3. The race of heroes is clearly incongruous, in that it is not denoted by a metal, and, unlike the previous two and the succeeding race, it gets a good write-up. Again, this is a problem if one is thinking in terms of progressive deterioration.

Where problem 1 is concerned, one can fit Prometheus and Pandora in if one really wants to. The scenario might run thus: Zeus usurps Kronos, and when Prometheus plays the sacrifice trick on him withdraws fire from the golden race; when Prometheus steals it back, Zeus hands out Pandora, the golden race gives up the ghost, and is replaced by the silver race. This basic compatibility is confirmed by the first appearance of women in the next section, as the mothers of the silver race; by the reference in their era to sacrifice as a custom of men; and by the belated advent of Zeus, as their destroyer and the creator of the next race (lines 130, 137, and 138). This perhaps makes the story strain a bit at the seams, but what it does reveal, I think, is that the two myths (very likely derived by Hesiod from two different sources) tell the same story and are juxtaposed by him for a very good reason. Both hark back to a time when there was no toil, disease, or death: both emphasise the fact that that happy era is over, and that we must reconcile ourselves to a new way of life, involving above all the need to work.

Problem 3, that of the heroes, is generally tackled through the plausible suggestion already referred to, that it represents the fusing of two separate traditions, a myth of four ages (probably imported from the Orient), and a vigorous home-grown tradition about semi-divine heroes who fought great wars. Hesiod (or possibly some predecessor) would have felt it incumbent on him to graft the local product onto the foreign stem. Since aristocrats in Hesiod's own day thought of themselves as descendants of the heroes, they had to come fairly late on in the scheme; they also had to come after the bronze race, since it was this generation that had seen the advent of war. So they were slotted in between the bronze and iron races. Later writers were offended by the incongruity, and unanimously eliminated the sore-thumb heroes from their schemes.

All this seems very probable: but it does not exclude the possibility that Hesiod (or whoever) in making the graft sought to hide the join as much as possible by formulating a structure in which the heroes could be put to good use. Toynbee in 1954 suggested that the heroes are an idyllic version of the bronze race. (5) Some time later Vernant went further, and tackled both problem 3 and problem 2, by linking not just the heroes with the bronze race, but also the silver race with the golden race. (6) He posited in fact a 3-tiered construction (gold-silver; bronze-heroes; present iron race-future iron race), in which each tier consists of two complementary and opposed aspects of reality: complementary, in that each of the three tiers represents a different function within society - kings, warriors, and workers; and opposed, in that each pair within the tier is determined by the same oppositional set of values, by the tension between <u>dike</u> (justice or righteousness) and hubris. Thus the history of the human race is made to conform with 'the model of a timeless hierarchy of functions and values' (p.20). The races can be interpreted, then, both diachronically and synchronically: and here it perhaps becomes significant that the Greeks speak of 'races' and not 'ages', a point not remarked on, I think, by Vernant; the importance of this can be better appreciated when we realise that the Greek word for race, <u>genos</u>, can also mean a 'clan', 'caste', or 'breed'.

Vernant's analysis is backed up by much ingenious argument, and is the most convincing resolution of the problems which I have read. It falls down rather on the factual point that the textual link between the gold and particularly the silver races and kingship is a tenuous one (for the arguments, see p.9-12); and perhaps on an interpretive point, that in stressing the synchronic aspect of the myth, it fails to bring out the unreality of the golden race, and the message about the present need for hard work which this quality transmits. Vernant's answer to the latter objection might be, I suppose, that even contemporary rulers and their idleness seem unreal to the majority of people: it need not, at any rate, be a fatal objection.

Fontenrose in his analysis does lay emphasis on the work theme of the poem. (7) While rejecting Vernant's tripartite structure, he accepts that there is a synchronic as well as a diachronic aspect to the myth. The myth, he says, is an <u>exemplum</u> of an argument about the necessity for work, and presents as history a pattern which must be supposed to exist synchronically: there are silver and bronze as well as iron men among Hesiod's own contemporaries. As far as the problem of the heroes is concerned, he suggests that it is not really a separate age, but represents rather the first and best part of the iron age. In support of this he cites the contemporary belief in descent from the heroes, and he makes use of the mutilated condition of the lines purporting to describe the creation of the fifth race (173 d-e): these should be removed, he believes, since the iron race was not a new creation but directly descended from the heroes. Hesiod himself was living in an intermediate period of the iron age, mid-way between the excellence of the heroes and the utter corruption to come.

This also is an attractive theory. One basic objection is that there is a reference to a fifth generation (line 174) which is not textually suspect. And Vernant's pairing of the heroes with the bronze race is perhaps more plausible, both on account of the warrior function which they clearly share, and because it may well have been deduced from Homeric epic that the heroes lived at a time when bronze was the basic metal in use; (although it is true that there are references in Homer to iron implements, no mention is made of iron weapons).

These are questions which are well worth considering, but cannot be decided. What one can say with some certainty, I believe, is that problems 2 and 3 rule out the notion that we are dealing here with a scheme of progressive degeneration. The main contrast which Hesiod wishes to draw is between the golden race and all the other races - as later Golden Age theorists recognised when they allowed the races intervening between the golden one and our own to become obscured. The golden race is the only one whose existence on earth was utterly idyllic, and the apparently motiveless ending of their era must carry the message that for us such bliss is out of the question.

There seems to be no doubt that for Hesiod his own era is one of mingled good and evil - 'nevertheless, for these too good things will be mixed with their evil.' (179) This puzzle, this never ending indissoluble bitter sweetness, is resolved in the myth by setting out the two polarities between which we hover. In the age of gold there was no sorrow, no war, and no miserable old age; at the end of the iron age there will be misery, endless strife, and grey-haired babies. In the age of gold, people were ruled by Kronos, they lived like gods, and were loved by the gods. At the end of the age of iron, people will pay no heed at all to the gods: they will live as the Greeks imagined animals to do, fighting with their parents, children, brothers and friends; and Aidos and Nemesis will depart for Olympus and abandon the human race for ever. We are in between, we have an intermediate status between the divine and the animal. This model is presented in the myth as a whole; it is also presented in the history of each individual race: each is created by the gods, each starts its existence on Olympus, but ends it under the earth, or at the far ends of the earth. In life we are halfway between heaven and earth, and again the pattern is one of descent.

The Theogony, we have seen, tells a similar story to this. At one time, before events at Mekone, gods and humans used to meet together: this state of affairs was brought to an end through Prometheus and Pandora, through the sacrifice trick, the theft of fire, and the deceitfulness of woman. In that work, meat-eating, the use of fire, and the institution of family life were highlighted as the items which effected a transition from blessed innocence to double-edged knowledge.

The story has been repeated in the Works and Days, and now, from the myth of the races, the hiding of corn and the need for agriculture can be added to the list of transitional items. For the golden race the earth bore corn spontaneously. But now 'the gods keep the means of subsistence hidden away from men' (42), they hide the corn in the earth (just as the defunct races are covered by earth): so the people of the silver race are nurtured by their mothers (131), instead of by the generous earth; the bronze race eats no corn or bread (146/7); and the iron race has to toil for its livelihood (176/7). Perhaps a fifth item in the transition can be cited: Kronos has been defeated and chained up; now the justice and laws of Zeus are imposed on the human race.

One point which must be stressed is that the ending of the age of gold does not signify either a drop or an improvement in cultural standards, only a deterioration in the methods by which they are maintained. Humans had corn before, and they have it still, but now they have to work for it; they had fire before it was withheld by Zeus, and they have it again now, thanks to Prometheus, but now they have to suffer for it; they had freedom from old age before, but now they have to have hungry wives and dependent children in order to avoid its worst rigours; (8) they had wealth before, and if that time could come again 'then soon in the smoke of the ingle the rudder would find its place' (line 45, trans. Way), but as it is they now have to sail ships to get it; and they had peace before, but now they need the laws of Zeus to maintain it. (And if Griffiths is right, they also had metals before, but certainly without mining). There is no suggestion here at all that we could do without the things provided by agriculture, fire, shipping, laws, and families (to the Pandora story in the Theogony, he has added the comment that the man who refuses to marry will have no-one to care for him in his old age - line 604/5). Technology, culture, society must be accepted; though they are double-edged and entail much suffering, they are also very necessary, because the age of gold is over. What life might be like without them now - without honest toil, caring children, and respect for the gods' laws - is graphically illustrated by the apocalyptic end of the iron race.

Hesiod is very far, then, from denying the value of present-day civilisation. We cannot believe for one minute that, in a poem which is dedicated to the theme of hard work, he is recommending a return to a Golden Age when work was unnecessary. Such a return is impossible. (9) We are not told why the Golden Age has ended, but we are told in no uncertain terms that ended it has: we must resign ourselves to the here-and-now, with all its drawbacks. 'Life could have been very much better', Hesiod is saying 'but on the other hand, it might be a whole lot worse'. People often seek consolation in such a thought.

Later poets who took up the story of the metal races tried to make it more coherent than Hesiod's version appeared to be, and to give it a more consistently moral significance. The next full-scale poetic treatment which we possess comes from the Hellenistic era, from the pen of the third century BC poet Aratus, who was probably a pupil of Zeno, the Stoic philosopher. He was the author of an astronomical poem called the Phaenomena, and when in this account of the stars he reaches Virgo, he repeats a story which he says 'is current among men', about how the Maiden (Virgo) once lived on earth among humans and was called Justice. At that time,

> people did not yet understand hateful wars or bitter disputes or the din of battle, but they lived in the same old way as ever. The cruel sea was concealed, and ships did not yet carry back our livelihood from faraway places; but oxen and the plough, and Justice herself, mistress of the

people, giver of just things, furnished all things a thousand-fold. This was maintained for as long as the earth nourished the golden race.

Next there came a silver race: Justice was still on the earth, but she frequented public places only in the evenings, and when she did she berated a crowd of onlookers for their wickedness (a fine picture of a soap-box orator, this). Finally, as Justice had predicted, a bronze race was born which was still worse. These people were the first to forge the sword and to eat the oxen which had formerly been used for ploughing. At this point Justice lost patience, and flew off to heaven in a huff, where she became the planet Virgo (lines 96-136).

Aratus reproduces here two of the features of transition highlighted by Hesiod: humans mix freely with the gods, the gods withdraw themselves partially, and then completely; and peace and goodwill are ousted by warfare. But leisure is not one of the features of Aratus' Golden Age: his primitives are farmers, and in their activities employ livestock and tools. This is almost certainly a reflection of the sophisticated urban society out of which Golden Age beliefs are now issuing: Hesiod could never have made an idyll out of the farming life, because he was a farmer himself and knew too much about it; but Aratus could. There is nothing realistic or attainable about his image of early bucolic life, which is furnished with an impossible plenty.

One item underlined by Aratus is the transition from vegetarianism to meat-eating. This can also be assumed for Hesiod - it fits in with the story of the sacrifice trick at Mekone; and the golden race lived off the produce of the earth, while the race of bronze 'did not eat bread', and can probably be taken to have introduced meat-eating. The rights and wrongs of vegetarianism have by now become a contentious issue in the ancient world, and the subject receives more emphasis than it did formerly. For Golden Age theorists, the abandonment of vegetarianism often goes hand in hand with a loss of divine status: meat-eating can be interpreted as something which sets the human race apart from the gods, which precipitates a descent towards the level of the animals.

Perhaps the most striking change made in the story by Aratus is the transfer to the past (from the future) of the departure of the goddess and the collapse of justice. His is a story which seems to offer little consolation to the human race: our

145

Golden Age Theories

severance from the gods and the morality they represent is complete. That leaves human beings on their own; but still the manner in which they have become eaters of oxen (the expression means literally 'they were the first to sprinkle salt on oxen') can be taken as an indication that their status, though no longer on a par with the divine, is nevertheless above that of the animals. They are not consumers of raw flesh or raw vegetation.

By the third century BC, the story of the metal races was clearly a well-known one, and the popularity of Aratus' poem carried it (and an interest in Hesiod's original) into the Roman world, where it was taken up with gusto at the end of the first century BC. Later on Greek poets were still harking back to it. One interesting twist to the theme of Golden Age vegetarianism is provided by the poet Babrius (who was writing in or before the second century AD) in the introduction to his version of Aesop's fables. Not only, in the time of the golden race, was there spontaneous production of crops and comradeship between gods and men, he says, but animals had the use of words and held assemblies in the middle of the woods, 'and the stones spoke, and the needles of the pine-tree, and the sea spoke, Branchus, to ship and sailor, and the sparrows held wise discourse with the farmer' (Fab.Aes. Preamb. 1-13). The absence of the need to eat animals is taken a stage further here, and now humans are hobnobbing freely with the natural world. But this is far from the close association perceived by 'evolutionists' between primitive human life and the plant and animal kingdoms (see chapter 4 above): humans here do not have a lowly status, but rather the world of nature has been elevated, by the gift of language, so that like the human race of that time it is almost divine. This represents a variation on the Golden Age response to the problem of the human relationship with animals. 'Progressivist' thinkers (as we shall see) identify primitive people with animals by making them savage, speechless, and eaters of raw food; Golden Age thinkers on the contrary almost invariably wish to associate the earliest human beings with the gods. They avoid any suggestion that humans might have resembled animals by making them into vegetarians (though animals may be used for wool or milk or ploughing) - vegetarians who eat 'cooked' and not raw vegetation (that is, corn, not grass, berries and acorns). Some go further, and recognising that primitive people must have had quite close communication with the animal kingdom, respond not by making humans as unthinking as animals, but by making animals as rational as humans. Here we see again (as with Hesiod) that civilisation is consistently maintained throughout the ages, but by different means: we are still as close to animals as we were in the Golden Age, but now we communicate by eating them, instead of chatting to them.

GREEK PHILOSOPHERS AND THE GOLDEN AGE

Philosophers are not immune from the idealisation of the past entailed in Golden Age beliefs, although sometimes their employment of the myth is more conspicuously metaphorical than with some of the poets. The earliest example is a poet as well as a philosopher: Empedocles, uniquely among the Presocratics, seems to have entertained a rosy view of the human race's early history. In one fragment he looks back to a time when 'they had no god Ares or Kudoimos, no Zeus as king or Kronos or Poseidon, but Cypris was queen. Her they appeased with holy gifts, with paintings of living things, and exotic perfumes, with offerings of pure myrrh and of sweet-smelling frankincense, pouring to the ground libations of yellow honey. Their altar was not drenched with the pure blood of bulls, but this was the greatest defilement amongst men, to tear the life out of the lovely limbs and eat them' (DK B128). A similar picture of mutual goodwill between humans and animals is conjured up by another fragment: 'all were docile and gentle with humans, both beasts and birds, and affection glowed between them' (DK B130); while yet another tells the opposite story of a different age: 'a father, with changed form, lifts up his dear son and, uttering a prayer slays him, the great fool. The people are at a loss as they help in the sacrifice of the imploring victim. But he, shutting his ears to its cries, slaughters it, and prepares in his halls an evil feast. And so in this way son seizes father, and children their mother, tearing the life out of the dear flesh, and eating it' (DK B137).

It is generally agreed that these fragments come from Empedocles' second poem, the <u>Purifications</u>, about the journeys of the soul. There seems to be little doubt that in the first two fragments he is looking back to a primeval Golden Age of vegetarianism - this would be the point of denying that Kronos was the king in those days. Like Aratus (who was a later writer, of course) and probably Hesiod, he associates the fall from grace with the onset of blood-sacrifices and meat-eating; like Babrius, he converts the animal kingdom into a civilised and good-tempered phenomenon. We cannot know whether Empedocles in his personal life was an apostle of vegetarianism; but it is interesting that elsewhere he is quoted as exclaiming, 'alas that the pitiless day of death did not destroy me before I committed the savagery of eating flesh with my lips' (DK B139), which suggests that he may have regarded vegetarianism as an escape-route for the individual from the corruption of the present age. But the fragment could equally well be interpreted as a sign that Empedocles saw himself as having irrevocably embraced his status as a meat-eater.

Just as the first two fragments recall to us the Golden Age, so the third one cannot fail to put us in mind of Hesiod's late-iron-age apocalypse (though here the horror is even greater). The fact that Empedocles uses the present and not the future tense suggests that we could be listening here to a colourful and exaggerated warning of the danger involved in meat-eating for a believer in reincarnation - the danger that one might unwittingly eat a member of one's family. For such a believer, that danger is a very real one, and does entail a genuinely terrible cannibalism. What we seem to be viewing, then, in historical terms, is a steady descent from vegetarianism, via meat-eating, to cannibalism - from the divine to the appallingly animal. And this is a picture which does not fit in at all with the suggestions of biological improvement which have been received from the fragments of the other poem, On Nature. If our interpretations are correct, Empedocles is the only Golden Age theorist to tell us that the human beings who lived in that happy era were the outcome of a cosmological accident, and had an identical origin to other animals.

Yet another problem presents itself. In fragment 128, he tells us that Cypris (or Love) was sole ruler then, and that the god Ares (or Strife) had not been invented. Strenuous efforts have been made on the strength of this to synchronise the fall from grace with the phases of the cosmic cycle. The time when Love was in complete control and Strife was utterly absent would be the time of the Sphere, and this has been suggested as the most likely setting for the Golden era. (10) If this is so, the Golden Age would have to be a purely symbolic one, since all the elements are fused together in the Sphere, and no world in our terms (with people and animals and

Golden Age Theories

altars) can exist. Another suggestion (11) is that the Golden Age occurred immediately after the Sphere, when Strife was only just beginning to enter the world, and Love was almost totally dominant. A world slowly coming under the influence of Strife would then be the suitable backdrop for progressive moral decline. This, of course, would be in accord with the 'two-world' interpretation of the cosmology, but would rule out the 'one-world-sudden-catastrophe' theory; whereas the 'Sphere-as-Golden-Age' view could be incorporated into both. One might add that in a cyclical view of history, everything is in the past (and in the future), and that the Golden Age could have occurred at the end of Love's last world-take-over (just prior to the Sphere, instead of just after it), with moral collapse and meat-eating being a feature of this world prior to the repeated conquest of Love. The cannibalism that took place in mythological families (e.g. that of Thyestes) might have led Empedocles to see this as a reality of the past, with present-day meat-eating representing a slight improvement. The scenario would then be one of gradual moral progress, and in such a world biological improvement would not be out of order. Perhaps one could also say that in seeking to describe a future vegetarian paradise, occurring when Love is again supreme, Empedocles would naturally hark back to the last one, as being at least notionally memorable.

All this must remain pure conjecture. The evidence is so difficult to cope with that one is tempted to conclude that Empedocles' two poems are incompatible. But all one can be truly confident in saying, I believe, is that the fragments appear to be incompatible.

The Golden Age does not seem to feature much in fifth century thought. The main evidence for its survival rests with the parodies which will be looked at later on in this chapter. It crops up again in the fourth century, in the dialogues of Plato, where it is incorporated in some consciously mythological representations. In both the Politicus and the Laws, accounts of primitive peoples are used as springboards for political and social theory. And, though the personalities of myth are rigorously excluded, most of the traditional Golden Age features are preserved in these accounts. In the Politicus, we are told that what people call the reign of Kronos in fact occurred during the first half of the cosmic cycle, when God was still in control of the world's revolutions. At that time, the bodies buried in the

149

earth came to life when fitted with new souls, and grew towards youth and babyhood - except for those whom 'God removed to another fate'. The people on earth had God as their shepherd. No animals were wild, or ate one another; there was no war or strife. Political states and family life were unheard of. The earth bore fruit of its own accord, without the need for agriculture. People lived mostly in the open air, and did not require clothing or bedding, since the weather was milder then, and the grass grew abundantly, and provided them with soft couches. It was perfectly possible to converse with animals as well as other humans. But in spite of all this the speaker is surprisingly reluctant to commit himself on the question of whether people were happier then than now.

The onset of the reign of Zeus represents the moment when God 'let go' of the world. The survivors immediately started to grow old and die in the normal way. And now they had to fend for themselves, since there was no God to care for them. They had to resort to sexual reproduction in order to maintain their existence. Some animals now were fierce, and what was more, the spontaneous food supply had been cut off, so they at first had great difficulty in staying alive. That is why the gifts of the gods which we hear about were presented to them - fire by Prometheus, technology by Hephaistos and Athene, plants by the other gods. From these arose 'everything which constitutes human life' (271A - 274D).

Practically all of the features of the Golden Age already remarked on are present in this story: it serves, in fact, as a comprehensive compendium of mythological motifs. These are: close association with divinity; a creation story which, while it makes use of the alternative earth-born explanation, preserves the notion of divine creativity by stipulating souls supplied by God; the reversal of the process of ageing (though it is hard to believe that he is not parodying Hesiod's apocalypse when he talks of people being born as grey-haired ancients); vegetarianism; peace; absence of government, family life, agriculture, private property; spontaneous fruits; and friendship with intellectual animals. Like Hesiod, he sees technology as a necessary compensation for the loss of these blessings. And like Hesiod, he believes that there is worse to come: in the phase of the cycle corresponding to ours, 'disorder prevails more and more' (273C), until the world is on the brink of destruction, and God takes

it in hand once more.
    We cannot believe that we are expected to take this story as a genuinely historical account - not the least, because Plato has told us that there is a little 'child's play' (<u>paidia</u> - 268D) in it. Its stated message is that the statesman, the shepherd of the human flock, while he should not be confused with the God who rules over the human race in the first part of the cycle, has nevertheless been shown by the comparison to be a person of singular responsibilities; and should be investigated with just as much care (274E - 275C). This message in itself is not a trivial one (as some have thought) (12) and it is backed up by the whole weight of the myth - which, occupying as it does a substantial part of the central section of the dialogue, one would expect to be of some importance. The conclusion which we are to draw from it is not that such a blissful era ever occurred in history; and not, I think, that the first half of the cycle represents a standard of perfection identifiable with the metaphysical and absolute Forms: we cannot believe this of a world which 'has produced a little evil and a great deal of good' (273C), and whose happiness-productivity the speaker refuses to assess. Rather, it is a world which comes very near to the perfection of the Forms: it cannot quite achieve it, because any world, while it has received from its creator many blessings, has a bodily nature, and cannot be free from change - absolute changelessness is an absolutely divine thing (269D-E). What I think the first half of the cycle does present us with is a picture of what the world would be like <u>if</u> it were very closely controlled by God. And here I would agree with Friedlaender (13), when he says that we are being asked to see our world (and to an even greater extent a world closely controlled by God) as 'an outgrowth of perfection'. Our own world, and any statesman in it, must be judged by the external standards which are present in the Forms and in God. As Dodds has said (14), in Plato's world there can be no open future and no genuine invention; one must be always harking back (or up) to a superior reality, which is outside of history and outside of change.
    Life in a world closely controlled by God would be easier than life in our world. The technology which has to be introduced in the second half of the cycle is a compensation for the withdrawal of divine rule, but it is clearly compensation at a price. Plato thus devalues technology, by making it second-best, and at the same time he robs human

beings of the credit for it by making it the gift of various gods, who are still doing the best they can for the world.

We should not, I feel sure, believe that the world of the first half of the cycle is, or ever was or will be, attainable. This is indicated by the stated message: 'we made a mistake when we compared a statesman in our world with the divine shepherd of that earlier world' - life is not ever going to be like that for us. It is indicated also by the unreality of its material features - old folks turning into babies, eternally warm climates, chats with animals, are, as Plato well knows and wants us to know, ludicrous. And finally it is indicated by the speaker's refusal to pass judgement on the happiness-content - 'it is all quite unreal, so there's no point in worrying about it', he seems to be saying. We never will live in a world which' is closely controlled by God, and we might as well reconcile ourselves to that fact. And for that reason technology is essential, and we cannot assume that we could do without it - this much at least Plato has learnt from the fifth century 'progressivists'. He makes room for technology in the same way as he allows for some earth in the composition of the human race.

What is our world like then? As with Hesiod's, it is a mixture of good and evil: it is not a world 'which has produced a little evil and a great deal of good', for that is unreal; nor is it a world which 'mixes a little good with a great deal of the opposite' (273D), because that is in the future and may well be unreal too. We are half-way between the two; but we should not forget about the mythical God-controlled world, nor about the world-on-the-point-of-destruction, because both are the parameters by which we measure where we are, and by which we know what we should aim to copy and what we should aim to avoid. That is why the stated message tells us that our statesman should be investigated 'neither the less nor the more' for the fact that he may resemble either a divine shepherd or a flock - the truth will be that like the world he is somewhere in-between. So Plato's message, like Hesiod's, is both a negative and a positive one. The world of Kronos is out of the question for us, but by knowing it, and its spur towards work and effort, we can help to keep ourselves on the right side of a great deal of wrong.

There is another reference to the rule of Kronos in the <u>Laws</u> which seems to spell out the same lesson with even more clarity. There we are told that in the distant past, demi-gods were appointed by Kronos to rule over the human race: they took care of us and made us happy, giving us peace, reverence, order and justice. 'And even today this tale speaks with truth, and tells us that cities of which some mortal man and not God is the ruler have no escape from evils and toils' (713B-E). Here in no uncertain terms is the message that we have put together from the myth in the Politicus - the age of Kronos tells us, because of its impossibility, that work, evil and human statesmen are for us inevitable. But like the Politicus it tells us also something more hopeful: 'we must do all we can to imitate the life which is said to have existed in the days of Kronos; and in so far as the immortal element dwells in us, to that we must pay heed ... and regulate our cities and our houses by law, meaning by this term 'law', the diffusion of reason' (713E-714A). A world ruled by Kronos may not have existed, but by imagining what it would have been like, we can bring ourselves closer to the perfect reason of the Forms. It is both a warning and an encouragement, a stick and a carrot. (15)

In the Laws we have another, longer, account of a primitive society. This is more realistic than the age of Kronos - for, I believe, a very good reason, which will be discussed in chapter 8.

Aristotle's view of the human race's early history is much more straightforward than Plato's. His analysis of the evolution of human society (Politics 1252 A24 - 1253 A40) may be genetic as well as historical (see chapter 7), but it is not metaphysical in the way that Plato's is, and it eschews any notion of a Golden Age; as far as Aristotle was concerned, primitive people were 'probably similar to ordinary foolish people today' (Pol. 1269 A6). Whether or not he could be described as a progressivist will also be discussed in the chapter that follows; what I will say at this stage is that he certainly comes closer to progressivism than his pupil Dicaearchus, who was writing at the end of the fourth century BC. In an account of the primitive age reproduced by Porphyry (who admittedly had a vegetarian axe to grind) Dicaearchus completely contradicts his teacher's theories of human history. In it, he claims historical validity for a reconstruction which, while it severely rationalises the traditional tale, retains some very definite Golden Age features.

Dicaearchus stresses, in good Peripatetic style, that the approach he has adopted in his treatment of primitive life is a thoroughly scientific one: 'If (life under Kronos) is to be taken as having really happened, and not just as an idle tale, when we remove the overly mythical aspect, we can, through the operation of reason, reduce it to a realistic account.' The earliest inhabitants of Greece, he says, were akin to the gods; they led the best kind of life, and are thus regarded as a golden race. They ate no meat. All things then must have grown spontaneously, since agriculture had not been invented; so people enjoyed lives free from toil, and also from disease - for there was no excessive eating or over-rich food (in fact they often went hungry). There was no war or feuding, because there was no private property to fight over. In short, life was full of leisure, health, peace and friendship. Later there came a pastoral wandering life, when people began to domesticate harmless animals, to attack fierce ones, and to obtain possessions. And at this point, wars made their appearance, along with society and political leadership. Next came the agricultural way of life. And so, Porphyry concludes, we can see that the onset of meat-eating also sees the start of war and competitive materialism (De abstinentia 4.1.2).

Obviously, this account is a lot more plausible than the other ones considered so far. It borders, in fact, on a 'hard primitivist' interpretation - 'life was tough but good.' But many of the motifs we have come to expect of Golden Ageism are present: kinship with the gods; vegetarianism; spontaneous food (though it is neither plentiful nor, one imagines, very nice); freedom from toil; absence of warfare, private property, society and government; and (a new item) freedom from disease, directly linked to the diet (a very modern touch, this one). Dicaearchus is not really prepared to draw the conclusion, freely admitted by most hard primitivists, that life must have been infinitely nastier and more painful then than it is now.

The fall from grace is linked, by Porphyry at least, to the use and abuse of animals. Whether Dicaearchus would have claimed that a return to vegetarianism would free us from the evils of civilisation is open to doubt. Men of the present day, he says, are made of base inferior matter (not of gold), so perhaps he accepted our current status as an inevitable one, linked to our constitution.

Among later philosophers there is a more realistic, less metaphorical, approach to cultural history, and hence a dearth of Golden Ages. It is sometimes suggested that the Stoic theory of ekpyrosis implies a belief in an early state of perfection, (16) followed by continuous deterioration, since the world when newly emerged out of divine fire will be in a better condition than at any later time. Seneca's vision of the onset of a new cycle and the short-lived innocence for which this is responsible (see above, p. 128) certainly points to a primitivist line of thought; but his, as we shall see in chapter 8, is more of a 'hard' primitivist response. And it seems likely that this was not an entirely orthodox Stoic view of cultural history, for a measure of progressivism seems to have been displayed by Zeno, the founder of the school, and even more so by the Stoic polymath of the first century BC, Posidonius. They will be discussed in the next chapter; but a preliminary reservation can be stated here, to the effect that for a Stoic, material things have no intrinsic value, and morals - the only element in civilisation that really matters - cannot be judged in accordance with a simple pattern of decline or improvement.

PARODIES OF THE GOLDEN AGE

That the rule of Kronos did not die the death in the fifth century BC is demonstrated by the frequency with which it is parodied in Old Comedy. This is indicative both of the fact that the tradition itself was still going strong (you do not parody something which no-one believes in anyway), and of the way in which progressivism was beginning to throw doubt over the soundness of such a pessimistic view of human history. So in Aristophanes, when the adjective kronikos (derived from Kronos) is applied to a person, it always means, not that he is happy, good and prosperous, but rather that he is old-fashioned to the point of idiocy. (17) It seems likely that it was used in the same sense in everyday speech.

In the full-scale parodies, the feature of the Golden Age most often satirised seems to have been, as one might expect, nature's artless provision of cultivated food. A character in one of Teleclides' plays (who seems to be Kronos, in fact) rapturises about the time when 'the earth bore neither fear nor disease, but all the necessaries appeared of their own accord. For every stream flowed with wine, and barley-cakes fought with wheat-cakes around men's mouths, pleading to be gulped down ... and fishes, coming to men's houses and baking themselves, would

Golden Age Theories

serve themselves up on the tables. A river of soup flowed by the tables, swirling hot meats. Pipes with sharp sauces were provided for those requiring them ... Roasted thrushes with milk-cakes flew down one's gullet. The war-cry was heard of pancakes elbowing each other aside at one's jaw ... men were fat then, like so many giants' (from <u>Amphictyons</u>, in Athenaeus <u>Deipnos</u>. 6.268).

Sometimes the absence of toil is lighted on as well:

> A. I shall make everything walk about.
> B. So what?
> A. Each object will approach of its own accord, when you order it to. Table, set yourself. Get yourself ready ... where is the wine-cup? Wash yourself! ... Fish, advance. 'But I'm not yet baked on the other side!' Then why don't you turn yourself over, and salt yourself, silly?
>
> (From Crates' <u>Beluae</u>, in Athenaeus <u>Deipnos</u>. 6.267).

Thus, the picture of a civilisation-without-pains is taken to its illogical conclusion. It was against this background that Plato wrote about his age of Kronos in the next century: and he knew, as clearly as the comic poets did, that a life like this was impossible.

ROMAN POETS AND THE GOLDEN AGE

It was in the Latin poetry of the late first century BC that the era of the golden race was translated into a golden age. Whether or not Rome had its own separate tradition of a lost paradise, we cannot say. It is true that Saturn makes frequent appearances in the story, but he too could have been a transplanted Kronos. Certainly, Roman poets are often following their Greek predecessors quite closely when the Golden Age pours from their pens. But with a certain shift of feeling, I think. For Hesiod and Plato, at least, the time of the golden race, though unreal, had an urgent significance for the present generation. In Latin poetry, this didacticism is often replaced by a conscious and elaborate fantasy about the past (or in one case, the future), which may explain why the golden race has now become an 'age': it represents an escape into another time.

One of the earliest references to a golden <u>age</u>,

whose metallic splendour became contaminated first with bronze and then with iron, occurs in a poem in which Horace is manufacturing a geographical escape for the present-day generation (Ep. 16.64-5; see below). At about the same time (it is probably no coincidence that these two poems were written during an uneasy lull in civil wars) Vergil was escaping into the future, but was still writing in Greek fashion of the advent of a golden race, and the disappearance of the iron breed. In the notorious Eclogue 4, he rapturously predicts the birth of a child whose lifetime will witness the return of Justice to the earth, and the renewal of the reign of Saturn. The child will lead a godlike life, and will himself mingle with gods and heroes; his growth to manhood will see a gradual accumulation of moral and material blessings, culminating in a full-blown Golden Age. All the traditional features are there, writ very large and very extravagant. The earth will pour forth flowers, goats will come of their own accord to be milked, the lamb will not live in fear of the lion, serpents will die, and grapes will grow from thorn-bushes and honey drip from oak-trees. And when at last the child has reached maturity, there will be no more sea-faring, no more commerce, and no more labour on the land. Even manufacturers of dyestuffs will be put out of business, since sheep will grow coloured coats, of purple, yellow and scarlet (1 - 45). With this surreal scene, the vision fades.

Much debate has centred, of course, on the identity of the unborn child, with no very convincing conclusions. These need not be discussed here; though I am happy to announce that the two most likely prospective candidates, the offspring of Octavian and Antony respectively, both turned out to be girls (one of them the splendid Julia, who might well have made a sheep blush). There has been much talk too of Messianic prophecies, and of whether Vergil had had a preview of Christianity, or could have read Isaiah. It seems pretty certain that there is a political message in all this somewhere, but we cannot fathom what it is, and it need not concern us now. Perhaps all we need to note here is (1) that Vergil was fed up with civil war, (2) that he needed a solace and hope for the future, (3) that he probably did think that things were going to get better, and (4) that a vision of a golden future might well have helped to reconcile him to a present which, while not as awful as the past, still had a lot of unpleasantness in it.

Once civil war in the Roman world had been

forcibly suppressed by Augustus, the metaphor of the Golden Age took on a very definite political meaning. So Aeneas on his guided tour of the underworld has pointed out to him all the future heroes of Roman history: 'And here, here is the man, the promised one you know of - Caesar Augustus, son of a god, destined to rule where Saturn ruled of old in Latium, and there bring back the age of Gold ...' (Aeneid 6.791-4; trans. C. Day-Lewis). The implication is that Vergil himself is now living in the Golden Age, and if so, he may have found it rather less brilliant than the one he had predicted some twenty years earlier. But it is interesting that it is still cast in the future. Not many people can bring themselves to say that they are actually living in it - for Horace, dragged out of retirement to celebrate the same political millenium, it is still in the past, though 'should time itself return/to the age-old Age of Gold', it would never produce anything better than Augustus (Odes 4.2.37-40). The metaphor is now reduced, particularly after Augustus' death, to a rather empty form of flattery. After another spate of civil war, Calpurnius reported a promise which had been found scratched on the bark of a tree: 'the Golden Age of untroubled peace is born again ... and the happy times are ruled by a youth ... When he reigns over the people himself as a god ... all wars will be buried in the prison-house of Tartarus ... and shining peace will appear' (Eclogue I. 42-54). The youth was Nero, and with him (though Calpurnius was not to know) the Golden Age metaphor reaches its nadir. We have come a long way now from the sober acceptance of present-day evils which the original myth implied; although the desperate clinging to hope which underlies these latterday prophecies is not, I think, a totally alien response.

The Golden Age of Latin literature also produced, appropriately enough, a plethora of past Golden Ages. Vergil in the Aeneid turns at one point from prophecy to history, when in Book 8 he has his hero visit king Evander on the site of the future Rome, and listen to a tale about the people who once lived there, a race 'born of tree trunks and the hard oak', who at first had no government or agriculture or food-storage, but lived by food-gathering and hunting. Then Saturn, fleeing from Olympus after Jupiter's coup, arrived there and gave them government and laws, and ruled them in peace: 'the age over which he reigned is called golden'; but later warfare and the lust for property set in (Aeneid 8. 314-327). The Golden Age here is not located at the beginning of history, but is achieved after a modicum of social and technological innovation. Saturn thus becomes a culture-hero, and a degree of progressivism is displayed. The message conveyed to the future occupants of the site (not always noted for their devotion to peace and simplicity) is perhaps a more dismissive one than usual: by making the Golden Age appear fairly realistic, Vergil is perhaps advising the Romans that they might do well to return to their former state of existence.

Tibullus in one of his poems gives a conventional picture of the negative blessings of a Golden Age under Saturn: there was no travel, no ships, no trade, no agriculture, and, above all, no private property: 'No dwelling then had doors, no boundary-stone stood on the land to mark out each man's own' (Elegies I.3.43-44; trans. Philip Dunlop). But now under the reign of Jupiter there are 'a thousand roads to sudden death'. In another poem, Tibullus adds a novel feature: one of the drawbacks of the present iron age, quite apart from warfare, pillage and horrendous greed, is that agriculture keeps women toiling in the fields. 'The acorn nourished our ancestors, and they made love whenever and wherever they wanted ...' (Elegies II. 3. 69-70). The absence of family life for Hesiod and Plato meant celibacy and a freedom from burdens: in Tibullus it is converted into a passport to free love. Here the Golden Age represents little more than idle wishful-thinking.

The Roman poet who gives the fullest account of the myth of the ages is Ovid, who omits the age of heroes but otherwise adheres closely to Hesiodic tradition. In the Metamorphoses he relates how the first human beings were either made by the creator from divine seed, or were fashioned by Prometheus in the image of the gods, out of an earth which still had particles of heavenly aether mixed with it. There ensued a golden age, when there was righteousness and faith, without justice, laws or punishment. There were no ships and no wars. Without the need for agricultural labour, and under an eternal spring, the earth gave plentiful supplies of wheat, and rivers flowed with milk and nectar. But when Saturn had departed, and Jupiter came to the throne, the silver race was born. The other seasons were introduced, and people had to provide themselves with simple houses, and to start to till the land. In the age of bronze, people were fierce and warlike, but not utterly wicked. That fate was reserved for the age of iron, when treachery, deceit, violence and greed were rife. Ships were invented, farming-land, hitherto a common possession, 'like the light of the sun and the breezes', was divided up among private owners; mining was introduced, and iron and gold both helped to intensify warfare. Then violence and murder were rife within families, and the maiden goddess Astraea left the earth (Metamorphoses I. 76-150).

Here Ovid has manipulated the Hesiodic scheme to produce a picture of progressive deterioration, with increasing technological sophistication going hand in hand with moral decline. Features from other poetic accounts of the ages have been incorporated; elsewhere in the Metamorphoses, vegetarianism and kindness to animals are added to the Golden Age characteristics - in that distant time, people were content with fruits and herbs, and birds, beasts and fishes could go about their business unharmed; but later meat-eating and blood-sacrifices were invented (15. 96-142). This second passage is of a more practical import - it ends with an exhortation to abstain from flesh, and we are led to believe that in this way we can recapture the Golden Age. The practising primitivism thus proclaimed (put, it must be said, into the mouth of the philosopher Pythagoras) is more akin to the 'hard' variety of primitivism. But in the first passage, the Golden Age and all the other ages are placed firmly in the past. For, Ovid announces, Jupiter destroyed the iron race with a great flood, so that we ourselves are the descendents of the humans subsequently recreated by Deucalion and Pyrrha. The link between these and the people of his own day and age is reinforced when Ovid makes a subtle comparison between the avenging Jupiter and Augustus (I. 199-206). So that, whereas Hesiod placed his own generation fairly and squarely between the best and the worst, giving it a share of both good and evil, Ovid removes his entirely from the scheme, setting it apart and refusing to impose on it value judgements which belong to the past. It is a kind of acceptance of the present, but it is one that is achieved by shutting one's eyes to the good and evil that is in us. Hesiod and Plato were much bolder than Ovid in facing up to the urgent implications of the myth.

THE ISLANDS OF THE BLESSED

Increasing knowledge of foreign lands may have inhibited somewhat the manufacture of geographical

Golden Age Theories

Golden Ages - of civilisations existing elsewhere in the world where life was considered to be ideally happy and good. But the myth about the Islands of the Blessed affords us one example of an imaginary happy country. In Hesiod and Pindar, these are islands at the extremity of the world to which specially favoured heroes (Hesiod) or the souls of just men (Pindar, in <u>Olympians</u> 2. 68-76) are translated at the end of their lives. But later on, some people liked to regard them as real places, identifying them apparently with the Canaries - and so here too the Golden Age comes to provide, not an illustration of an extreme to which we ordinary mortals cannot aspire, but a credible mental refuge from the miseries of the real world. Someone who took the story seriously, apparently, was <u>Sertorius</u>, a Roman revolutionary of the first century BC, who succeeded for quite a long time in unlawfully controlling the provinces of Spain. According to Plutarch's biography, at a time when he had been temporarily dislodged from his Spanish stronghold, he contemplated escaping to some islands described by passing sailors. The Islands of the Blessed, they said, were beyond Libya and had a wonderful temperate climate, so that they 'bear spontaneously fruit in such quantity and of such sweetness as to feed the people without toil and trouble, providing them thus with plenty of leisure' (<u>Sertorius</u> 8-9). Horace is less credulous: anticipating a renewal of civil war he urges an escape to an impossible country, the Fortunate Islands, where there is food-without-tears, where animals are friendly and the weather persistently mild, and where disease is unknown (<u>Epodes</u> 16). Horace knows perfectly well that no such country exists; he is simply trying to highlight by contrast the awfulness of the age in which he lives.

Like many another myth, the Islands of the Blessed are extravagantly parodied by Lucian, a satirist of the second century AD. In his <u>True History</u>, he describes how a group of adventurers come to an island which is bathed in sweet perfumes and wafted by soft breezes, where the natives dance and sing to the music of flute and harp. Being taken prisoner and bound with festoons of roses, the seafarers are tried and condemned to spending no more than seven months on the island. Later on they learn about its delights - its buildings of gold and ivory and precious stones, its gossamer garments, the absence of old age and of day and night, its climate and its miraculous harvests; and they are entertained at a banquet where cups of wine grow from the trees, musical accompaniment is provided by choruses of birds, and the winds wait on at the flower-strewn couches (2. 4-16). (18)

The myth of the Golden Age contributes a cultural dimension to the anthropogonic myth about the divine origins of the human race - indeed, the two are often combined. It adds circumstantial detail to the story of how human beings began their existence living very close to the gods, and describes a life-style which is very similar to the divine one, encompassing freedom from toil, freedom from suffering, disease and old age, and freedom from government and family life. The fall from grace, the fall towards an animal status, is effected by the onset of meat-eating, by the loss of fire, by the advent of women and sex, by the withdrawal of cultivated food, and by the tyrannical rule of Zeus. But we never sink to the level of animals, because the reacquisition of fire and its associated technology, the ability to cook our meat instead of eating it raw, the institution of family-life, the invention of agriculture and the ability to 'cook' our vegetation, and the system of law and order instituted by Zeus, all help to keep us above that level. We have an intermediate status, and our culture is vital in that it keeps us in that position - it is a distinctively human attribute. A fall and a partial rise is the movement implied by the Golden Age myth. We do not have to believe that any mythographer really thought of it as a historical event. What it teaches us is that our culture (not the least, our technology) has a lot of potential for good, but even more potential for evil. It will never restore us to a Golden Age situation, but it will keep us hovering above the level of the beasts. On the other hand, if not handled carefully, it could send us hurtling down again. (In this respect, it is rather akin to the Epicurean notion of pleasure: a little bit of food will take away the pain of hunger, but too much will give you indigestion). 'Nothing to excess' is a well-worn Greek cliche, but it seems appropriate here. It is even appropriate, I believe, when we come to consider the Golden Ages of the Roman poets, though I think that they dwell with rather more yearning on the excessive sweetness of the lost paradise than do their Greek counterparts.

NOTES

1. H.C. Baldry, 'Who invented the Golden Age?', C.Q. N.S.2. (1952), p.83-92.
2. For a discussion of Saturn's ancestry, see H.J. Rose, Ancient Roman religion (London, 1949), p.76-78.
3. J.G. Griffiths, 'Archaeology and Hesiod's five ages', Journal of the history of ideas 17 (1956), p.109-119.
4. Works and Days, edition and commentary by M.L. West (Oxford, 1978), p.173-177.
5. A.J. Toynbee, A study of history VIII (London, 1954), p.76.
6. J.P. Vernant, 'Le mythe hesiodique des races. Essai d'analyse structurale', Revue de l'histoire des religions (1960), p.21-54; and 'Le mythe hesiodique des races', Revue de philologie (1966), p.247-76; reproduced as chapters 1 and 2 of Mythe et pensee chez les Grecs (1965); English translation Myth and thought among the Greeks (London, 1983), p.3-72.
7. J. Fontenrose, 'Work, justice and Hesiod's Five Ages', Classical Philology 69 (1974), p.1-16.
8. The silver race's child, that stays by its mother's side for a hundred years, and dies soon after leaving it (131-2), must, I feel sure, be an understandable hyperbole on the part of a peasant-farmer who spends years raising a child, only to have it die from war or disease just as it becomes capable of helping on the farm. A risky investment. The contrasting counterpart in the age of gold is the absence of old age: now in order to avoid the miseries of old age, people have to have children who hopefully will support them when they grow old (this is where Pandora comes in); and the counterpart in the future iron age is the children who will refuse to 'repay their aged parents for their nurture' (187/8). That really would be the last straw.
9. Hesiod is reluctant to dismiss the Golden Age altogether from present reality. A select group of non-humans - the departed heroes - continue to enjoy in the Islands of the Blessed a life which has three Golden Age features - it is free from sorrow, the earth is super-fertile, and they are ruled over by Kronos (167-173a). But once again, this is not an option that is open to us ordinary mortals - there is no question of our achieving it on our departure from this life. Like the Golden Age of the past, this one just serves to remind us that some people have to work for a living.

10. Most recently by Schofield, in Kirk, Raven and Schofield, p.318.
11. Made, for example, by Wright, p.282.
12. Guthrie, Greek philosophy, Vol. 5 (1978), p.182-3, is rather dismissive about the serious content of the myth. P. Friedlaender, Plato, trans. H. Meyerhoff, vol. 3 (London, 1969), p.284, thinks the stated message trivial, but finds a more serious hidden meaning.
13. Vol. 3, p.285.
14. p.15.
15. The Golden Age theme is probably relevant also when one considers the lengthy account of proto-Athens and proto-Atlantis given in the Critias (108E-121C) - an account which deserves more analysis than there is room for here. Proto-Athens can be contrasted both with what Atlantis became in that distant time, and with what Athens has become now (as Vidal-Naquet, op.cit., has shown, latterday Atlantis and latterday Athens have much in common). Thus the model is both a synchronic and a diachronic one. Both proto-Athens and proto-Atlantis have two 'Golden Age' features - they are close to the divine (in those days the gods looked after humans as shepherds do their flocks) and their soil is exceptionally fertile; but on the other hand they both have arts, crafts, agriculture, armies, and governments. The diachronic relationships are in fact very complicated, since there is a movement in time which is confined to the past (proto-Atlantis to latterday Atlantis) and one which reaches the present (proto-Athens to latterday Athens); while synchronically proto-Athens is related both to proto-Atlantis and to latterday Atlantis. I suspect that the model might be this: as proto-Athens is to (proto-Atlantis changing into latterday Atlantis); so a hypothetical God-controlled world is to (proto-Athens changing into latterday Athens). Thus proto-Athens would have a dual function - the timeless and the pseudo-historical - and this would explain why it has both 'Golden Age' and technological features.
16. See, for example, Lovejoy and Boas, p.261.
17. See, for example, Pluto 581.
18. For an account of other geographical Golden Ages, see J. Ferguson, Utopias of the Classical world (London, 1975), p.122-129.

Chapter Seven

THEORIES OF PROGRESS

J.B. Bury in his definitive work The idea of progress (p.1-7) delineates three distinguishing features of a thorough-going theory of progress. These are:

1. The belief that civilisation has moved, is moving, and will move in a desirable direction; which for most people means in a direction which ensures that a condition of society develops which promotes human happiness.
2. The belief that the movement in this direction will be maintained for a lengthy period in the future: so that the idea contains not just an analysis of the past but also a prophecy for the future.
3. The belief that this process is the outcome of human nature and human intellect, and not of any external will. For a guarantee of its continuance, it must be a human achievement. If any external controlling force - like a god - were involved, it would lapse into an idea of providence.

These demands are pretty stringent, and few of the accounts of progress reviewed in Bury's own history of the idea are able to match up to it. As Bury himself admits, the belief in progress must be an act of faith; and even among the nineteenth century apostles, there is a great tendency for faith to crumble when it is confronted with particular historical conditions and events. We should not be surprised, then, if ancient thinkers seldom, if ever, make the grade.

Bury himself believed that the idea of progress was scarcely to be found in ancient thought. And certainly on one of the conditions - the second one - it falls down rather heavily. Greek and Roman thinkers are much more inclined to speculate about the past than to make predictions about the future. This fact is scarcely surprising, since most people know (or think they know) rather more about the past than they do about the future, and even today history still predominates over science fiction. Most of our own futurism has been prompted by the forward-looking inventiveness of scientists and technologists, which was not such a factor in the ancient world. So full-scale treatments of the future are rare in ancient authors - we are often left in the position where we have to guess, from little hints dropped here and there, their attitude to the time-to-come. But there certainly is not a total dearth of predictions of future (limited) progress. As one might expect, scientists were more aware than others of future possibilities: Archimedes was quite prepared to admit that later thinkers would discover theorems that had not occurred to him (Method. p.430, Heiberg); and the astronomer Hipparchus in the second century BC knew that his list of fixed stars would enable future astronomers to understand better the workings of the universe (Pliny, N.H. 2.95). Other practitioners too had an eye to future generations: both Thucydides and Polybius thought that their work would be of value to people trying to cope with similar problems, or trying to understand historical change; while Seneca looked forward to a protracted extension of knowledge - 'no-one born in a thousand years time will be short of an opportunity to add to the store of knowledge' (Ep. Moral. 64.7). Much rarer, though not entirely absent, are the more detailed visions of the future: these, however, tend to be apocalyptic (like Hesiod's) or rose-coloured (like Vergil's). Our own futurism is not always so very different; but it is, undeniably, encountered far more frequently than is the futurism of ancient literature.

Another objection which is often made to the ancients as thorough-going progressivists relates not to their failure to examine the future, but to their conviction that the future, as a series of unique events, did not even exist. The widespread belief, still maintained, (1) that the ancients had a concept only of cyclical time, has already been dealt with in chapter 5. The theory of cosmic cycles was by no means the majority view in the ancient world; and the belief in minute repetition was even rarer. But I would admit that those who do think in terms of cycles tend not to want to pass value judgements on the process of time. Other thinkers again, like Democritus and Lucretius, simply believe that sooner or later our world will be destroyed, without giving much thought to the possibility of its being recreated. Judgement is perhaps not absent from their accounts of cultural change, but it is not really extended into the future.

Clearly ancient thinkers are not, with regard to condition (2), going to fit easily into Bury's definition of progressivism. For us, the definition will have to be modified. Nor does this seem to me to be a fatal alteration: I believe that it would be possible to think that the world was going to be destroyed tomorrow, and still to count oneself as a progressivist. If the destruction was to come about through the human race's own actions, then one's judgement would probably not be so favourable: but in the ancient world this possibility had not yet materialised.

Bury's third condition is one that introduces all manner of complications. The notion of a purely secular and unplanned progress is in fact quite common among ancient thinkers. But again, its presence is perhaps not essential: modern theologians would argue that progress involves the idea of movement towards a specified 'good', and that only religion can supply us with a stable and absolute criterion of 'goodness'. The goal towards which society is moving would thus be divinely determined, and the laws governing the process of change would be laws put into the system by a god. This too is a concept which is not altogether foreign to ancient thought. Perhaps the one idea which one can exclude from the definition of progress is that of intermittent and arbitrary improvements bestowed by some extra-mundane power. To qualify as progress, the process of change for the better (whether inherent in human nature or injected by some deity) must be endogenous and dependable.

Condition (1), of course, is really the most difficult of all. Who knows what is productive of overall human happiness? Who is prepared to assert that all changes in all societies are desirable? Certainly no ancient thinker that I know of is prepared to commit himself unequivocally to a steady and inevitable increase in human happiness. Qualifications or limitations always exist, and for this reason it often becomes necessary to separate the changes reviewed into various strands, in an attempt to judge whether or not an author's commitment to one form of advance is outweighed by his rejection of another. Included among these strands are: technology and material improvement;

the development of the human intellect; social and political change; linguistic competence; juridical and moral change; and artistic developments. Some writers look at the strands separately, some combine them into full-scale treatments of cultural evolution (and often begin their accounts with a description of biological origins). It is not always easy to decide what judgements are being passed on the various changes which are being outlined; and it is even harder to discern what <u>explanation</u> is being given for cultural change, other than a historicist 'this is how it happened' explanation. Moreover, where we think we know what judgements are being passed, these are sometimes contradictory. So an author's inclusion among the progressivists is sometimes a touch-and-go affair. My general rule-of-thumb has been that where an author's perception of the adverse moral effects of technological change (to take the most common example) is offset either by his enthusiasm for that change or by the length with which he treats it, then he has been included. And my one fairly consistent parameter of progressivism has been an account of primitive human life which brings out its unpleasant, bestial qualities.

Edelstein's work, coupled with that of Dodds (<u>op.cit.</u>,) has provided us with a wealth of detail on anything which might be termed progressivism in ancient thought. In this chapter I will confine my attention by and large to those accounts which deal with wholesale cultural evolution since the primitive age.

MYTHOLOGICAL REPRESENTATION OF PROGRESS

The outstanding mythological figure associated with human progress is Prometheus - who is also in Hesiodic myth the principal agent in the human race's downfall. For Prometheus is a trickster, and like the technology he bestows on the human race, he is thoroughly ambiguous. In Hesiod, he introduces humans to meat-eating and to fire, and in this way he ensures the separation of the human race from the race of gods. In this we can read a consciousness of the double-edged character of the fire he has brought us. Fire gives us warmth, it gives us the ability to cook our food and to make sacrifices to the gods, and the ability to mould metals. But fire also destroys; it emphasises our separation from the gods by giving us a food which they do not need, and a channel of communication which would not be necessary if we were still at one with them; and the metals it moulds are the source of the wealth and the weapons which promote warfare. In addition, Prometheus brings down on our heads Pandora, who is also thoroughly ambiguous: she is lovely to look at, she has been instructed in the art of weaving, and she enables us to marry and to gain a kind of immortality through procreation; but she brings with her toil, disease, and the burden of supporting the families which we would not need if we had personal immortality and a guaranteed food-supply.

Thus at the very heart of the myth, in the twin figures of Prometheus and Pandora, lies the ambiguity which can be manipulated to give a reversible perspective on the history of human civilisation. Prometheus and Pandora, with identical gifts, either rob us of the Golden Age, or help to raise us from savagery. They can do both these things at the same time because the gifts they bring are a mixture of good and evil, and their myth serves to remind us that we are living in a mixed-up world.

In the Hesiodic version of the story, the technological and social innovations for which the two are responsible are evil because they are second-best and remind us of the blessings of which we have been deprived; but we need them, and in that they are good. However, in the course of time, the myth is adapted and retouched, so that the picture is inverted: when the Golden Age blessings are removed from the representation of primitive life, and savagery is substituted, then the gifts which Prometheus bestows on us become more obviously good; but they still, as we shall see, involve almost inevitable evil.

Though he is the most prominent, Prometheus is by no means the only culture-hero offered to us by Greek mythology. Numerous other deities appear from time to time in the guise of benefactors, of inventors and technicians who pass their skills on to the human race. Among the earliest are Demeter, who taught humans how to sow corn and thus introduced them to agriculture; Athene, who instructed them in the technique of weaving; and Hephaistos, who taught them metal-working. Sometimes the benefaction is seen as unalloyed and uncontroversial: so Hephaistos, along with Athene,

> taught men on earth glorious crafts - men who before used to live in caves in the mountains, like wild beasts. But now through Hephaistos, the renowned technician, they have learnt

crafts and easily live lives free from care the whole year round in houses of their own. (Hymn to Hephaistos 2-7).

Here we have in brief a typical progressivist scenario, picturing the human race raised through technology from an animal condition. The poem may be of a fairly late date (possibly fifth century); undoubtedly early are the ones that tell a more ambiguous story. So in Hesiod, the art of weaving is passed on by Athene to the human race, but via the disastrous Pandora (Work and Days 63/64). And probably of the seventh century BC is the hymn which first tells us the story of how Demeter guaranteed the human race fruitful fields, but only after the seed-corn had been kept hidden for a whole year, and abundant crops had been reinstated for a limited season only - the period of Persephone's return to the earth (Hymn to Demeter). Here too the message seems to be about the ending of a Golden Age, and the bestowal of a mixed blessing.

Divine or semi-divine culture-heroes continue to be employed in later mythology to dole out compensation for the withdrawal of a Golden Age (as in Plato's Politicus myth); or at the least to reinforce the notion that what advances the human race has achieved have been enjoyed only as a result of divine beneficence. From the fifth century on, when interest in technology and in origins generally was on the increase, whole catalogues of culture-heroes (and heroines) were produced, and their activities were extended to social and political innovations, as well as to some rather specialised techniques. The longest list of all is given by the elder Pliny, who provides us with the names of no less than 139 divine, heroic and human inventors: among the inestimable boons for which they are responsible are wells, ships, fishing-lines, the saw, axe, awl and plumb-line, and vegetable-and-fish glue (N.H. 7.56). By this time (the first century AD), the idea of progress as a purely human achievement had been around for some time, and with some of these lists we may be witnessing attempts to rationalise mythological culture-heroes, by suggesting that they were in reality exceptionally gifted humans who had been accorded divine or semi-divine status because of the benefits conferred by their inventions. So Pliny launches his exhaustive list by telling us that 'Ceres gave men grain, before which they ate acorns; she also taught them to mill and prepare it for baking, and on this account was judged to be a goddess.' The most famous attempt at rationalisation had been made by Euhemerus, in the fourth/third centuries BC, who wrote a pseudo-autobiographical novel about the discovery on a remote island of a monument which showed that Ouranos, Kronos and Zeus had once been great kings who were worshipped as gods by their grateful subjects. (2) This could be interpreted as providing a historical justification for the ruler-worship instituted by Hellenistic kings; or as a piece of propaganda in the cause of humanistic atheism. It was the latter idea that was the more favoured among Roman readers, and the result was a number of 'euhemerising' accounts, the best-known being a lost work by the poet Ennius, which challenged (among others) the divinity of the head of the Roman pantheon, Jupiter. It was an approach to the pagan religion much prized by the Christian fathers. (3)

THE ATTIC TRAGEDIANS

Paradoxically enough, one of the earliest progressivist accounts of any length which we possess comes from the pen of an Attic tragedian (4). In the Prometheus Bound, we are presented with a moving picture of the renowned culture-hero, chained to a rock on the orders of Zeus as punishment for his theft of fire, and pouring out a defiant justification of his actions. With passionate force, he claims for himself the credit for having raised human beings from a condition in which they resembled 'swarming ants', living in caves under the ground, having no way of marking the seasons, and being incapable of making use of their sense-perceptions through the power of reasoning. It was Prometheus who taught them how to construct houses and to measure time; how to make use of numbers and writing, of beasts of burden and of ships; how to make medicines; how to read the signs for predicting the future, and to perform sacrifices to the gods; and how to mine metals - so that 'all the techniques known to mortals came from Prometheus' (436-506). Here Prometheus has developed from a mere fire-robber into the bestower of a whole range of intellectual and technical accomplishments. It is through the invention of devices and techniques that the human power of reasoning is actually developed - 'mortals were witless before I gave them intelligence and minds' - for humans were not created fully-equipped with all the powers of the intellect. Indeed, they were once like animals, but through technology and the stretching of their minds they have been brought to a point where they can <u>use animals</u> - in divination and sacrifice - in order to get close to the gods and rival them in their ability to read the future. Thus the picture is an inversion of the Golden Age one: humans move away from animals and towards the gods, instead of vice versa. But at least some of the steps on the route are the same - fire, a settled domestic existence, agriculture (referred to obliquely in the yoking of animals), and meat-eating appear both here and in Hesiod.

One of the problems presented by this passage is whether we should see Prometheus as a symbol of the human race's intellectual and inventive struggle against the savagery which the divine order of things has bequeathed to them; or whether Prometheus' own divine status should be taken as signifying that civilisation is a gift from god. The question would probably not have occurred to a primitive myth-maker; but to a fifth-century Athenian one it may well have been important. The very unfavourable picture painted in the play of Zeus' tyranny encourages us to interpret civilisation as a battle against the gods; but on the other hand, the impression we gain of the human race from Prometheus' speech is of a passive and helpless tribe, with no innate lust for self-improvement. Our uncertainty is intensified if we continue to ascribe the play to Aeschylus, as most people probably do, since we know him to have been a poet of strong religious convictions, who was probably not disposed to see human achievements as occurring outside the orbit of divine control. Numerous resolutions of the play's supposed contradictions have been suggested by commentators committed to Aeschylean authorship, many of them involving reconstructions of the two missing plays of the Promethean trilogy, and a surmised evolutionary presentation of either the personality of Zeus, or of the Greek concept of the divine (5). If we are prepared to abandon Aeschylus as author, then the contradictions become more easy to cope with, and we can perhaps see Prometheus as symbolising that element in the human psyche which is opposed to passive acceptance, and is prepared to do battle with a hostile natural order. But these are the kind of questions which can never be resolved. One thing that seems more certain is that the poet does not intend us to see civilisation as conferring on us an existence of unmixed blessings - the profound suffering of Prometheus suggests that quite strongly; and Prometheus himself makes it clear that only 'blind hope' enables human beings to shut their eyes to their miserable mortality (250-252). Like Hesiod, he accepts that we are living in a world of good and evil mixed. This ambiguity encouraged some nineteenth century commentators to go so far as to interpret the play as a repudiation of the benefits of technology. Such a conclusion is an unjustifiable one: Prometheus' powerful speech tells us in no uncertain terms that without technology humans would lead miserable unthinking lives, far from that of the gods. But technology brings with it inevitable suffering, and ensures that our existence, though better than that endured by animals, can never encompass the freedom from pain and anxiety which is characteristic of the divine.

In the Prometheus Bound, divine power could be interpreted as either promoting or opposing human aspirations; from Sophocles we get instead an impression of divine indifference, transformed only in certain circumstances into active opposition. In the Antigone, a stirring choral ode presents us with a celebration of a species which has conquered the seas, brought the earth under the plough, won mastery over birds, beasts and fishes and forced them to be useful, and invented language, laws, society and houses (332-375). All this has been achieved by a human race that has freedom of will and is responsible for its own destiny:

> Wonders are many on earth, and the greatest of these
> Is man, who rides the ocean and takes his way
> Through the deeps, through wind-swept valleys of perilous seas
> That surge and sway.
>
> He is master of ageless Earth, to his own will bending
> The immortal mother of gods by the sweat of his brow
> As year succeeds to year, with toil unending
> Of mule and plough.
> (332-340; trans. E.F. Watling)

Again, the movement is away from the animals (symbolised by our use of them for food and labour) and towards the divine - humans have even conquered the immortal Earth, oldest of the gods. But again, the picture is not one of unalloyed good: the sea is stormy, agriculture involves endless work, and humans cannot conquer death; what we should remember above all is that our wisdom 'creeps now towards evil, now towards good' (366), and that the laws of the gods have imposed a limit on our aspirations.

> ... Great honour is given
> And power to him who upholdeth his country's laws
> And the justice of heaven.
>
> But he that, too rashly daring, walks in sin,
> In solitary pride to his life's end,
> At door of mine shall never enter in
> To call me friend.
> (368-375; Watling)

Here we see the human race very much on its own, shaping its own environment, controlling its own progress. That Sophocles had been touched by the new ideas of the fifth-century anthropologists seems evident. But they evoke from him a reaction: yes, the gods have given us the freedom to develop, but we must not use that freedom for evil purposes and against the will of the gods. This is the message of the concluding verses of the ode, and of the play as a whole. There is no Prometheus here, then; but otherwise Sophocles tells much the same story as the author of the Prometheus Bound - we are not going to be allowed to advance too far, we will always be trapped in a world where good and evil go together.

From Sophocles, such caution in the face of divine control is not surprising. It is rather more unexpected when it comes from the pen of Euripides, whose attitude towards the gods could be interpreted on occasions as being distinctly hostile. He of the three tragedians is in fact the one who expresses most clearly the idea of progress as the working-out of some divine plan for the world. In The Suppliants he makes Theseus recite a heavy speech in which he argues that the human race enjoys more blessings than misfortunes. Some praiseworthy god, he says, has raised human life up from a 'bestial state', and has bestowed on it intelligence, language, the ability to construct shelters, navigation and trade, and the power of divination. We should be grateful for these benefactions, and not show discontent; but in fact, we humans seek to outmatch the gods in our wisdom (195-218). Again we have a progression from the animal to the divine; and again a warning that we should not aim too high and offend the gods: we must be content with a life in which there is more good than evil. But this time the credit for the progression is handed fairly and squarely to some divine power, and no room is allowed for human ingenuity. It is a view of progress which some of Euripides' contemporaries would certainly have contested; but we need not believe that Theseus' views echo Euripides' own: the former comes over as a somewhat stuffy representative of the more conservative side in a current debate.

None of the tragedians' accounts of human progress fully answer Bury's demand for the absence of an external will. In this, the poets show themselves to be less radical than some other fifth century thinkers. But what is most remarkable about them is that all three present an exact inversion of the Golden Age picture of a move from gods to animals; and all three show the human status as being midway between these two outer poles of existence. Like Hesiod, they tell us to make the best of a mixed-up world: we are warned off aiming at divinity as roundly as Hesiod's iron race is exhorted to keep on the right side of future bestiality. So the tragedians' progressivism leaves us in the same position as Golden Age primitivism, a view of things which will be repeated in some of the later accounts of humanity's rise.

PRESOCRATICS, SCIENTISTS AND SOPHISTS

While tragedians were reflecting in this way the development of a new perspective on cultural history, philosophers and scientists were in the thick of the controversy. In the previous century, the Presocratics had been producing theories of biological origins which suggested a rise from an animal-like condition; they may have examined also the implications which this had for cultural evolution, but if so we lack most of what they wrote on the subject. The one sure indication which we possess of a new attitude in this area is vouchsafed to us by Xenophanes, who said that 'the gods have not revealed all things to mortals from the beginning, but they in the course of time by seeking discover something better' (DK B18). The gods do indeed, as Hesiod says, 'hide men's livelihood'; but they have done this since the beginning of creation, so there has never been a Golden Age; and it is human beings themselves who, through their researches, are responsible for the upward movement away from ignorance.

By the latter half of the fifth century, some of the citizens of Athens, at least, had begun to take seriously the human race's potential for self-improvement, and there arose a great demand for the kind of all-purpose teaching which the Sophists could provide. We know that lectures and treatises on prehistory became popular, and we cannot doubt that these anthropological studies taught the lesson mirrored in Sophocles' choral ode - that human beings have always had the freedom and the capacity to make enormous advances. That a new spirit of humanism and progressivism was beginning to make itself felt seems very clear; and it is also evident who some of the leading figures in this intellectual movement were - the Presocratic scientists Anaxagoras, Archelaus and Democritus, and the Sophist Protagoras. Unfortunately - and this is one of the saddest losses from Greek literature - we possess only a few fragments of their work, plus two debatable longer testimonies to the thought of Democritus and of Protagoras.

Anaxagoras' assertions that the human being is the most intelligent of the animals because he possesses hands (Aristotle De part. an. 687 A7), and that 'we make use of our own experience, memory, wisdom and technology' (DK B21b) suggest a study of the way in which the human race's peculiar physical and mental attributes, coupled with time and experience, have gradually raised it above the level of the animals. Our knowledge can be supplemented a little from the thought of his pupil Archelaus, who described how humans, whose biological origins were much the same as those of other animals, became gradually differentiated from them by the development of 'political leaders and laws and technology and cities, and so on' (Hippolytus Ref. 1. 9. 6.): technological, political, social (and by implication, moral) change were part-and-parcel of the historical process that gradually separated us from animals, and were not god-given or god-directed.

The possibility of our reconstructing Democritus' anthropological thought with anything approaching thoroughness rests on our acceptance of the thesis that it has been preserved for us in Diodorus' preface to his Universal history, (6) where an account of cultural history is added to that of biological origins. Many of the concepts employed in this account, and its overall progressivism, certainly seem to hark back to fifth century thought; and Diodorus himself acknowledges a debt to 'the best authorities on scientific and historical questions' (1. 6. 3.). But the relationship with Democritus is open to doubt, and it seems best for us to look at Diodorus in his chronological place, while bearing in mind that his cultural history probably carries numerous echoes of the late fifth century. For Democritus, we will have to fall back once more on fragments. These testify to an interest in the development of weaving, house-building, music (DK B154 and B144), stock-breeding (DK A151), and divination (DK A138); and to a belief that human nature can be shaped by education (DK B33), and that the education of the human race as a whole is based on observation (DK B154), chance (DK A151), need (DK B144), and economic surplus (DK B144). This all points to a detailed analysis of the <u>causes</u> of cultural transformation, and its fragmentation is a great loss. What we can be fairly sure of is that human progress as far as Democritus was concerned was not a god-directed exercise, but one maintained through the experience and suffering of humans themselves.

In the Platonic dialogue that bears his name, Protagoras appears as an opponent of both contemporary and chronological primitivism. With some irony, he utterly rejects the notion of noble savagery:

> he who appears to you to be the worst, out of those brought up under laws and in the society of other men, would appear to be a just man - indeed, a master of justice - if one were to judge him in comparison with men who have no education, nor courts, nor laws, nor anything compelling them to practise virtue - in comparison for example with savages like those the poet Pherecrates exhibited at last year's Lenaea. (327C)

His own interpretation of the origins of justice is given in the parable already outlined (see chapter 4). This tells how Prometheus, by stealing fire and technical skill from the gods and giving them to humans, bestowed on them the means of life. After that, people set to work creating the apparatus with which to worship the gods, on account of their 'divine kinship'. They also developed speech and language, and invented houses, clothes, shoes, bedding and agriculture. Then, in order to defend themselves against wild beasts, they came together in fortified cities; but they soon began injuring each other because of their lack of political skill, and scattered again. Then Zeus, in order to prevent their

177

extinction, gave them the qualities of respect for each other and justice, as the basis for urban life, friendship and society. Of these qualities, all people were given a share (321C - 322D).

Again, we have the problem of deciding how much of this is Protagoras and how much is Plato. There are some striking progressive features to the account: the difficulty which Prometheus has to face in stealing fire could be interpreted as emphasising the fact that technological progress represents a struggle against divine order (as in Prometheus Bound); the importance, in technological, social and moral development, of the instinct for self-preservation is clearly recognised; a link is made between language and technology; and morality is depicted as growing out of social intercourse rather than preceding it - morality is a product of history like any other human invention. All in all (particularly if we remove Prometheus and Zeus from the scene, as I think we may), I believe that Plato may in this section have done a fair amount of justice to Protagoras' beliefs. The major reservation lies with the attribution of 'divine kinship' to the human race (which is at odds with the preceding picture of divine opposition to human survival), and with the statement that religion was the very first human invention, instead of one of the last (as in Prometheus Bound and Euripides). Some contamination by Plato may be suspected here, but I think that he has left us with enough genuine material for us to form a reasonable notion of Protagoras' anthropology. (7)

Some of the most unequivocal examples of classical Greek progressivism exist for us in the medical literature which circulated in the fifth and fourth centuries BC. Scientific research and practice are naturally the themes most commonly to be encountered there, but cultural history is not entirely absent. In the treatise On ancient medicine generally attributed to the fifth century, the author rejects primitivist doctrines, and sees the gradual discovery of a decent diet as one of the developments which has helped to rescue the human race from primitive squalor and suffering:

> I am of the opinion that the kind of diet and nourishment used at present by healthy people would not even have been discovered if the human race had been satisfied with the same food and drink as the ox, the horse, and every other animal apart from the human - such as the things

> that grow from the earth, fruits, wood and
> grass. On these, animals are nourished, grow,
> and live without suffering, having no need of
> any other kind of diet. I am of the opinion that
> in the beginning the human race used this kind
> of nourishment. Our present diet has, I believe,
> been discovered and elaborated over a long
> period of time. For many and terrible were the
> sufferings caused by a crude and animal-type
> diet, when humans consumed raw food, unmixed and
> of great strength - the same sufferings as they
> would experience today, falling into pains and
> diseases and speedy death. In those days, they
> probably suffered less because they were used to
> it, but still they suffered severely. The
> majority - the ones with a weaker constitution -
> probably perished, while those who were
> stronger lasted longer ... For this reason it
> appears to me that people looked for a
> nourishment which harmonised more with their
> constitution, and discovered what we use now.

He goes on to describe how they would have learnt to treat wheat and barley in order to produce bread and cake, and how they would have experimented with mixing, boiling and baking.

> To this discovery and research what name could
> be more justly or appropriately applied than
> divine medicine, since it was discovered with a
> view to the health, survival and nourishment of
> the human race ...? (I.576-578).

This is, for a number of reasons, a remarkable account. It traces the rise of the human race from a condition which was shared with animals, to a state which in its implementation deserves the epithet 'divine': so, as with the tragedians, the perspective is from animal to god; and though none of the tragic warnings about not going too far are applied here, it is interesting to note that the right diet is seen as one achieved by 'mixing strong and untempered ingredients with weaker ones, adapting all to the nature and capacity of the human being' - which calls to mind the mixture of good and evil with which it is the human lot to live. As in Plato's Protagoran account, it is the physical incapacity of the human race - here, their inability to cope with food that other animals find quite acceptable - which acts as a spur to progress: physical weakness is one of the chief things that distinguishes humans from animals, and to this weakness can be attributed the suffering (cf. the tragedians), the need (cf. Democritus) and the struggle for survival (cf. Protagoras) which presses the human race upwards and onwards. And the account is notable for its overriding humanism - not least in the way it extrapolates <u>divine</u> medicine from <u>human</u> health and safety; the go<u>ds</u> have no role to <u>play</u> at all in human dietary researches - it is by their own unaided efforts that humans approach the level of the gods. All in all, this is one of the most complete documentations of fifth century progressivism which we possess. It is also the first account of cultural history available to us which elaborates on the crucial contrast between a raw and a cooked diet - cooking (which necessarily involves fire) is the technique which has given the human race its distinctive status. In this it provides a direct contradiction of the Golden Age situation, where cultivated food is provided by the gods: so for the first human beings 'cooked' vegetarianism, which places them on a level with the gods, is replaced here by 'raw' vegetarianism, which is very much the diet of animals.

It is noteworthy, but perhaps not surprising, that the same writer shows not only admiration for past discoveries, but a confident expectation of future advances:

> many beneficial medical discoveries have been made in the course of time, and the rest will be brought to light if an able man who is familiar with past discoveries takes them as the basis for his researches. (I.573)

I cannot leave the fifth century without making a brief mention of the interaction between progressivism and the contemporary historical researches of Herodotus and Thucydides. Both of them are well aware of improvements made in the past, and Thucydides in particular discerns a strong humanistic element in the process of historical change. The works of both writers include strands which might be termed progressive, but neither is by any means committed to the idea of an overall movement in a desirable direction, and a detailed examination of their convictions is outside the scope of this work.

Theories of Progress

PLATO AND ARISTOTLE

Plato in his analyses of social development could not sweep aside the conclusions of the fifth century anthropologists. He recognised that there had been cultural progress in the past; but he did not believe that these improvements could render our world anything other than a poor second-best in relation to an imaginary god-controlled world (see chapter 6, on the Politicus myth). Nor did he believe that cultural advance should be carried too far. In his pseudo-historical dissection of an existing state in the Republic, he maintains that the state

> springs, as we have seen, from our needs ... and our first and greatest need is for food to be provided which will keep us alive ... Our second need is for shelter, and our third for clothing of various kinds.

The meeting of these basic needs will produce the technologies of agriculture, stock-breeding, building, weaving, shoe-making, metallurgy (for the manufacture of tools and equipment), trading and seafaring (for the acquisition of the necessary imports - presumably metals), and retailing (in order to ensure the maximum specialisation among craftsmen). A state thus provided would be the 'true norm', and the acquisition of cumulative luxuries - furniture, perfumes, sculpture, painting, music, poetry, drama, jewellery, confectionery, cows and pigs (not previously needed in a vegetarian state), and medicine (ditto) - would produce greed and imperialist aggression, thus necessitating, as a crowning touch, an army (369B - 374E).

Thus basic physical and economic need is seen as the spur to a healthy progress; and the suggestion is even made (but not elaborated on) that morality is a product of the relationships established to satisfy those needs (372A). This much would satisfy the most radical of progressivists. But as far as Plato is concerned, every state reaches an optimum point of development beyond which it is dangerous to proceed. So for Plato there can be no open-ended improvement. Two limits are imposed on it - a metaphysical limit derived from the theory of Forms, which interprets even the very best that can be achieved in the physical world as a feeble imitation of an eternal and unchanging absolute; and an idealistic 'physical world' limit which sees the best in our world as occurring at an early stage in technological and social development, at the point where basic needs have been satisfied. This cultural primitivism is of the 'hard' rather than the 'soft' variety, and will be looked at again in the next chapter. If Plato had ever unveiled a plan for the achievement of this primitivistic ideal (which as far as we know he did not), then such a scheme would certainly have involved progress in his terms, but it would have been progress towards a predetermined and finite end.

Similar objections could be made to Aristotle as a progressivist, though the end which he envisages, the culminating point of the process of improvement, is not a historically retarded one, as it is with Plato. But the teleology which discerns in all natural phenomena an inherent principle of orderly development is obviously going to confine all change within predetermined channels, and limit it to the realisation of pre-existent ends. In addition, a restriction in time is imposed on all future progress by Aristotle's theory of recurrent disasters. This said, Aristotle did at least postulate, within these limits, a process of improvement in the broad fields of cultural and social evolution; and to that extent he could be called a progressivist - indeed, his thinking is quite close to that of later thinkers, like Descartes and Leibniz, who saw change for the better as a necessary law of nature, which will operate continually providing nothing occurs to hinder it. Beneficial changes, Aristotle said, have been achieved in sciences like medicine and physical training, and in general in 'all the techniques and faculties': for 'generally all people seek what is good, and not what is handed down to them by their ancestors' (Politics 1268 B36 and 1269 A3-4). Elsewhere, he writes of the advances made in philosophy and the arts prior to each cyclical destruction (Metaphys. 1074 B10-12). Constitutional improvements, like technological ones, have been discovered 'infinitely often': this is why we must study the past, so that we may 'make full use of what has already been discovered, while endeavouring to investigate things that have been hitherto passed over' (Politics 1329 B33-35). Here we learn that Aristotle was even prepared to envisage improvements in the future which had not been accomplished in some previous cultural cycle; though his teleological principles would have made it inevitable that novelty would be confined to detail, and that the broad patterns of social and cultural change would be endlessly repeated.

The subject of social development is the one on

which Aristotle provides us with most detail. In the Politics, he proposes to analyse the polis or city-state by reducing it to its component parts, and he suggests that the best method of doing this is by studying its development 'from the beginning'. His analysis is thus both a genetic and a historical one - his view of change as an orderly unfolding of inherent potential makes it almost certain that he would have seen what he describes as a genuine historical process, and not just a convenient way of dissecting the state, as is possible with Plato. The first 'necessary' forms of human association, he says, are the mating of male and female, and the coming-together of master and slave (that is, of the natural ruler and the natural subject): from these two associations we get the formation of the household, which is an institution designed for the satisfaction of basic needs. Next several households, brought together by kinship, unite to form a village. Finally, a number of villages come together in the form of a polis.

> For the polis is the end of the other associations, and nature comprises an end, for what each thing is when its genetic development has been completed we speak of as being the nature of each thing ... Again, the purpose and end of a thing is its best condition. Self-sufficiency is an end and a best condition. From these things it is clear that the polis exists by nature, and that man is by nature a political animal ...
> (Politics 1252 A20-1253 A3).

At the stage of the self-sufficient polis, humans become capable of enjoying, not just life, but 'the good life' (1252 B30).
The polis, then, is regarded as a natural phenomenon, which in its development passes, like a living organism, through a finite and predetermined number of stages. The limit of this development is reached when the institutions created by human association are self-sufficient, and the polis represents this limit or end - it is the best condition of human society. So in Aristotle's terms, there can be no natural political development beyond the point of the polis - and certainly no unlimited or unforeseeable progress. Since he cannot have been blind to the fact (though he never mentions it) that the polis in his own day was on the verge of being submerged within much larger political institutions,

183

what Aristotle is virtually saying is 'what we have now is best, it represents the ultimate fulfilment of the human capacity for association'. Any further development (such as the absorption of the <u>polis</u> into the Hellenistic kingdoms) would have been regarded by him as a chance interference with a natural process. So, like the Attic tragedians, he offers a view of progress (albeit in more scientific terms) which advises acceptance of the here-and-now, and implicitly warns against unlimited change. For the tragedians, the limit is imposed by divine law; for Aristotle, it is part-and-parcel of a natural law. Like the tragedians too, he recognises that human beings exist on a scale between the animal and the divine. Not only do humans share many of the psychological traits of animals (see above, p.74-75), but they also have the gregarious instincts of bees and herd-animals, and they have in common with all of them the faculty of vocalisation (<u>Politics</u> 1253 A7-14). On the other hand, only humans 'and whatever beings may be superior to them' possess the power of thought (<u>De anima</u> 414 A29 - B19), and 'thought alone ... is divine'. (<u>Gen.an.</u> 736 B27-28). Thought it is which makes humans political, and not merely gregarious; thought it is which allows them to develop the capacity for vocalisation into the power of speech.

> Speech is designed to indicate the expedient and the harmful, and therefore also the right and the wrong; for this is the peculiar characteristic of humans as distinct from animals, that they alone have a perception of good and bad, of right and wrong, and it is the sharing of these things that makes a household and a <u>polis</u>
>
> (<u>Politics</u> 1253 A14-18).

It is thought, and the power of speech to which thought is linked, and the formation of the <u>polis</u> to which this ultimately leads, which positions the human being between the animal and the god: 'the man who is by nature, and not merely by chance, without a <u>polis</u> is either of lowly status, or greater than a man' (<u>Politics</u> 1253 A3-4); 'the man who is incapable of entering into associations, or who has no need to do so because of his self-sufficiency, is no part of a <u>polis</u>, so that he is either a beast or a god' (<u>Politics</u> 1253 A27-29). Being in that intermediate position, he has the potential for both good and evil: 'as man is the best of animals when perfected,

Theories of Progress

so he is the worst of all when severed from law and justice' (Politics 1253 A31-33). The government of law is like the government of God and reason, whereas government by a human being alone can be compared with government by a wild animal (Politics 1287 A28-30).

Aristotle is in agreement, then, with Golden Age theorists and with the 'progressivist' tragedians alike in seeing the human race as existing halfway between the animal and the divine, and thereby as living in a world where good and evil are mixed. In his conviction that, in historical terms, humans have acquired their status by a rise and not by a fall, he is in accord again with the tragedians. Where he differs from them, and most definitely from the fifth century anthropologists (who also believed that humans started out as animals) is in his belief that human beings have always been inherently superior. It was not by virtue of physical need, or the instinct for self-preservation, or physiological qualities, or chance, that humans assumed their intermediate status - it was through thought and the moral sensibility to which thought gives rise. Humans were never really like animals and Aristotle nowhere suggests that they were. They have always been distinguished from them by their rationality: this develops gradually, it is true, but it is always there in embryo, and it develops not through force of circumstances, but rather because it is part of human nature for it to do so. Like Aristotle's physical world, the human status is for him fundamentally eternal and changeless, and there can be no true progress where that is concerned. Even the social progress which serves to bring out the latent human capacity for enjoying 'the good life' cannot be maintained: all forms of government, even the best, are liable to 'perversions' because of the weakness of human nature, and 'perverted' forms of government are necessarily subsequent to correct ones (Politics 1275 B1-3). And so the cycle of inevitable growth and decline adds another serious qualification to our assessment of Aristotle as a progressivist.

PARODY

As in the fifth century, so too in the late fourth or third, the satire of the comic dramatists can be taken as an indication of popular feeling on the subject of cultural history. The Golden Age parodies of Old Comedy suggest a contemporary reaction against soft primitivism; later on New Comedy seems to be dealing a few blows at the fashion for progressivist reviews of cultural transition, perhaps indicating that in the Hellenistic era progressivism was a well-known phenomenon that was beginning to be questioned. By Athenio at any rate, we are treated to a long satirical disquisition on the art of cooking, reminding us that this item in cultural evolution was seen by a medical writer, and presumably by others too, as a significant step on the route from a primitive to a civilised way of life. Cooking, we are told, has alone been responsible for the human race's rise from unruly cannibalism to their present condition of urban association:

> when cannibalism and many evils existed, there appeared a certain man - no fool - who first roasted sacrificial meat as an offering. And since this flesh was sweeter than the flesh of men, they didn't chew each other up, but sacrificed and roasted cattle ... After this, in the course of time someone invented the stuffed sausage; he boiled a kid; he cut up meat for a stew ...; he secretly introduced a disguised fish, greens, costly smoked delicacies, salt, honey. And as each of them, on account of the pleasure I'm speaking of now, abstained from eating even dead people, they all desired to live with each other, a community was formed, and inhabited cities grew up; on account of the very art of cooking which I have described ... We cooks take the lead in the sacrifices ... because the gods listen to us most of all, on account of the discovery of the things which more than anything else promote good living
> (in Athenaeus, Deipnos 14.660-1).

The eating of raw vegetation is seen by some authors (like the anonymous medical writer) as one of the factors that links primitive humans with animals; but for others the same link is established by the eating of the uncooked flesh of one's fellow creatures i.e. cannibalism. The ability to cook and eat the flesh of other creatures - meat-eating - is interpreted as an important step in the assumption of a fully human status, marking as it does a distinction between us and animals. Athenio's satire, while it has highlighted the ridiculous aspects of this analysis of culture, is by no means an extravagant fantasy, for it clearly found its mark among current anthropological speculations.

THE HELLENISTIC AND ROMAN WORLDS

In the Greek world, the philosophies that flourished in the third century BC – Stoicism and Epicureanism – ceased to offer their followers communal dreams or aspirations, but concentrated rather on more personal routes to salvation. Progress was for the individual, and the early thinkers in both schools seem to have given little attention to the general trends of civilisation. The idea of progress was maintained during this period by thinkers like Archimedes, in the specialised field of scientific knowledge, and more generally by playwrights. The fragments of the tragic poet Moschion include a long piece on the evolution of civilisation. In this he tells us that humans originally lived like animals, without houses or cities, agriculture or technology. Cannibalism was rife, and force rather than law was the ruler. But in the course of time, agriculture, the eating of cultivated food, the drinking of wine, city life and houses were introduced, and a savage way of life was replaced by a civilised one. A law was introduced that the dead should be buried in tombs, so that people would not be reminded of their cannibalism (In Stobaeus, *Ecl*. 1.8.38-70).

This is a short but classic account, laying stress as it does on the rise from an animal condition, effected by the transition from the eating of raw food (here, the raw flesh of one's fellows rather than raw vegetation) to the production and eating of cultivated food. Moschion in a brief explanation of the causes of the rise combines a number of the explanations given by fifth century thinkers: either the rationality of Prometheus, or necessity, or the copying of nature coupled with long practice, may have been responsible for the change, any one of these factors operating with the passage of time, 'which brings forth and nourishes all things.'

In the course of the second century BC, the centre of the literary world began to shift to Rome, where a new self-confidence was developing. One of the first tentative expressions of progressivism to emerge from that city came from the pen of Polybius, who was in fact a Greek emigre. He describes how after one of the periodic catastrophes which wipe out the majority of humankind, the survivors gradually come together in a group, like other herding animals (who need the group on account of their constitutional weakness); and, as is also the way with bulls, boars and cocks, once they are in a group a leader emerges who surpasses the others in physical and psychological strength. This was the primitive way of life. But then in the course of time there developed among them fellowship and common customs, and the notions of right and wrong were born - they grew out of the intellectual capacity to recognise harmful behaviour and to anticipate that it might one day be directed against oneself, or conversely out of the recognition of the expediency of noble behaviour.

In some ways this is orthodox progressivism: again, primitive humans are compared with animals; and the evolution of society and morals is seen as the product of both natural necessity, and of the human faculty of reason - a firmly utilitarian concept of morality is propounded. But we cannot be sure that Polybius is expressing a favourable judgement on these early changes: he has made no criticism of the first 'natural' group (other than a comparison with animals); and certainly when he goes on to outline the successive forms of government within the group (discussed on p.123) it is clear that he envisages neither progressive improvement nor decline. Like other disciples of cosmic cycles, his attitude to cultural history appears to be a neutral one.

In the first century BC, philosophical interest in cultural history seems to have increased. The early Stoics appear not to have been too concerned by it, though Zeno, we are told, had admitted that human life would have been impossible without the arts and sciences, some of which he recognised to be of quite recent origin (Philo, De incorr. mundi 24). But for a Stoic, the material things of this world, along with health, pleasure and beauty, were 'indifferent', though some at least were 'to be preferred' rather than 'to be avoided' (Diogenes Laertius 7. 102-7). Later Stoics, however, seem to have taken advantage of this concession in order to uphold the value of cultural evolution. Such a one was Posidonius, whose exhaustive researches into history, geography, natural science and anthropology may well have led him to speculate on the origins of civilisation. A record of his theories in this direction is preserved in Seneca's ninetieth Moral Letter, though it is much disrupted by the frequent injection of the author's own comments. But what does emerge fairly clearly is that this is far from being a classic text of progressivism. Posidonius certainly was aware of the benefits of technology, and seems to have given a detailed account of the invention of a large number of techniques, including building, tool-making, mining, weaving, agriculture, milling and baking, ship-building, pottery-making, and the construction of arches (7-32). Like the fifth century progressivists, he recognised that chance, the physical environment, and the imitation of natural processes were significant factors in technological advance: the possibility of mining was realised when forest fires melted veins of ore (12); milling and baking were modelled on the human eating and digestive systems (22-23); and ships were constructed to resemble fishes (24-25). But much more importance was accorded by him to the quality of human rationality - and not just the common-or-garden rationality shared by all human beings, but the special wisdom of the philosopher: his contention (much disputed by Seneca) was that philosophers were the fathers of invention. And when we turn to his somewhat bizarre analysis of political development, we encounter a distinct note of primitivism. Posidonius believed that at some stage in human history (obviously an early one, though Seneca's account does not make it clear exactly when) people had been ruled by philosophers, who maintained a just, benevolent and peaceful dictatorship. But later on kingship was transformed into tyranny, and to combat this, laws were devised, again by philosophers (5-6). For Posidonius, the rule of law cannot possibly have compensated fully for the loss of government by the wise, and we are forced to the conclusion that he would have placed the happiest epoch for the human race at an early (though not the earliest) stage of their existence. Seneca indeed compares it to 'the age which people call Golden'. This attitude to cultural evolution perhaps resembles Plato's, in that social and technological advance are seen as a necessary but second-rate compensation for an ideal situation; perhaps for Posidonius too the ideal is purely imaginary and unattainable - it certainly sounds unrealistic enough to us. But whether real or not, it puts progress in the shade, by setting up a divine and utterly rational standard by which all our achievements are to be measured. This, to be sure, is what one would expect from a Stoic.

Epicureanism, like Stoicism, promised personal happiness to its disciples. In its early days it too may have shown relatively little concern for the historical trends from which it sought to provide an escape; though one of the letters of Epicurus which has been preserved does indicate that he had given some attention to the history of language, at least, and his general statement that

> nature has been taught to do many things of all kinds by force of circumstances, and reasoning later on developed the things passed on by nature, and made further inventions ...
> (Letter to Herodotus 75)

speaks of an interest in the causes of cultural change. Hermarchus, Epicurus' successor as head of the school, wrote a brief account of the origins of the law against homicide (preserved by Porphyry in De abstinentia 1. 7-11), in which he gave a utilitarian explanation of the evolution of society and law. But it is in the work of an Epicurean of the first century BC, Lucretius, that we find the most detailed of all the ancient accounts of cultural history. In Book 5 of the De rerum natura, having described how animals emerged from the earth and how natural selection ensured the survival of the best-equipped species, he goes on to give a picture of the primitive human condition, and to analyse its subsequent social and technological transformations. Primitive people, he says, were hardier than now, and lived a wandering life like wild animals. There was no agriculture or cultivated food: they ate the acorns and berries which the earth provided spontaneously, and drank from streams, just as animals do. They had no fire or primitive clothes, but took shelter in caves and woods. Communities, customs and laws were absent: each person lived for himself alone, and sex was a promiscuous haphazard affair. They hunted animals with stones and clubs, and slept on the ground 'like bristly boars'. The departure of the sun at night did not disturb them, but attacks from wild beasts did, and many lost their lives in terrible pain. But deaths through warfare, shipwreck, over-indulgence or murder were unknown (925-1012).

Then the acquisition of huts, skin-garments, fire and family life began to produce a softening of the human race. At this point neighbours began to form compacts 'neither to harm nor to be harmed', and in the course of this language came into existence. Fire, which had been introduced to them through natural occurrences, enabled them to cook their food. Kings (men of superior intelligence) began to build cities, and divide up the land. But they were overthrown, and disorder threatened, so magistrates and laws were devised, and with them came the fear of punishment. Religious belief and worship came into

Theories of Progress

existence (1011 - 1240).

Mining and metallurgy were taught to them by a natural event - a forest fire - and so weapons and tools were manufactured. At first, gold and silver were used, but later bronze and iron. The technology of warfare was developed. Weaving was invented, based on looms made from iron. Agriculture, initially copied from nature, progressed by leaps and bounds. Music too was something which people learnt from the natural environment. Calendars and the planning of the year were introduced. Shipping, treaties, writing, poetry and the visual arts all came into existence, all taught by experience and the power of reasoning (1241 - 1457).

In many ways this seems to be a traditional account; leaving aside for the moment the question of whether Lucretius' value judgement on cultural history is a truly 'progressivist' one, we can see that it does incorporate many of the motifs of mainstream progressivism. It is interesting to note that many features of Lucretius' primitive age do in fact match but at the same time oppose many of the classic Golden Age/pre-Prometheus features. Eternal youth is replaced here by superior physique; whereas in the Golden Age humans are close to the gods, here they are compared in three instances with animals; in both ages, there is no agriculture, and human beings are vegetarians (the hunting of animals in Lucretius' account seems to have been purely for purposes of self-defence), but in the Golden Age people eat cultivated vegetation, whereas in the primitive age their food is raw; in the Golden Age people use fire, but only at the dispensation of the gods, here they do not have it at all; there is no family life in either age, but whereas in the Golden one this is because there are no women, or because sexual reproduction is unnecessary, here we have promiscuous sexual relations; and the absence of law, which is compensated for in the Golden Age by the benevolent despotism of the gods, in the primitive age produces unconstrained individualism. These inversions are vital - they make all the difference between a primitivist and a progressivist explanation of cultural history, since in either account the steps between the earliest age and our own are necessarily the same. If in that earliest age we lived like gods, then these steps serve to accomplish and to emphasise our fall from grace (though they may at the same time compensate for it); if on the other hand we lived like animals, then the steps represent an elevation in status. In either case, we end up as human beings, and this is not an unmixed blessing.

The steps in the acquisition of a fully human status outlined by Lucretius are the same as those described both by Golden Age theorists and by progressivists. Absolutely crucial here (as in Hesiod, to mention the obvious alternative theory) are the use of fire, which is vital in the development of all the subsequent technologies - cooking, mining and metallurgy, warfare, weaving, and agriculture; and the onset of family life, which gives rise to society, language, government and laws. So Prometheus (fire) and Pandora (family life) are the mediators here to, though we should not forget that for Lucretius there can be no question of any divine intervention: human need, along with human reasoning, the experience gained with time, and the assistance of chance events, account for all cultural changes. But here too both fire and family life produce a softening of the human race, just as with Hesiod's silver race domestic life and fire (if we marry the myth of the races with the Prometheus/Pandora myth) give rise to a prolonged period of immaturity. A lengthy childhood or softness is something that distinguishes humans from animals; and Lucretius is well aware that softness (i.e. humanity) can be an ambiguous thing. It is synonymous with physical weakening and it also has psychological drawbacks - the burden of supporting a family and the loss of a proud independence; but at the same time, love for one's children and the willingness to form friendships are two of the benefits of softness (1017-19). Finally, we noticed how in other progressivist accounts, the ability to communicate with the gods came very low down in the list of inventions; here too it is one of the later developments. (8) So the move is away from animals and towards the gods. But the Attic tragedians in their accounts of the same move warned us that we would never be able to reach the level of the gods, and should not attempt to do so: we are forever in-between. And so here too Lucretius lets it be known that our beliefs about the gods and our manner of worshipping them are far from satisfactory (1194-1240). For an Epicurean (we know from other texts), (9) belief in the gods' existence is a true belief, but belief in their control of the world is false. Contemplation of the happy images of the gods will assist us in emulating their perfectly peaceful, perfectly painless lives; but the kind of worship which seeks to influence and propitiate them is misguided and only augments our anxiety. It is the latter form of religion which Lucretius describes in his cultural history, and so we see that in trying to reach the gods we go wrong, and are left very much shackled to the human world, and its mixture of good and evil.

Lucretius' 'progressivist' account may be the longest which ancient literature affords us, but it is also the most ambiguous. His expression pedetemptim progredientis ('moving forward step by step', line 1453) has been seized upon by modern commentators as a motto for the ancient doctrine of evolutionary progress; but there are very many qualifications to the notion of uninterrupted advance, both in the account itself, and in the Epicurean philosophy as a whole. The primitive era is described in terms which, though the extent of physical suffering is not disguised, perhaps tend to dwell a little on the advantages of that life-style. And technological advance brings with it the violent greed and ambition familiar to us from the modern age (999-1010, 1113-1135), the effects of which Lucretius describes in all the graphic and gory detail which he can supply so well. The frenetic and insane elaborations of large-scale warfare are also brought home to us in stupendous verse (1308-1349). Law is necessary, but introduces us to a horrific fear of punishment (1151-1160), and the fear of the gods is a perfectly frightful and ruinous evil (1194-1240). Moreover, the Epicurean cosmology to which Lucretius subscribes by no means allows for a belief in indefinite future advance. Atomism imposes very definite limits on every process of change, since every atomic compound, great or small, must come to a peak of development when it reaches the limit of its capacity for absorbing new atoms, after which it goes into steady decline (2.1105-1174). This is as true of the world as a whole as it is of every object in it; it may also be true of cultural phenomena (it is hard, though not impossible, to imagine what the atomic basis for this might be), since the last two lines of Book 5 announce to us that 'people saw one thing after another grow clear in their minds/until in their arts they reached the utmost limit' - cacumen, the word used here, being also Lucretius' expression for an atomic limit. Elsewhere, Lucretius impresses on us the fact that many human skills are relatively new - he mentions epic poetry, improvements in ship-building, music, and philosophy (5. 324-337) as providing evidence that the world is young and fresh; he even seems to

193

allow for future developments - some arts, he says, are still growing (333). But in other passages he seems to see the end of the world as frighteningly close: the earth is in its old age and has lost most of its creative power (2. 1150-1152, 5.826-827), and perhaps 'in a little while you will see earthquakes arising and the whole world shaken to its very foundations' (5. 105-106).

Lucretius' world, then, is in some ways new and in some ways old; some of the things that have been invented are good and some are awfully bad. Prometheus and Pandora have done their trick again, and left us with a deal of mixed blessings. This outcome has been detected in other progressivist accounts which we have studied; we do not know enough about the crucial fifth century texts to know whether they too would have left us with this conclusion, but it would not have been too surprising if they had.

I should not leave Lucretius without mentioning a possible hint of primitivism in his account. In attributing the origins of music to the shepherds who invented pipes, he describes a pleasant scene where in springtime the rustics, after a simple meal by a stream, used to amuse themselves with talking and joking, with music and clumsy dancing (5. 1390-1404). We cannot be sure of the chronology, but it seems likely that this event should be assigned to the period when the earliest communities, based on the social contract, had been established. It was a time, clearly, when the simple pleasures advocated by Epicureanism were readily available. Do we detect here a note of idealising nostalgia? One might well be tempted to say so, except that the same scene, with a few alterations, is described in Book 2 of the poem; only here the present and not the past tense is used (lines 29-33). The 'Epicurean picnic' serves to remind us that for those who direct their lives by true reasoning, the simple pleasurable life of bygone days is always attainable. And herein lies another objection to Lucretius as a progressivist: in the last analysis, cultural trends can be of no significance to an Epicurean, since it is open to every individual to embrace the escape from history represented by the 'divine discoveries' of Epicurus. The route from the animal to the divine becomes a personal one.

Diodorus Siculus, in the introduction to his universal history, follows up his account of creation with a brief summary of prehistoric cultural advance (1.8). This description, written at about the same time as Lucretius' longer version, has much in common with it, but there are enough differences to suggest that the immediate sources at least were separate. (10) The primitives, Diodorus says, led bestial lives, and existed entirely as individuals. They ate raw vegetation - herbs and fruit - and were in a miserable condition, having no clothing, houses, fire, or knowledge of food-storage: consequently, many died from cold or starvation. But eventually, expediency made them come together, since they were driven to help each other fend off attacks from wild beasts. Then social life and language developed. Houses, food-storage and fire in particular were discovered, and gradually the technologies generally and the ramifications of social life were introduced. It was necessity that was responsible for these changes - but necessity acting on a creature which was naturally well-endowed, with hands, speech and an intelligent mind.

Again, humans start off as animals, and again they are 'raw' vegetarians. Social life (which presumably embraces family life) and fire are the two key steps in the rise towards civilisation. The gods are nowhere to be seen, and necessity, coupled with the human race's distinctive physical and psychological qualities, accounts for all changes. Diodorus' summary thus embraces some of the familiar motifs of progressivism; it also, as is the way with progressivism, shares some of the items of change specified by Golden-Ageism. But there is no intimation in this account that civilisation is a mixed blessing; Diodorus is indeed quite unequivocal about the miseries of primitive life, much more so than Lucretius. There is also no suggestion that the human race, having started out as animals, has tried to reach the gods.

A mythological version of the early history of Egypt which follows this account supplies, however, some of the missing detail. According to the Egyptians, Diodorus says, some of their gods were mortals who as a reward for their wisdom and their services to humankind were promoted to immortality. The god whose name can be translated as Hephaistos was the discoverer of fire and Egypt's first king. Osiris, the third king, was the first to make the human race give up cannibalism, when his sister-wife Isis introduced cultivated cereal crops. Isis also established laws which through fear of punishment had the effect of suppressing violence and crime. Copper and gold mines were discovered, and thus implements for killing wild beasts and tilling the soil were invented. Images of the gods and golden shrines were manufactured. Osiris discovered the vine, and taught humankind to make and store wine. And under his rule, Hermes introduced language, writing, sacrificial practices, astronomy, music, wrestling, and the olive-tree (I. 13-16). Here, some of the technologies familiar to us from other progressivist accounts are mentioned, and some new ones are added. In this survey, one animal eating-habit (cannibalism) replaces another one ('raw' vegetarianism) mentioned in the earlier account. Thus the move is still away from an animal-like condition; and here the opposite pole of existence is established: certain exceptional humans become divine, and late on in the list of inventions religious worship and sacrificial practices are mentioned. The human race rises, then, from the animals towards the gods, but only a few make it all the way - the rest stay in-between. This, it must be said, is one of the few indications given by the account of the intermediate status of the human race: that our world is one of good and evil mixed is suggested only by the information about the need for laws and the fear which they engender. Diodorus is among the most optimistic of all our progressivists, and if his account really does hark back to fifth century sources, we perhaps have evidence here of the more self-confident quality of anthropological speculation in that crucial century.

It is the ambiguity of Lucretius, rather than the straightforwardness of Diodorus, which seems to set the tone for much later Roman thought on the subject of cultural history. In the first centuries BC and AD, it became commonplace to celebrate humankind's rise from squalor and savagery to a state of technological and social grace. Cicero, in one of a number of passages in which he gives thanks for civilisation, (11) tells us that oratory is one of the arts which has led people away from 'an animal-like and savage life-style, towards a human and urbane refinement' (De or. 1.8.33). Horace expresses his disgust with the primitive species which, 'a dumb and squalid herd, fought over acorns and dens with nails and fists': later, through language, they achieved urbanism and legal codes (Satires 1.3.99-114). And even the Golden Ageist Ovid can at times reflect that a pre-agricultural human race must have eaten acorns and grass (Amores 3.10.1-15). One should not underestimate the impact of a change in thought which made the brutal reality of primitive life common knowledge, and which allowed people to recognise with gratitude the benefits of civilisation; but Cicero, Horace and Ovid all wrote

Theories of Progress

too of the corruption and demoralisation of the modern age, and were clearly aware that progress had its drawbacks.
Technologists and scientists could perhaps afford to be less equivocal in their appreciation of human history. The two classic progressivist accounts which remain for us to consider are those of Vitruvius, the architect and engineer, who was active in the latter half of the first century BC, and Manilius, who was writing about astrology in the early years of the first century AD.
Vitruvius takes his history of architecture right back to the days of old, when people lived in the woods like animals and ate raw food. Then lightning caused a forest fire, and people gathered round the embers and laid wood on them to keep the warmth alive. In this group primitive communication began, and so gradually language developed and established the foundations of society. As people came together, they began to construct houses, some using leaves, some caves, some twigs and mud. In time better and better dwellings were built, and techniques were circulated, emulated and constantly improved (De architectura 2.1.1-3 and 6-7). The reasons which Vitruvius distinguishes for the civilising process are chance; the erect posture of human beings, 'so that ... they gazed on the magnificence of the universe and of the stars'; their possession of hands; their power of thought; their imitative and teachable nature; their competitiveness; and time and experience. Again, gods are far from the scene. Again, fire and social life are pictured as crucial, and as closely linked. There is no hint anywhere here of any evil consequences of civilisation: someone who concentrated his attention on the building industry probably found it easier than most to maintain a positive frame of mind. Manilius is similarly sanguine. In his poem Astronomica, he tells us that primitive humans had no power of reasoning, but responded only to their sensations. They were terrified by the disappearance of the sun at night, and had no way of measuring time. There was no agriculture, mining or sea-faring; there was no thirst for knowledge. But time, the human mentality, hard work, adversity and experiment all combined to produce improvements. Language grew up, laws were devised, and agriculture and trade were developed. People learned to practise divination, and even how to 'turn day into night and night into day'; they were not satisfied until 'reason had scaled the heavens and ... seen the causes of all

existence' (I.66-98). And so, according to Manilius, humans do indeed, by their own unaided efforts, seem to succeed in reaching the divine.

Technological progress had become almost a literary cliche by the end of the first century AD; but scarcely anyone after Manilius wrote about cultural history with such a lack of reservation as he had. Ever present, and growing stronger, was the sense of inevitable and inextricable evil which cultural sophistication brought. No-one could now deny that technology had conferred many benefits, but there were some who seemed prepared to renounce those benefits in the hope of recapturing innocence. 'Hard' primitivism, to be surveyed in the next chapter, became from now on a noticeable element in Roman thought.

THE COMPARATIVE METHOD

Golden Age theorists derived little of their material from contemporary races, though imaginary countries like the Islands of the Blessed offered some opportunities for flights of fancy. But for progressivists, the comparative method was, of course, far more productive. The Greeks and Romans knew full well that there were groups of people elsewhere in the world whose culture was very different from their own; and from at least the sixth century BC, it was the practice to use these foreign cultures as points of comparison with one's own civilisation. Sometimes the message is one of neutral relativism. (12) But often contemporary races provide progressivists with the contrast they need to throw into relief their own achievements. Thucydides combines the comparative and historical methods, when, in looking for evidence for the prehistory of Greece, he turns to the foreigners and backward Greeks of his own day. Piracy, armed robbery, the effeminate practice of wearing clothes for athletics - these are the features of early Greek life for which he finds support among contemporary peoples; 'and indeed a number of other examples could be quoted to prove that the way of life of the ancient Greeks once resembled that of foreigners today' (1.5-6). Ephorus, writing in the early fourth century BC, points out that some tribes of Scythians are cruel and cannibalistic: they provide one point of comparison: but other Scythian tribes, who do not eat animals at all, provide another, oppositional one - we, as animal-eaters, are between the two. (13) A

Theories of Progress

similar kind of duality had been set up by Homer in his account of an imaginary race of foreigners, the Cyclopes: one of them, Polyphemus, was bestial and ate human flesh, whereas the rest of his tribe were looked after by the gods, enjoyed cereal crops and vines produced without benefit of agriculture, and lived without government, laws and sea-faring; again, we, the humans who might journey to that land if ships were permitted, are in-between – not cannibals, but workers of the soil (Odyssey 9, esp. 106-135). But opposition of this kind within a foreign race, is unusual: generally the opposition is between them and us. Aristotle is consistently rude about contemporary foreigners – 'And among foolish people, those who are irrational by nature and live only by sensation are like animals, as indeed are some of the races of distant foreigners' (N.E. 1149 A9). Lucretius, on the other hand, not always a good progressivist, uses the same method to show that civilisation (unlike the Epicurean philosophy) is not really necessary: corn-cultivation and wine-making cannot be terribly vital, for we hear that other races manage to do without them (5.14-17). Vitruvius, as one might expect, is not so dismissive of the benefits of civilisation: primitive types of building, much inferior to modern ones, are still in use with some barbarous races (2.1.4).

The ancient idea of progress by no means meets the demands which Bury would make of it. Greek and Roman progressivists rarely do more than glance at the future – and when they do so, it is sometimes to offer a warning that we should not attempt to go too far, or to remind us that the inevitability of change implies also the inevitability of decay and destruction. For many writers, improvements in the past, though absolutely necessary if human life was to be rescued from misery, have nevertheless brought with them problems for the present: few thinkers succeed in evading this conclusion, though among those who do we can count Diodorus, Vitruvius and Manilius, and possibly the fifth century anthropologists about whose theories we have only an incomplete notion. Where the ancients are probably most successful in matching up to the modern definition is over the question of humanity's responsibility for its own advance: only Euripides, and possibly the author of the Prometheus Bound (if we exclude Plato from consideration) introduce the element of divine will into the process; though

199

Sophocles advises us to pay heed to the gods in considering how to make use of progress, and Posidonius' handing over of responsibility to philosopher-inventors suggests a strong injection of divine reason. Perhaps a more significant rift is to be discerned between a thinker like Aristotle, who sees progress as a natural law, requiring little active co-operation on the part of the human race; and those theorists who distinguish chance, the interaction with the environment, need, physical aptitude or deficiency, experience and expediency (in conjunction with human rationality) as elements in our rise from savagery. The idea that we are battling both against and along with the environment, both against and along with our own constitutions, produces, together with birth from the earth and an original animal status, a strong conviction that we are a self-made race and have something to be proud of. Aristotle makes us fall back on our genealogy, like complacent aristocrats; other thinkers - such as Anaxagoras, Democritus, Lucretius, Diodorus - tell us on the contrary that we have risen from the gutter.

But the ambiguity, in all save a few accounts, remains. It is an ambiguity which is present in the myth. Kronos may have administered a Golden Age, but he was also a cannibal who consumed his own children, and like Hesiod's iron race he foully mistreated his father; (14) and so in his own person he represents also an original animal-like state of existence. And Prometheus may have caused the human race's downfall, but he also enabled it to survive separation from the gods. Golden Age theorists adopt one aspect of the myth, progressivists another; the former choose the gods as our progenitors, the latter the earth - but there are gods in the earth, and there is earth in the gods, and neither primitivism nor progressivism succeeds very often in escaping ambiguity. Both of them more often than not tell us that we are not animals, but neither are we gods. This is something we should constantly bear in mind when considering Greek and Roman ideas about progress: perhaps after all, we should abandon modern criteria, and judge ancient progressivism solely by what it was opposed to. It often delivered the same message as primitivism - 'be reconciled to a life that is less than perfect' - and it described a route to our current location which was in many ways the same as the route described in Golden Age theories. But it did at least tell us that we started out from a situation which was a complete inversion of the

Golden Age: so its perspective was the more optimistic one, and it gave people some cause for rejoicing.

NOTES

1. See, for example, J. Baillie, The belief in progress (London, 1951), pp. 45-67.
2. See Eusebius, Praep. evang. 2.2. 52-62; and Sextus Empiricus, Adv. math. 9.51.
3. See, for example, Lactantius, Div. inst. 1.1.12.14, and Minucius Felix, Octavius 21.1.
4. See p.21 n.21 above, for a reference to the authorship of this play, generally attributed to Aeschylus. M.L. West, 'The Prometheus trilogy', J.H.S. 99 (1979), p.130-148, who agrees that the play is not by Aeschylus, suggests a date of about 440 BC for its composition, which would mean that it was in fact written at about the same time as Antigone, the next text to be discussed.
5. See, for example, The Prometheus Bound, ed. G. Thomson (Cambridge, 1932), p.18-38 of the introduction; F. Solmsen, Hesiod and Aeschyxus (Ithaca, N.Y., 1949), p.124-147; G. Grossmann Promethie und Orestie (Heidelberg, 1970), p.73-78; Dodds, Progress, p.26-44. As far as the trilogy is concerned, we know of the existence of plays called Prometheus Unbound and Prometheus the Firebearer, included in the ancient catalogue of Aeschylus' plays, but we have no direct evidence that the three plays formed a connected trilogy.
6. See above, p.68 and p.72 n.22.
7. For an opposing view, see Havelock, p.91-94. In trying to understand what Protagoras is really being made to say, a lot depends on how one interprets the figures of Prometheus and Zeus. Perhaps Plato deliberately used the mythological form in order to leave the implications of Protagoras' thought vague and open to different interpretations.
8. The order of inventions is somewhat disrupted in Lucretius' account by his subdivision of them into socio-political, religious, and technological categories. We can assume that at least some if not all of the technological developments he describes came before the advent of kings and laws. Religion comes after kings and laws in the text, but we cannot be sure that Lucretius believed that it did so in chronological terms. However, I feel reasonably convinced that, whereas belief in the gods' existence would have arisen before then, belief in their power

over the world and their ability to punish humans could not have been formed until the experience of rule by kings and the punishment ordained by laws had produced a concept of power and punishment – this in accordance with Epicureanism's empirical theory of knowledge. Hence belief in the gods (a true belief, according to Epicurean theology) would come before kings etc., but belief in their power (a false belief) would come after. Religious worship would thus be a late phenomenon, and would be a product of socio-political developments.

9. See Epicurus, Letter to Menoeceus 123-4; and Principal Sayings 1; and Lucretius D.R.N. 2. 646-51 and 1090-92, 3. 18-24, 5. 156-234, 6. 68-75 and 379-422.

10. For the theory that the ultimate source for both was Democritus, see above, p.68 and p.72 n.22.

11. See also Pro Sestio 42. 91-92; and De officiis 1.4. 11-14 and 2. 4.15.

12. See Xenophanes, DKB16, and Herodotus 3.38.

13. See Strabo, Geog. 7.302.

14. See Hesiod's Theogony. Saturn, Kronos' Roman counterpart, is also accused of cannibalism by Ennius (Euhem. frag. 9, quoted by Lactantius in Div. inst. 1. 13.2), and is chosen by Q. Curtius Rufus as the recipient of a human sacrifice (Hist. Alex. 4.3.23). Similarly, the planet Saturn was considered by some to have a malign influence (see Apuleius, Florida 10).

Chapter Eight

HARD PRIMITIVISM AND THE NOBLE SAVAGE

Though the Golden Age theories which were examined in Chapter 6 highlighted many of the unsatisfactory features of contemporary civilisation, the very unreality of the primitive age which they described showed up the impossibility of living in any other way. Their message was one of awareness, to be sure, but it was also one of acceptance. I have occasionally applied the term 'soft primitivism' to this brand of cultural history; but primitivism is perhaps not an entirely appropriate term in this context, since Golden Ageism was far from providing a practical ideal. There was no question of these theorists advocating a return to the life-style of an earlier age: that age, whether historical or imaginary, had a lesson to teach us, but it was a lesson to be applied to the here-and-now, and one important aspect of it was that we should not hope to enjoy a Golden Age type of existence.

A more realistic picture of the primitive age, and one which does have implications for contemporary morality, is presented by the class of cultural history which Lovejoy and Boas have christened 'hard primitivism'. The common theme of this type of analysis is the corrupting effect of modern technology and modern society. Life in the earliest years of the human race's existence, the hard primitivist readily admits, doubtless involved considerable material deprivation and physical suffering. No techniques, or at the most only very rudimentary ones, had been acquired. The diet was grim and severely limited, clothing was either non-existent or consisted of animal skins or roughly-woven pieces, and people lived in the open-air, or at the most in caves or huts. They often suffered tortures from the cold, particularly if fire had not been discovered. And they certainly had no knowledge

203

of metallurgy, which meant that they had no efficient weapons with which to ward off the attacks of wild animals. Nevertheless, in the opinion of hard primitivists, it was the very absence of sophisticated devices for alleviating discomfort which enabled people to lead better and happier lives than they do today. The multiplicity of material goods which modern civilisation has made available has produced the necessity for hard work, the misery and violence of unquenchable greed, the concept of private property, and the horrible spectre of warfare. The primitive age lacked all these evils - it was characterised by freedom, simplicity, friendship and harmony. For all its discomforts, its passing must be regretted: often the message, either implied or openly stated, is that we should as far as possible return to the practices of that far-distant age.

The dividing-line between this kind of cultural history and the Golden Age variety is sometimes a fine one, since an appreciation of the beneficial moral effects of material poverty can occasionally lead to a romanticising of its physical aspects. But it is safe to say that among Greek and Roman authors, hard primitivism is not nearly so common as the Golden Age approach. Perhaps it is understandable, in an era when even the wealthier classes were more familiar with physical hardship than we are today, that few people should have indulged in nostalgia for a time when suffering and pain were at an optimum. Again, technology was not so pervasive as it is now, and consequently its evils may not have been so thoroughly apprehended. Hippyism, 'back to nature'ism, the frenetic consumption of wholefoods - these all had their equivalents in the ancient world, but there is no evidence to suggest that they were at all widespread. And the cultural histories which might have lent them support are few and far between. It is in the more sober thinkers that we generally encounter the more rigorous demands of hard primitivism, and consequently my first four examples are derived from philosophy. The conclusions which are reached are sometimes rather more complex than those of latterday primitivists.

THE SOPHISTS AND THE 'NATURE VERSUS CONVENTION' DEBATE

In the latter years of the fifth century BC, a controversy grew up about one particular aspect of cultural values which continued to exercise the minds of serious thinkers for several centuries to come. This was the physis versus nomos, or nature versus convention, debate: the question of whether civilisation as a whole, or certain individual facets of it, was (or should be) based ultimately on nature, that is, on a permanent and unchanging reality, existing outside of human beliefs and human actions; or whether on the contrary, it was (or should be) a purely human phenomenon, something which humans had arranged between themselves because it was convenient, and which they might alter at will when the balance of convenience shifted. Before we can begin to understand all the complexities of this debate, some analysis of the key words on which it centred must be attempted.

The word physis had by the fifth century come to mean the essence or real constitution of a person or thing. (1) The Presocratics Heraclitus, Parmenides and Empedocles all seem to have used the word in this sense; and Aristotle may have reflected their meaning quite accurately when he wrote of Presocratic philosophers:

> By some, the nature and essence of natural things is said to consist in the primary element inhering in each thing when it is reduced to its basic condition: for example, wood is the nature of a couch and bronze of a statue ... the essence of a thing being the aspect of it which continually abides while it is undergoing changes ... Wherefore some say that fire, some that earth, some that air, some that water, some that more than one of these, and some that all of them, constitute the nature of things
> (Physics 193A9-23).

For Presocratics, then, physis represents the permanent material constitution of physical objects. Any other transitory qualities which objects possess are, as Aristotle again says, 'merely properties and states and conditions of things'; whereas nature is eternal, properties etc., 'are perpetually coming into existence and passing out of it again' (193A25-28). Physis thus comes to denote one side of an antithesis between true constitution on the one hand, and superficial appearance on the other. Democritus, for one, seems to have used the word in this way, to mark the distinction between the ultimate reality of atoms and void, and the perceptible qualities of the objects which they constitute.

> As for the other perceptible qualities, (Democritus) holds that none of them has _physis_, but that all of them are experiences of the senses ... For not even for heat and cold is there, according to him, any _physis_ ... Proof that these qualities do not exist by _physis_ is found in the fact that they do not appear the same to all living creatures
> (Theophrastus, _De sensibus_ 63).

The word which came in the fifth century to be used to denote the other, impermanent side of the antithesis was _nomos_, or convention. So again Democritus could say of physical objects, 'By _nomos_ things possess colour, by _nomos_ they are sweet, by _nomos_ they are bitter; but in reality there exist only atoms and the void' (DK B125). But this meaning of _nomos_ - a subjective standard of judgement - was one that had grown up only in the fifth century. Prior to this, the word had been used to signify the behavioural or moral norms operating within human society - norms which were regarded as authoritative and legitimate because they were based on long-established custom. Some _nomoi_ were thought of as having been introduced ultimately by the gods, others were seen as purely human in their devising. But whatever their origin, their validity seems to have remained for a long time unquestioned: thus late in the sixth century or early in the fifth century, the philosopher Heraclitus could still write that 'all human _nomoi_ are sustained by one divine _nomos_' (DK B114). At some stage in the fifth century, the word began to take on the additional meaning of formal statute; and these three meanings - divine law, customary law, and formal statute - are all commonly encountered in that century. So Democritus himself is able to advise us that 'it is proper to be obedient to _nomos_, to the ruler, and to the wiser' (DK B47); but at the same time he could use the word to signify the subjective appearance of matter, divorced from its ultimate reality. That the word could now have this dual significance is indicative of the revolution in ethical thinking which had taken place in the latter part of the century. Faith in the established morality expressed in custom or law was being rapidly undermined; people were beginning to realise that different populations had different customs and laws, and that what was regarded as good by one state was not necessarily upheld by another. Even within a single state, hallowed customs might be in conflict with each other, as Aeschylus had forcibly demonstrated in the Oresteia. And customs and laws were very far from being permanent - few people in Athens at the time could have been in any doubt that new laws might be introduced which would radically alter the working of long-established institutions. By the end of the fifth century, all thinking people would have been obliged to accept that human laws were artificial and fallible. As Aristotle said, 'things that are right and just ... are characterised by so much diversity and variability that they are believed to exist only by convention (nomos), and not by nature (physis)' (NE 1094 B14-16). Nomos thus came to denote (as well as a transitory physical state) an institution, code, or set of beliefs which was temporary and subjective, with no foundation outside of the realm of human perceptions.

Some people were quite content to accept the fundamental impermanence of all our social and moral institutions; but others were anxious to discover a basis for human relations and for the laws by which they were regulated which was permanent, universal, and objectively real. And, as the antithesis expressed by Aristotle indicates, the concept which seemed to provide the best contrast to the artificial character of nomos was the concept of physis. The word was already being used by Presocratic scientists to denote the ultimate physical reality of things; at the same time medical writers were probably beginning to employ it as a way of describing the basic condition of the human body, when it is unaffected by disease and has characteristics in common with all other human bodies. (2) So physis came to suggest something that was universal and utterly real, and in this capacity it was transferred to the cultural and ethical field, where it was applied to the moral absolutes that people were seeking outside of the world of changing human experience. 'Nature', then, came to signify the normal and best condition of any phenomenon, including psychological and moral ones. (3)

We have perhaps come rather a long way from cultural history, but the excursion has not been an idle one - it is vital to an understanding of the values which people at the time were beginning to attach to their past. For the word physis retained of course its old meaning of an innate condition of people, animals or things, achieved without conscious human intervention; and so by an understandable association of ideas, some people began to believe that what was 'natural' or instinctive was also what was good. Hence, to discover the good in human beings, they thought that one must strip away the refinements accrued in the course of a civilised existence, and study only the basics. Some thinkers imagined that one could do this by distinguishing what was 'natural' in present-day behaviour from what was learned and superficial; others sought to plumb the depths of the human condition by studying foreign and less civilised races; and others again, the hard primitivists, tried to do it by picturing the very earliest phase of our existence. We behaved 'naturally' then, the argument went, so we must also have been good, because 'nature' represents the unsullied essence of every being, its most perfect condition. Every change which has taken place since then, which has led us steadily away from our natural condition, must have been for the worse.

It was among the Sophists that the debate about nature and convention began to come to the fore; but there is not a lot of evidence to show that cultural history was exploited by them as a way of reinforcing a primitivist message. However, we do learn in the Platonic dialogue the <u>Greater Hippias</u> (said by some not to be the work of Plato) that the well-respected Sophist Hippias had made a study of primitive times (285D), and that he was an admirer of the 'ancients' (282A). In another dialogue, he demonstrates a primitivistic attitude towards social evolution when he announces,

> I consider all of you present here to be my kinsmen, family and fellow-citizens - by nature (<u>physis</u>), though not by convention (<u>nomos</u>). By nature, like is kin to like, but convention is a tyrant over the human race, and does much violence to nature
>
> (<u>Protagoras</u> 337 C-D).

The implication here is that the development of distinct political states marked a deterioration from a condition of natural kinship between humans. Hippias may in fact to some extent have been a practising primitivist, since another story about him is that he once appeared at the Olympic games boasting that everything he was wearing had been made by himself (the <u>Lesser Hippias</u> 368 B-C): since the accessories included a ring, a strigil, an oil-flask and a costly girdle, this hardly points to a primitivistic rejection of superfluous goods, but it does at any rate indicate a William-Morris-type attempt to reverse the process of the technological division of labour. And the fact that some people felt the need to have sexual intercourse with their children led him to discountenance the ban on incest as a law of the gods (Xenophon's Memorabilia 4.4.20). That Hippias interpreted cultural history from a hard primitivist viewpoint seems very likely; but for more complete treatments, we will have to turn to writers of the following century.

PLATO

We have already discerned in Plato's work elements of Golden Ageism and of limited progressivism. His appreciation of progress was confined to the distant past, and his Golden Age was a purely imaginary one. A more credible historicity may be accorded to the hard primitivism which he displays in Book 3 of the Laws, where he makes what appears to be a genuine attempt to reconstruct the evolution of a typical community from its earliest beginnings. As an introduction to a study of constitutional and legal principles, he asks the question, 'What is the origin of political organisation?', and in seeking an answer invites us to think back to the time when one of the periodic catastrophes which decimates the human race has just occurred - in this case a post-flood era. The only people to escape drowning must have been shepherds living on the mountain-tops. In this initial epoch they kept herds of oxen and flocks of goats, which (perhaps after an initial shortage) kept them provided with meat and milk, and their food-supply was supplemented by hunting. They had plenty of clothing, bedding, houses and dishes, both fired and unfired; for God had granted them the two technologies, weaving and pottery-making, which would furnish them with all the necessities. But there was no knowledge of urban life, of constitutions, or of legislation. They had no metals, and none of the technologies based on the use of metals. There was no transport, and no system of writing. And there was a complete absence of warfare, and of the peculiarly urban forms of warfare which go by the names of law-suits and political factions. This was for two reasons: people led isolated lives and so were eager for friendship; and there was no excessive poverty or wealth, either one of which can lead to bickering and envy. People then were simple-minded, and believed what they were told about good and evil, about the gods and about humankind. The only form of government to be met with was 'patriarchal rule and the kingship which of all kingships is the most just', that is, the kingship which proceeds from rule by the parent, and which exists in households and clans (677A-680E).

Perhaps some of the material features of soft primitivism are still to be detected in this account – the ample supplies of food and of domestic comforts certainly seem to be unduly optimistic. But we are a long way here from the extravagant fantasy of the *Politicus* myth: on the whole, where material conditions are concerned, Plato presents us with what we may imagine to be a fairly realistic picture of the pastoral way of life pursued in the later Stone Age, when some basic technologies had been acquired. Plato's primitives, however, are not the products of a progress achieved after a long struggle against a hostile environment; they are the earliest generation, living at the beginning of a time which is measured from the onset of a new terrestrial cycle. Many of the features of their existence are down-to-earth adaptations of the blessings enjoyed by that other group of originals, the golden race. Instead of spontaneously produced cereals, they have meat and milk; instead of generalised plenty, they have an amplitude of the true necessities; instead of having fire dispensed to them by the gods, they are allowed to use it on their own account; instead of the companionship of the gods, they have technologies supplied by a benevolent deity, and a received knowledge of gods and humans; and instead of the rule of Kronos, they have patriarchal kingship. The ludicrous splendours of the Golden Age have here been transmuted into a realistic assessment of past privileges; so that, whereas the *Politicus* myth erected between us and an imaginary past a warning about the impossibility of living in a near-perfect world, the account in the *Laws* invites us to look on the past as something that is both viable and superior. On the other hand, this primitive era is an inversion of the one described by progressivists, when there was no fire, no meat-eating, no use of animals, no domestic comforts, no conception of divinity, no morality, no families and no government. What Plato is in fact saying is that all the characteristics of *humanity*, which according to progressivists were only slowly and painfully achieved, have been present in the human race since the beginning of its existence. In the Golden Age myth, we fall from the level of the gods to the human level; in the progressivist accounts, we rise up to it from the level of the animals; but in the Laws, we are already there from the word 'go'. We come into the world as fire-users and meat-eaters, we come into the world knowing about good and evil, and about gods and humans (679C) - we have always existed in a state of moral ambiguity, we have always had the ability to distinguish ourselves from gods on the one hand, and to make use of animals on the other. In other words, we have always had the intermediate status of human beings. It is a profoundly anti-evolutionary view of cultural history.

It is also, I believe, a primitivistic view. There is some uncertainty about the moral judgement which Plato is passing on his primitives, since in one passage he asks, 'Do we imagine that those who are ignorant of the many evils of cities, but also of their many goods, can have achieved their full development in either virtue or vice?' (678B). This reinforces the message that the mixture of good and evil which it is the human lot to encounter has been with us from the very beginning, for it is from these primitives that 'there has arisen the whole of our present condition - cities, constitutions, techniques and laws, and a great amount of evil, and a great amount of good' (678A). But the suggestion is also being made that, whereas the primitives escaped the worst of our excesses, they also knew nothing of the full-scale virtue which urban life makes possible. On the other hand, we are told later on that 'it is in the community which has no communion with either wealth or poverty that the noblest characters almost always arise' (679B), the reference being to the community of primitives; and that our earliest ancestors were 'more straight-forward, and brave and temperate, and altogether more righteous' than we are (679E). Though we urbanites, it seems, have more potential for virtue, the primitives in actual fact were, on average, far better behaved than we are. Plato at this point passes on to a consideration of how the pastoral household developed into the small agricultural community, and later on into the city; and how at the same time custom law was subsumed within written law, and patriarchy was supplanted, first by aristocracy or monarchy, and later by the mixed urban constitution (680E-682C). Again, the judgement passed on later developments seems to be an unfavourable one, since it is this type of constitution, the polymorphic type that exists in democratic societies, which Plato most despises (see Republic 557D-562A). But the primitives get rather

lost in all this, and Plato does not return to them.
What then does he intend us to make of them? It is difficult to say, but I would suggest that they are being held up as a kind of practical ideal - more attainable than the purely imaginary ideal represented by the Golden Age of the Politicus myth. What seems to emerge from Plato's works is a four-tiered scheme of societies. There is (1) the near-perfect society of an imaginary God-controlled world, as described in the Politicus, which hypothetically is the nearest approach which can be made in a physical world to the metaphysical absolute of the Forms, but which, while it is something to be aimed at, is forever beyond our grasp. Then (2) there is the technologically and politically innocent society of the primitives outlined in the Laws. At the bottom of the scale, there is (3) the technological and urban society in which we live, which has the capacity to bring to fruition the seeds of good and evil existing in (2), but which generally exploits the evil rather than the good. Existing potentially somewhere between (2) and (3) is an ideal society (4) which, while it makes use of the technology and the urban organisation of (3), manages by imitating the material restraint and patriarchal government of (2) to capitalise on the basic elements of the good which are present in all of us. Somewhere on the route from our earliest to our present condition, Plato seems to be saying, we have gone wrong. We must try to go back - we cannot go all the way back, for there are certain technologies which we could not now live without, and what is more, the polis is an institution which could serve to bring out our finest qualities. But we can go part of the way there. The ideal society which he would thus construct perhaps resembles most of all, in pseudo-historical terms, the arrested community described in the Republic (referred to by one of the participants in the dialogue as a community of pigs), which enjoys the basic technologies (including metallurgy), plus overseas trade and retailing, and has achieved division of labour, but does not possess any of the luxury industries, and above all has no economic need for warfare (369B-374E; see above p.181-2). What the government of that community would have been like Plato does not inform us, but of course for his ideal government we can turn to the declared utopias which are the subject of the Republic and the Laws. The latter are certainly based on the institution of the polis, and we can easily imagine that they enjoy the same technologies as the

community of pigs; but they also have a number of features in common with the primitive era described in the Laws - the simplicity of the life-style ordained for the guardians, the absence of excessive poverty or wealth, the lack of political factions, the dearth of legislation, the patriarchal government which the guardians provide, and the instruction which they mete out to their subjects on questions of morality and theology. There are, then, many characteristics of primitive life which Plato believes we should copy: a complete return would not be possible (few hard primitivists would demand that) or even desirable, but a return in some degree is essential. This is true primitivism, and brings a total clamp-down on any possibility of future progress.

THE CYNICS

An even more rigorous hard primitivism than Plato's was the one produced by the group of philosophers known as the Cynics. The founder of the sect may have been Antisthenes, who like Plato was a pupil of Socrates; but its most famous member, and the one who provided it with its name, was Diogenes, beloved by story-tellers for his barrel. His nickname was ho kuon, or 'the dog', because he rejected all conventions and lived an animal-like existence. His philosophy was based on the principle that happiness is to be attained by living in accordance with nature, and by seeking to satisfy only one's most 'natural' needs, in the cheapest and easiest way possible. What is natural cannot possibly be indecent, and can and should be done in public. The result was a life of stringent self-sufficiency, since little is required for the satisfaction of basic needs; and also, in some people's eyes, a certain shamelessness - it may have been Diogenes' habit of meeting some of his more intimate bodily needs in public which helped to earn him his nickname.(4) What especially distinguished the Cynics from other primitivists was that they did not just draw a theoretical ideal from the life of primitive humans, they actually lived it. And they lived it in the midst of civilised society. Unlike some modern adherents of alternative life-styles, they did not see the necessity for retreating into rustic obscurity. The biographer Diogenes Laertius has described their way of life thus:

> The Cynics maintain that we should live simply, eating only such food as is required for nourishment, and wearing only a single garment. They despise wealth and reputation and high birth. Some are vegetarians, and drink only cold water, and make use of any shelters that happen to be handy - even barrels, as Diogenes did, who used to say that the characteristic of gods is that they need nothing, and of people who are like gods, that they want only a little. (6.104)

Apart from the legendary barrel, there are dozens of entertaining anecdotes which illustrate the paucity of Diogenes' wants; such as the one about him seeing a boy drinking out of his hands, and then taking his cup out of his knapsack and throwing it away (Diogenes Laertius 6.37).

One fundamental difference between Plato's primitivism and that of the Cynics is that, whereas Plato lauded an original race of beings who had already acquired a fully human status and a few basic technologies, the Cynics believed, like the progressivists, that the original condition of the human race was an animal-like one, and, unlike the progressivists, that we should endeavour to return to this. Time and again, the life which we should aspire to is compared to that lived by the animals. So Diogenes likened his nomadic habit of shifting himself to where the climate was most favourable to the migratory behaviour of storks, cranes, deer and rabbits (Dio Chrysostom Orat. 6.32-33). An anonymous Cynic is described in one treatise as picking up food here and there, like a dog, and like a dog 'laying himself down on the hard ground' (pseudo-Lucian, Cynicus 1 and 5). Diogenes denied the value of family life, and thought that women and children should be common to all (Diogenes Laertius 6.72). Even incest was seen by him as permissible - 'cocks do not see anything wrong in such relationships, nor do dogs or asses' (Dio Chrysostom Orat. 10.30). And, whereas among Plato's primitives one of the foremost features of a fully human existence - the eating of cooked meat - was present, the Cynics adopted diets which were seen as characteristic both of animals and (by the progressivists) of the first humans: either they were vegetarians (as noted above by Diogenes Laertius), or they ate raw flesh: the Roman emperor Julian records Diogenes' belief that

> if one can eat meat without going to any trouble over it, as can all the other animals to whom

> nature has granted this diet, and if one can do so without harm or discomfort ... then, he thought, eating raw meat is quite in accordance with nature ... Why on earth, if we make use of cooked meat, do we not use it raw too, answer me that. You have no answer, except that this is our custom and practice. For obviously it is not that meat is by nature disgusting before it is cooked, but becomes pure by cooking ...'
> (Orat. 6. 191-2)

Cannibalism too is not out of order, 'as is evident from the practice of other races' (Diogenes Laertius 6.73). In all these items of dogma, the appeal which the Cynics would make to animal behaviour, as being the most natural, is obvious. What is interesting is that the Cynics also saw their life-style as typical of the gods: '(Diogenes) imitated for the most part the life of the gods. For they alone, Homer says, live at ease ... Animals too, he said, have the right idea about such things ...' (Dio Chrysostom Orat. 6.31); 'Moreover, if it seems to you that because I need and use only a few things, I live the life of an animal, then according to your argument the gods live worse than the animals, for they have no needs at all ... The gods need nothing, and those men who are nearest to the gods need very little' (the anonymous Cynic, pseudo-Lucian, Cynicus 12). Repeatedly in Golden Age and progressivist accounts, an antithesis has been suggested between animals and gods, with humans between the two; and when animals have been brought into contact with a divine way of life (as for example in Plato's Politicus myth), they have been made ultra-civilised. Here, on the contrary, the gods are brought down to animal level - and so the two outer poles of our existence, the two counterweights which keep us as human beings in balance, are removed. The effect is a rejection rather than an acceptance of our status, an insistence that we are out of line with the rest of the universe, and can only achieve conformity and happiness by freeing ourselves from the appalling demands of the humanity that distinguishes us.

The belief in self-sufficiency, in independence from the need for economic goods, was a prominent strain in Cynic thought. They sought to persuade people that nearly all possessions are useless, and that to feed one's desire for them gives rise to insatiable cravings which can only reduce one to misery. It is not surprising, then, that the Cynic judgement on cultural history is an adverse one.

Diogenes, we are told, saw urban life and technology as the source of all our evils: 'people first came together in cities so that they might not be harmed by those outside; but then instead they harmed each other, and did all kinds of dreadful things ...' The discovery of fire is also seen as a watershed, since 'that was the origin and starting-point of softness and luxury among humans'. It was not Zeus' desire to withhold fire that hurt us; but rather our own inventiveness and cleverness, which instead of being used to promote virtue, has led to the wearisome and anxious pursuit of pleasure. 'Thus it was altogether right that Prometheus, so the story goes, was bound to a rock and had his liver torn out by an eagle' (Dio Chrysostom Orat. 6.25-30). Here Diogenes makes use of familiar progressivist arguments about the utilitarian origins of society, and turns them upside down by pointing out that society has actually created the disadvantages it was designed to overcome. And whereas Plato's admired primitives already had the crucial use of fire, this essentially human attribute is also denied to us by Diogenes.

Maximus Tyrius, a philosophical essayist of the second century AD, reveals himself as a supporter of the Cynic creed in a piece in which he equates the life of the true Cynic with life in the Golden Age. Here the gold is most definitely metaphorical, for the primitive existence is not one of cushioned comfort, though it is perhaps a touch romanticised: the member of the golden race is an animal, but has a mind 'very near to that of the gods'; the earth furnishes freely an unlimited supply of food - grass, leaves and fruit; he spends his life 'naked, without a house, without techniques, but with the whole earth for his city and his household'; his existence is quiet, peaceful and healthy; he can 'lift his eyes to the rising sun, look at the stars, distinguish night from day, look forward to the changes of the seasons, feel the winds and breathe the pure free air'. To him the life of the 'civilised' man would appear as life in a dreadful prison (Diss. 36). So once again the primitive life, equated with an existence which is both animal and divine, is said to be at its best when it is devoid of even the most basic technologies.

THE STOICS

The Stoic school of philosophy was in its early days much influenced by Cynicism. Some of the beliefs attributed to the founder Zeno suggest that at that stage the Stoics were prepared to adopt even some of the more shocking of the Cynics' tenets - the acceptability of communal marriage (Diogenes Laertius 7.33), of incest (Stoic. vet. frag. 1.256 Arnim), and even 'in certain circumstances' of cannibalism (Diogenes Laertius 7.121), was, we are told, maintained by the upright and respectable Zeno.

The Stoic attitude to cultural history may, as we have seen, have been an equivocal one, but for some thinkers at least the doctrine of cycles seems to have reinforced the primitivism derived from the Cynics, by suggesting that the life of simple self-sufficiency was more easily attainable at the beginning of a cycle, when the world was newly created. It is in the writings of the Roman Stoics, and particularly in those of Seneca, that this hard primitivism receives its fullest expression.

Ancient literature's most eloquent and rapturous evocation of the primitive era is to be found in the Moral Letter (90) in which Seneca sets out and refutes Posidonius' interpretation of cultural history. The admiration which he voices here for the primitives seems at first unbounded. Nature, he says, has not treated us worse than other animals, for she has made it possible for us to live without techniques. 'We were born with everything ready made for us ... Houses, clothes, food and bodily comforts ... were ready to hand, and free, and obtainable with just a little effort' (18). If God should give us the task of fashioning earthly creatures and ordaining their life-style, the condition of the primitives is exactly the one we would choose. 'What race of men was ever happier than these?' They lived without agriculture or private property; there was no poverty, for the earth was fertile and produced abundant food. People were generous and cared for others as for themselves, and the only violence was directed against wild animals. There were no metals. People wore skins, and when necessary took refuge in caves or rough shelters. They slept on the hard ground, and 'as they lay beneath the open sky the stars swept noiselessly above them' (37-42).

Seneca, like Plato, believes that right from the beginning of our history we have possessed the only technologies which we need; like Plato again, he suggests that we have always had a fully human status, defined by the ability to master wild animals. His primitives may have enjoyed a food-gathering rather than a pastoral subsistence; but they seem not to have been accorded the utterly

217

animal existence which the Cynics wished upon their human race. His appreciation of the primitive lifestyle seems unqualified; indeed his enthusiasm for their outdoor life cannot at times be prevented from boiling over into what may seem to us to be an idealisation of the wonderful world of nature, with

> the air, the breezes blowing freely among the open spaces, the gentle shade of a rock or tree, the glistening springs, the streams ... flowing where they will, the meadows lovely without art – among these they made their simple homes, adorned by rustic hand (43).

One might expect that the moral condition of these people would also win Seneca's unqualified admiration; but when he goes on to examine the state of their souls, he draws back.

> But however excellent and free from crime their life was, they were not wise men, for that title goes to the highest achievement. Yet I would not deny that they were people of lofty spirit, and, so to speak, fresh from the gods. For there is no doubt that the world produced better things when it was not yet worn out ... Well then? They were innocent through ignorance. It makes a great difference whether a person is unwilling to sin, or does not know how to sin. Their life lacked justice, prudence, temperance and fortitude. Their simple existence had features resembling all these virtues: but virtue is attained only by a soul which has been educated and trained and brought by constant practice to perfection. To this, but without this, we are born ...' (44-46)

Here we have a classic illustration of the reason why most philosophers cannot be whole-hearted primitivists, since for them virtue can only be acquired intellectually, as a result of conscious reflection. (The Cynics are exceptions here – they despised most forms of learning, and Antisthenes is even reported as saying that people should not be taught to read: Diogenes Laertius 6.103). So Seneca cannot accept that the primitives possessed true virtue: he even implies that evil has to come into the world before virtue can exist, and to that extent evil must be seen as a necessity. It is only through knowledge of evil that we come to learn the conscious discipline of the emotions and of conduct which Seneca considers

to be indispensable to the good life: the virtue
which comes from the inner struggle against evil is
more complete than the goodness of innocence. In this
respect, Seneca's thinking comes close to that of
Plato: though Plato did not see virtue as arising out
of the conquest of evil, like Seneca he wanted to go
back only so far in his attempt to escape the evils
of a technological civilisation. For him, the basic
form of the urban community, while it produces much
evil, also makes possible the attainment of true
virtue, and it is to this that he would return. For
Seneca, the high point of civilisation had been
reached at the point when the Greek masters of the
Stoic school had discovered the essential moral
truths, which thus required no further investigation. Both would have seen future progress only in
terms of the recreation of an ideal thrown up by the
past: Plato aspired to the collective recreation of a
community; while Seneca aimed at teaching the
individual how to make progress through the
recreation of a system of morality.

JUVENAL

An embittered poet, living in an age when economic
and technological development were reaching a peak in
the Roman world, came closer than any other Latin
author to the rigorous primitivism of the Cynics. In
his Satires, written in the early years of the second
century AD, Juvenal makes savage attacks on the
luxury, vice, corruption and greed which he sees as
rampant in Roman society. One of the best-known of
these, (Satire 6) takes as the target for its
seething invective the immoral wives of the city; but
by way of contrast, the introduction tells us about
the chaste women who lived in the age of Saturn:

> I believe that under the rule of Saturn, shame
> lingered on the earth and was often seen, in the
> days when an icy cave provided a little home,
> and enclosed the fire, the household gods, the
> animals and their masters in common darkness;
> when a mountain wife spread a woodland bed of
> leaves and stalks and skins of the nearby
> beasts. She wasn't a bit like you, Cynthia, or
> you whose shining eyes were clouded by a dead
> sparrow. She bore breasts to feed great
> children, and was often more savage than her
> acorn-belching husband. (6. 1-10).

The world was new then, and the people were born of oak-trees or made out of mud. At first under the subsequent rule of Jupiter people still lived in an open garden, with no fear of theft. But later on in the silver age, adultery appeared - 'it is now an ancient custom to defile the bed of another' - and in the iron age every kind of crime was discovered (11-24).

No attempt at all has been made by Juvenal to idealise the life of these primitives - he refuses to wax even faintly lyrical about the imagined pleasures of the outdoor life. The spontaneous fruits of the earth are acorns, and there are no couches of grass, but only a pile of leaves in a freezing cave shared with goats. Juvenal is rare, even among hard primitivists, in his ability to face up to the crudity and squalor of primitive life. His people are coarse and ugly, but he is in no doubt about their moral superiority, and he emerges as an eloquent member of the school of thought that sees the only hope for virtue in renunciation and poverty. Unlike Plato and Seneca, he is fully prepared to go all the way back: but we should note that even for him the first phase of human existence (an existence which had started in the earth, as in progressivist accounts) is characterised by those thoroughly human attributes, the use of fire and animals, and the enjoyment of family life. We were human then, he tells us, and should not have attempted to advance any further. (5)

THE NOBLE SAVAGE

The primitivism which sees peculiar virtues in the original generation of humans is of course closely akin to the primitivism which holds up as ideals contemporary races of 'uncivilised' peoples. The comparative method of formulating value judgements was used by Golden Age theorists largely in relation to imaginary countries, but by progressivists with real groups of people. This latter source of material was the one adopted in the main by hard primitivists, and their exploitation of the comparative method is perhaps the most common of all. Actual contact with the peoples concerned would certainly have prevented excessive idealisation of the Golden Age type; but it is interesting that admiration rather than disgust seems to have been the more usual reaction when the 'uncivilised' way of life was studied. Of course, the writers, by and large, were not the people who had

had the contact, and a fair amount of romance may have crept into these travellers' tales; but it does seem to be the case that when hard primitivists wished to express their rejection of contemporary civilisation, they were more likely to choose the comparative method, whereas the theorists who taught acceptance of our status generally went for the historical method.

Mythological hard primitivism is not unknown - Homer's Cyclopes lived in caves, and, as Plato pointed out, enjoyed an uncluttered patriarchal government; but there were Golden Age features too in their existence (see above, p.199). From the fifth century BC on, however, real noble savages began to be enormously popular. The accounts of these remote tribes generally dwell with approval on their lack of economic and technological sophistication, and on their superior justice and temperance; some are meat-eaters, while others are vegetarians; some maintain family life, but others are promiscuous in their sexual relations, and share their wives and children. Many and far-flung are the races seized on as models for a better life-style, by writers disillusioned with their own civilisation: the Ethiopians, the Albanians, the Illyrians, the Hebrideans and the Germans are among the peoples who receive their share of eulogy. (6) But none are so universally acclaimed as the nomadic Scythians, who lived in the steppes of Southern Russia. From the fifth century onwards they appear regularly in literature as exemplars of a rigorous but virtuous way of life. Of them the Augustan historian Pompeius Trogus writes:

> There are no boundaries among those people, for they do not work the land; they have no houses or shelters or fixed dwellings, but wander through the solitary wastes, feeding their herds and flocks. They carry their wives and children with them in wagons, which, covered with hides on account of the rain and cold, they use as homes. Justice is maintained by their character, not by laws ... They despise gold and silver as much as other mortals seek it. They live on milk and honey. The use of wool and proper clothes is unknown to them, though they are tortured by continual cold; but they use the skins of wild animals and rodents. This restraint has introduced justice into their way of life, for they crave nothing that does not belong to them ... Would that other mortals had similar restraint ... there would not have been

so many wars through the centuries ... How wonderful that nature has given to them what the Greeks through the long teaching of their philosophers cannot achieve.
(in Justin <u>Hist. Phil. epit.</u> 2.2)

Another writer of the first century BC, the Greek geographer Strabo, describes the Scythians in similar vein, and is particularly impressed by the communism of a people who 'live entirely without contracts and money-making - who, indeed, possess all things in common except their swords and drinking-cups, and in particular have wives and children in common, in Platonic fashion.' He goes on pessimistically to throw doubt on the continuance of this happy existence,

> for our way of life has caused the degeneration of nearly all peoples, producing among them softness, and the love of pleasure, and perverse technology, and greed in countless forms. Much of this corruption has now reached even the nomadic barbarians ...' (<u>Geog.</u> 300-302)

But not everyone is complimentary about the Scythians. In a treatise attributed to the fifth century medical writer Hippocrates, they are discussed from a disinterested medical viewpoint, as an example of the influence of climate on temperament - the climate, of course, is severe, and we are given a gloomy view of their country and of their character. 'From the north there are constantly blowing winds that are chilled by snow, ice and many waters ... A thick fog envelops by day the plains, and it is here that they spend their lives. So winter is perennial, and summer lasts only a few days, and is not very warm.' Contradicting the normal image of robust and hardy nomads, Hippocrates says that the harsh climate has a debilitating effect on the Scythians. They scarcely have the strength to draw a bow or throw a javelin; and worst of all has been the effect on their sex lives: the men, because of their feeble constitutions and the fatigue induced by cold, and also as a result of their continual horse-riding and the wearing of trousers, often become impotent, while the women too are frequently infertile because they are fat and lazy (<u>De aere, aquis, locis</u> 19-23).

The Scythians fare even worse at the hands of the Roman poet Ovid, who perhaps knew them better than most, since he spent the last ten years of his life in exile among them, and had an opportunity to judge at first hand the primitives he had once admired. He complains bitterly of the climate – 'before one fall of snow has melted another has come' (Tristia 3.10.15) – and sometimes wonders whether the cold or the Scythian arrows will get him first: 'whether it's the waters of the sea or of the mighty river that have been frozen by the savage force of the great north wind, as soon as the Danube has been flattened by a dry north-easterly the barbarian horde presses forward on swift horse; an enemy, powerful with steeds and far-flying arrows, plunders far and wide the neighbouring land' (Tristia 3.10.51-56). Amid the ice and the hail, the butchery and the pillage, little survives of the noble savage, still less of the carefree Golden Age peasant whom Ovid lovingly described during happier days in Rome.

Golden Age and progressivist accounts of cultural history both tell us that the human status (as contrasted with a divine or animal status) is something which has been acquired with time: both teach us to accept what we have become and (in the main) to be cautious of becoming anything else. Only hard primitivism carries the message of regress and whole-hearted renunciation. Of the thinkers who subscribe to it, Plato, Seneca and Juvenal all tell us that we have always possessed the technologies which define our status as humans, and that we can renounce what we have become today and return to an existence enjoyed in the past without fear of losing our humanity. The Cynics are unique, I think, because they agree with the progressivists that we started out as animals, but they do not shrink from the conclusion that we should try to recapture that condition. This they can do, it seems, because they would also agree with the Golden Agers that we began our history living like gods – animals, gods, humans are all one to them, and we have been perverse in trying ever to part company with that blessed and uniform state of nature. Something similar, though not the same, is, I believe, conveyed by the Orphic message. The Orphic anthropogony (outlined in Chapter 1) can be seen as positing an initial fall, followed by a rise from the earth – like Golden Age and progressivist theories, it suggests that the human race currently occupies an intermediate status in the world. But the Orphics are not happy with that situation – in telling us to go back in time, they want us to endeavour to recover only our divine status, and to renounce as far as possible the earth that is in us. This, at least, seems to be the import of their vegetarianism, which refutes the cannibalism (the eating of Dionysus) which has placed us in our present position. If we can get back to a condition that preceded cannibalism, we can perhaps recover our divinity. For the Cynics, on the other hand, vegetarianism, and the eating of raw flesh (or even of human flesh) are both paths to virtue, because both lead back to gods and animals, which are indistinguishable and equally at one with the supreme good of the natural order.

NOTES

1. This may, indeed, have been its original meaning: see Guthrie, Greek philosophy, vol. 1, p.82-3; and Kirk, Heraclitus, p.227-30.
2. The uncertainty about the dating of most of the medical writings makes it unclear whether or not the medical usage predated the ethical usage, though it seems quite likely that it did. For an example of such a usage, see On ancient medicine I.578.
3. For fuller discussions of the physis-nomos debate, see, among others, F. Heinemann, Nomos und Physis, (Basel, 1945); M. Pohlenz 'Nomos und Physis', Hermes 81 (1953), p.418-38; Guthrie, Greek philosophy vol. 3, p.55-135; M. Ostwald, Nomos and the beginnings of the Athenian democracy, (Oxford, 1969): for the history of the word, see especially p.20-54.
4. See Diogenes Laertius 6.69.
5. Juvenal's sincerity as a primitivist may be questionable: he could even here be exercising his satire. See in general H.A. Mason 'Is Juvenal a Classic?', Arion 1 (1962), p.8-44 and 2(1962), p.39-79.
6. For a full account of the relevant texts, see Lovejoy and Boas, p.315-367.

CONCLUSION

Many questions and many channels of thought are created by an examination of Greek and Roman ideas about biological and cultural development; and I am well aware that I have not answered all the questions, or pursued all the channels of thought. Nor am I dogmatic about any of the conclusions which I have reached in the course of this study. But among the points which I hope to have demonstrated, and which seem to me to be worthy of consideration, I would emphasise the following:

1. In the ancient world there was (as there is today) an intimate connection between beliefs about the human race's biological origins, and appraisals of the direction and value of cultural change.
2. The two parameters of human development which were present in mythological thought - divine existence and animal existence - continued to be a significant element in non-mythological accounts of both biological and cultural change. Even those writers who were at pains to relieve the gods of any responsibility for human advance could not always (or did not always wish to) free their minds of the concept of divinity as a criterion by which to evaluate our status in the world.
3. A broad dichotomy exists between those thinkers who present a 'Golden Age' view of cultural development, and those whose analysis might be termed 'progressivist'; and these are categories which cut across the mythological/non-mythological distinction. The fundamental difference between them is their assessment of our origins; and this could be expressed in non-historical terms as their assessment of the most significant criterion by which we are to be judged. Were we once (or should we be compared with) gods? or were we once (or should be

be compared with) animals? When the answer to the first question is in the affirmative, then the problem of biological origins becomes immaterial: our attention is fixed only on our fall from metaphysical grace. When it is the second question which receives the affirmative answer, then we can begin to think in terms of biological evolution, since we have been given something concrete and physical by which to measure our biological/intellectual development.

4. But in many examples of these two contrasting versions of cultural history, we are referred not only to the point from which we have come, but also (albeit obliquely) to the point towards which we are moving. If we started out as gods, then we have animals as the opposite pole of our existence; and vice versa. Two oppositional standards of judgement are thus erected, with the result that human beings are assigned in both versions to an intermediate status between the two. No matter which of these a writer would prefer to compare us with (god or animal), he does not often forget that there is something worse or better (animal or god) against which we <u>could</u> be measured. The conclusion to be drawn in either case is that our status is a characteristically human one, which involves an inevitable mixture of divinity and bestiality, of order and chaos, of good and evil. We might be urged to strive beyond this mid-way point, or we might be warned not to attempt this: but we are told pretty firmly in either event that there is not much hope of our escaping, within the physical confines of this world, the ambiguities of our human constitution.

5. This idea of ambiguity and balance is expressed also (though from a wider angle of vision) in the cyclical interpretations of world history. Cyclical theories tend thus either to reinforce or (more often) to act as a substitute for cultural history.

6. Hard primitivism differs from both Golden Ageism and from progressivism in that it does not advise conformity to our present cultural standards: it represents therefore the only truly primitivistic and regressive version of cultural history. But in advocating a renunciation of the fruits of civilisation, it does not generally advocate at the same time a renunciation of our humanity. This is achieved by picturing the human race as being neither god-like nor animal-like in its origins, but as being sempiternally and unalterably human. Cultural advance can be dismissed as an aberration by hard primitivists, because humanity is seen by them as a

Conclusion

static entity whose basic needs can best be satisfied from resources which exist outside of the confines of an impermanent physical world. Hard primitivists are in fact the only theorists whose judgement on history is unequivocal enough for them to be willing to do away with it.

SELECT BIBLIOGRAPHY

Alderink, L.J. 'Creation and salvation in ancient Orphism', American Classical Studies 8 (Chicago, 1981).
Barnes, J. The Presocratic philosophers (London, 1982).
Bignone, E. Empedocle (Torino, 1916).
Burnet, J. Early Greek philosophy (London, 1892; 4th ed., London, 1930).
Bury, J.B. The idea of progress (London, 1920).
Cole, A.T. Democritus and the sources of Greek anthropology (Cleveland, 1967).
Cornford, F.M. Principium sapientiae (Cambridge, 1952).
De Lacy, P.H. 'Limit and variation in the Epicurean philosophy', Phoenix 23 (1969), p.104-13.
Detienne, M. and Vernant, J.-P. Cunning intelligence in Greek culture and society, trans. J. Lloyd (Hassocks and Atlantic Heights, 1978).
Diels, H. and Kranz, W. Die Fragmente der Vorsokratiker (Berlin, 1952).
Dodds, E.R. The ancient concept of progress (Oxford, 1973).
Edelstein, L. The idea of progress in classical antiquity (Baltimore, 1967).
Empedocles. The extant fragments ed. M.R. Wright (New Haven and London, 1981).
Fontenrose, J. 'Work, justice, and Hesiod's five ages', Classical Philology 69 (1974), p.1-16.
Friedlaender, P. Plato, trans. H. Meyerhoff (3 vols., London, 1969).
Furley, D.J. and Allen R.E. (eds.), Studies in Presocratic philosophy (2 vols., London, 1970).
Gordon, R.L. (ed.) Myth, religion and society (Cambridge, 1981).
Griffith, M. The authenticity of 'Prometheus Bound' (Cambridge, 1977).

Bibliography

Griffiths, J.G. 'Archaeology and Hesiod's five ages', Journal of the History of Ideas 17 (1956), p.109-19.
Guthrie, W.K.C. The Greeks and their gods (London, 1950).
Guthrie, W.K.C. A history of Greek philosophy (5 vols., Cambridge, 1962-1978).
Guthrie, W.K.C. In the beginning (London, 1957).
Havelock, E.A. The liberal temper in Greek politics (London, 1957).
Heraclitus, The art and thought of Heraclitus ed. C.H. Kahn (Cambridge, 1979).
Heraclitus, The cosmic fragments ed. G.S. Kirk (Cambridge, 1954).
Huxley, J. Evolution in action (Harmondsworth, 1953).
Kahn, C.H. Anaximander and the origins of Greek cosmology (New York, 1960).
Kirk, G.S. The nature of Greek myths (Harmondsworth, 1974).
Kirk, G.S., Raven, J.E. and Schofield, M. The Presocratic philosophers (Cambridge, 1983).
Levi-Strauss, C. Structural anthropology, trans. C. Jacobson and B. Grundfest Scheopf (Harmondsworth, 1977).
Linforth, I.M. The arts of Orpheus (Berkeley and Los Angeles, 1941).
Loenen, J.H. 'Was Anaximander an evolutionist?' Mnemosyne series 4, 7 (1954), p.215-232.
Long, A.A. 'Empedocles' cosmic cycle in the sixties', in A.P.D. Mourelatos (ed.), The Pre-Socratics: a collection of critical essays (Garden City, N.Y., 1974).
Lovejoy, A.O. and Boas, G. Primitivism and related ideas in antiquity (Baltimore, 1935).
Lloyd-Jones, H. The justice of Zeus (Berkeley, 1971).
O'Brien, D. Empedocles' cosmic cycle (Cambridge, 1969).
Ostwald, M. Nomos and the beginnings of Athenian democracy (Oxford, 1969).
Popper, K.R. 'Back to the Presocratics', in Conjectures and refutations (London, 1963); reproduced in Furley and Allen, vol. 1, p.130-53.
Pritchard, J.B. (ed.) Ancient Near Eastern texts relating to the Old Testament (Princeton, 1955).
Sikes, E.E. The anthropology of the Greeks (London, 1914).
Solmsen, F. 'Love and Strife in Empedocles' cosmology', Phronesis 10 (1965), p.109-48; reproduced in Furley and Allen, vol. 2, p.221-264.
Sorabji, R. Time, creation and the continuum (London,

1983).
Vernant, J.-P. Myth and thought among the Greeks (Eng. trans., London, 1983).
Vernant, J.-P. The origins of Greek thought (Eng. trans., London, 1982).
Walcot, P. Hesiod and the Near East (Cardiff, 1966).
West, M.L. Early Greek philosophy and the Orient (Oxford, 1971).
West, M.L. The Orphic poems (Oxford, 1983).

INDEX

Aeacus 7
Aeneas 6, 158
Aeschylus 7, 11, 172, 206
Aesop 146
Albanians 221
Alcmaeon 74
anti-evolutionary beliefs 74-9
Anaxagoras 45-47, 77, 80, 81, 85, 86, 176
Anaximander 26-32, 33, 39-40, 66-67, 80, 84, 115, 116, 118
animalitarianism 96
animals and humans,
    distinction between 74-5
    affinities between 79-83, 147
Antisthenes 213, 218
Antony 157
Apollo 93
Apollodorus 11
Aratus 144-6, 147
Archelaus 47-8, 58, 67, 80, 81, 85, 176
Archimedes 166, 187
architecture 197
Ares 19
Aristophanes 10, 83, 93-4, 155
Aristotle 62-4, 70, 74-5, 76-78, 89, 121-3, 153, 182-5, 199, 200, 205, 207
Asius 7
Athene 9, 11, 150, 169-70
Athenio 186
atomism 48, 65, 92-3, 125-6, 193-4
Atlantis 119-20, 164n15
Augustine 65, 127-8, 131 n24

Augustus 158

Babrius 146, 148
Babylonian Creation Epic 15, 16
Baldry, H.C. 136, 139
biological transformation 28, 73, 80, 84, 92, 94, 97,
Boas, G. 105, 203
bronze race 138, 139, 140, 141, 142, 145
Burnet, J. 25
Bury, J.B. 106, 113, 165, 167, 175, 199

Cadmus 7, 19
Callimachus 11
Calpurnius 158
Canaries, the 161
cannibalism 148, 186, 187, 195-6, 200, 202 n14, 215, 217, 224
charter myths 7-8, 19
Cicero 112, 196-7
circle-people 93-5
communism 222
convention 205-8
cooking 97, 180, 186, 215
Cornford, F.M. 25, 29-31
culture heroes 169-171
cycles, cosmic and cultural 111-129, 166, 188, 226
Cyclopes 199, 221
Cynics, the 96, 213-6, 216, 217, 218, 219, 223-4

Darwin, C. 28-9, 73, 87, 92, 95, 96

231

Index

Demeter 169-70
Demiurge, the 60-61
Democritus 48, 65, 68, 80, 81, 86, 166-7, 176-7, 180, 205-6
Descartes 182
Detienne, M. 103
Deucalion 6, 10, 17, 114, 119, 160
Dicaearchus 153-4
Diodorus Siculus 12, 64, 67-8, 80, 83, 86, 176-7, 194-6, 199
Diogenes (the Cynic) 213-6
Diogenes Laertius 213-4
Dionysus 12-13, 20, 224
Dodds, E.R. 151, 168
Dryops 6

Ea 15
Earth and Sky 4, 8-9, 10, 40, 47, 70
earth-born men 7-9, 17
Edelstein, L. 168
Egypt 64, 119, 195
Egyptian anthropogonical myth 14
ekpyrosis 117, 124, 128, 155
elements 36-7, 43, 60, 61, 63, 69, 83
Empedocles 35-45, 49, 80-1, 84, 86, 89, 90, 91, 92, 94-5, 112, 118-9, 128, 147-9, 205
Enki 15
Ennius 171
Ephorus 198
Epicurus and Epicurean philosphers 48, 65-7, 80, 83, 90, 125-6, 187, 189-90; see also Lucretius
Epimetheus 9, 10, 56-7
Erechtheus 7
Ethiopians 221
Euhemerus 171
Euripides 7, 8-9, 47, 174-5, 199

family life 137, 143, 144, 150, 159, 162, 169, 172, 191-2, 214, 220, 221
fire 4, 9, 11, 31, 57, 139, 140, 143, 162, 168-9, 172, 180, 190, 192, 195, 197, 211, 216, 220
fish 27-9
Florus 112
Fontenrose, J. 141-2
fossils 33

Gaia 4
Gellner, E. 103, 108
Germans 221
Golden Age 105, 107, 108, 126, 129, 191, 192, 195, 196, 200-1, 203, 204, 209, 210, 215, 216, 220, 221, 223; and chap. 6 passim
golden race 22 n27, 115, 136, 138, 139, 140, 141, 142, 143, 145, 146, 154, 156, 157, 216
great year 112, 117, 120, 122, 126
Griffiths, J.G. 139, 144
Guthrie, W.K.C. 7
gypsum 13

hard primitivism 105, 154, 155, 160, 182, 194, 198, 226-7; and chap. 8 passim
Hebrideans 221
Hephaistos 9, 32, 150, 169, 195
Heraclides Ponticus 11
Heraclitus 112, 117-8, 205, 206
Hermarchus 190
Hermes 196
Herodotus 180
heroic race 138, 140, 141, 142
Hesiod 4-5, 6, 7, 8, 9-10, 13, 17, 18, 30-31, 61, 74, 114-5, 128, 136, 138-144, 146, 147, 148, 150, 152, 156, 159, 160, 161, 166, 168-9, 173, 175, 192, 200
Hipparchus 166
Hippias 208-9
Hippocrates 222
Homer 3-4, 5-6, 7, 26, 104, 108, 114, 137-8, 142, 199, 221,
Horace 157, 158, 161, 196-7

Illyrians 221
instinctive behaviour 78-9
Io 19
iron race 138-9, 141, 142, 143, 144, 160, 200, 220
Isaiah 157
Isis 195
Islands of the Blessed 138, 161-2, 163 n9, 198
Isocrates 8

Julia 157

232

Index

Julian 214-5
Jupiter 158, 159, 160, 171, 220
Juvenal 219-20, 223
Kahn, C. 117
Khnum 14
Kingu 15
Kirk, G. 14-15, 116
kronikos 155
Kronos 4, 22, n27, 59, 136, 138, 140, 142, 143, 147, 149, 152-3, 154, 155-156, 163 n9, 171, 200, 210

larvae 64
Leibniz 182
Linforth, I.M. 13
Lloyd-Jones, H. 17-18
Lovejoy, A.O. 105, 203
Lucian 11, 161
Lucretius 65-8, 70, 80, 86, 89-93, 125-6, 166-7, 190-4, 195, 196, 199
Lykaon 5

Manilius 197-8, 199
Marcus Aurelius 125, 127, 128
Marduk 15
Maximus Tyrius 216
meat-eating 4, 13, 97, 137, 143, 145, 148, 154, 160, 162, 168, 172, 186, 210, 214-5, 221
medicine 55, 109, 178-180, 222
Mesopotamian anthropogonical myth 14-15
Momigliano, A. 124
monsters 40-2, 86-9, 90-1
Moschion 187
mutation 73, 76, 78, 92
Mycenean Greece 14, 108
myth to philosophy 24-6

Nammu 15
nature 205-8
Nero 158
Neoplatonist philosophers 12, 126-7
Nestor 103
Ninmah 15
Noble Savage 220-3
nomos 205-8

Oceanus 3

Octavian 157
Odysseus 6
Olympiodorus 12-13
Origen 127
Orphism 11-13, 20, 112-3, 223-4
Osiris 195-6
Ouranos 4, 171
Ovid 6, 11, 64, 70, 159-160, 196-7, 222-3

Pacuvius 70
Palaephatus 6
Panaetius 125
Pandora 9-10, 11, 14, 18, 31, 138, 139-40, 143, 144, 163 n8, 169, 170, 192
Parmenides 36, 205
Pausanias 11
Pelasgus 7
Pelops 5
Penelope 6
Pericles 104
Persephone 170
Phaeton 44, 119
Phanes 22 n27
Philemon 11
Philodemus 12
physis 205-8
Pindar 161
Plato 54, 58-62, 70, 74, 76, 81-2, 83, 93-5, 107, 108, 112, 119-21, 128, 149-153, 156, 159, 178, 181-2, 189, 209-13, 214-5, 216, 217, 219, 221, 223
Pliny the Elder 91, 96, 170-1
Plotinus 126-7
pneuma 63, 69
polis 183-5, 212
Polybius 123-4, 166, 187-8
Polyphemus 199
Pompeius Trogus 221-2
Posidonius 155, 188-9, 200, 217
Presocratic philosophers 24-53, 55, 56, 57, 60, 61-2, 63, 67, 70, 81, 83, 103, 107, 109, 115, 147, 175, 176, 205, 207; see also Anaxagoras, Anaximander, Archelaus, Democritus, Empedocles, Heraclitus, Parmenides,

233

Index

Pythagoras, Thales, Xenophanes progressivism 95-6, 105-6, 107, 108, 110, 129, 146, 152, 153, 155, 159, 209, 210, 214, 215, 216, 220, 223, 225; and chap. 7 passim
Prometheus 4, 9, 10-11, 14, 16, 17-8, 31-2, 56, 81-2, 138, 139-40, 143, 150, 168-9, 171-3, 177-8, 187, 192, 200, 216
Protagoras 56-7, 80, 81-3, 85-6, 176, 177-8, 179-80
Pyrrha 6, 160
Pythagoras and the Pythagoreans 34-5, 58, 62, 115, 116-7, 124, 160

Saturn 136, 156, 157, 159, 202 n14, 219
Schofield, M. 45
Scythians 197, 221-3
seeds 46
Seneca 78-9, 125, 128, 155, 166, 188-9, 217-9, 220, 223
Sertorius 161
Sextus Empiricus 65
Sibylline books 126
Sikes, E.E. 17-18
silver race 22 n27, 138, 139, 140, 141, 142, 143, 145, 159, 192
Socrates 8, 47, 54, 57-8, 75, 76, 120, 213
soft primitivism 105, 203, 210; and chap. 6 passim: see also Golden Age
Solmsen, F. 44
Solon 119
Sophists 56, 103, 176, 208-9; see also Hippias, and Protagoras
Sophocles 173-4, 200
Sorabji, R. 124, 127
spontaneous generation 62-5
Stoic philosophers 68-9, 70, 75, 78-9, 107, 108, 117, 124-5, 126, 128, 155, 187, 188-9, 216-9; see also Panaetius, Posidonius, Seneca and Zeno
stones 5-7
Strabo 222
survival of the fittest 44, 86-95

Tantalus 5
technology 107, 109, 135, 137, 144, 150, 151, 152, 162, 167, 168, 170, 173, 178, 188-9, 198, 209, 210, 223
Teleclides 155
teleology 75-79, 84, 87-8, 182-5
Thales 24, 26
Theophrastus 64, 65
Theseus 174-5
Thucydides 104, 108, 123, 166, 180, 198
Thyestes 149
Tibullus 159
Titans 12-13
Toynbee, A.J. 141
transmigration of souls 34, 36, 59, 112-3, 116-7, 131 n25, 148,
trees 5-6

vegetarianism 36, 75, 97, 137, 145, 146, 147, 148, 150, 153-4, 160, 180, 191, 195, 214, 221, 223-4
Vergil 6, 64, 126, 128, 157, 158-9, 166
Vernant, J.-P. 15-6, 141-2
Vitruvius 197, 199

Walcot, P. 14
West, M.L. 13, 139
woman 4, 9-10
wombs 65-7

Xenophanes 32-4, 80, 115-6, 175
Xenophon 75, 76

Zeno 68, 69, 133 n43, 155, 188, 217
Zeus 4, 6, 9, 12, 15, 16, 19, 22 n27, 74, 94, 137, 138, 140, 144, 150, 162, 171, 172, 178, 216